ESSENTIALS
OF AN EFFECTIVE
MARKETING
PROGRAM :

READINGS

ESSENTIALS OF AN EFFECTIVE MARKETING PROGRAM :

READINGS

John L. Kraushaar
Louis H. Vorzimer

University of Bridgeport
College of Business Administration
Bridgeport, Conn.

D. H. MARK PUBLISHING COMPANY / braintree, massachusetts

Printed in the United States of America.

Library of Congress Card Catalog Number: 75-134305

Preface

It is believed that the following readings contain strategies and ideas which are especially useful and which, if more widely understood and practiced, would improve marketing efficiency. In the classroom, the editors have experimented with these readings and have found them useful in two principal ways: first as a supplement in the basic marketing course to introduce students to the content of some important journals and to give examples of new applications and concepts; second, as a supplement in a case-method course in marketing management where the articles were analyzed and discussed in some depth in symposiums. The latter approach proved to be very rewarding for students.

By approaching the subject with the question, "which marketing ideas or strategies can we use *now*?", the editors believe that the discipline can be brought into sharper focus, hence awakening interest. Therefore, only readings have been included which contain strategies or ideas which can be utilized to some extent in the current operation of business. No attempt was made to cover every functional area.

In the belief that knowledge is advanced by the consideration of new structural frameworks, the editors have used a somewhat different arrangement which groups the readings under three general headings:

> Consumers
> Utilities
> Operations

Under "Consumers," readings have been grouped which are concerned with various aspects of consumer behavior. The "Utilities" section describes the formation of the consumer want-satisfying utilities:

Form (production)
Time
Place
Possession

Creation of form or production utility sometimes, is not considered to be within the province of marketing. But to the extent that it is the responsibility of marketing to determine the type of form utility desired by the consumer, it must be considered a partial function of marketing. The third section of the book, "Operations," is the force which coordinates the previous "Consumers" and want-satisfying "Utilities" sections.

In the interest of bringing some understanding of marketing strategy and knowledge to as wide an audience as possible, articles of a very technical nature have been avoided. On the contrary, this book is intended to act as a partial indication of the body of knowledge which exists. The main concern has been to illustrate the role of marketing in recognizing want-satisfying utilities for consumers and in delivering them with effective operations.

The 1970's will be a period of even greater change than the 1960's. Our space explorations have given tangible evidence of a changing world. To keep pace, changes of a great magnitude in marketing will take place in the 1970's. A group of articles are included, as an introduction, from a symposium arranged by the *Journal of Marketing,* which explores the pathways of marketing's potential.

Hopefully, a student faced with specific marketing problems, perhaps a year or two from now, may be able to recall something he read in this book which will give him the added insight he needs for the solution of problems.

Foreword

Objectives and methods for using a book of readings vary with each instructor. It may be used as supplementary collection of readings for a marketing text, or it may be treated as an independent unit. There is no one perfect approach for utilizing a book of readings in marketing. The editors have found the symposium effective in their classes. The description of the symposium format which follows, represents the editors' experience in the use of the readings and, as such, is a starting point toward teaching approaches which might help to vitalize the marketing discipline.

Description of the Symposium Format

A committee of three or four students is selected to manage the marketing symposium, one member being designated as chairman. Working with the instructor, the committee divides the class into small groups of about five or six students. Presentations are scheduled for class periods in the closing weeks of the semester. There are no written assignments, as students are evaluated on the basis of their class presentations.

Each group is assigned a topic for discussion, such as:

1. The contribution of anthropology to marketing.
2. The contribution of sociology to marketing.
3. The contribution of psychology to marketing.
4. Current product development strategies.
5. Current product promotion strategies.
6. Current product programing strategies.
7. Marketing as a science.
8. Types of marketing segmentation.
9. Controlling the marketing function.

The articles and the reading lists are only the nucleus for group research. In practice, each group usually shows resourcefulness in locating other valuable related references. The students are asked not only to summarize but to evaluate their findings. They are asked to consider "why" in addition to "how."

The student committee is responsible for:

1. Naming the discussion leader within each group of five or six students.
2. Assigning a committee member to act as advisor to each group.
3. Determining the length of time each group member will speak and the time available for class questions and comments.
4. The student committee makes the first presentation. They discuss the meaning, sources, and current state of marketing thought and knowledge, drawing on such references as:

Bartels, Robert, *Marketing Theory and Metatheory,* Homewood, Illinois: Richard D. Irwin, Inc., 1970.

Halbert, Michael, *The Meaning and Sources of Marketing Theory,* New York: McGraw-Hill Book Company Inc., 1965.

Schwartz, George, *Development of Marketing Theory,* Cincinnati, Ohio: South-Western Publishing Company, 1963.

Schwartz, George, *Science in Marketing,* New York: John Wiley & Sons, Inc., 1965.

When presentations are made, the group discussion leader calls on each member of his group. Then after each presentation the committee may ask questions of the group member to clarify points before the discussion is opened to the class.

Objectives of the Symposium Format

1. To bring into focus the continuing development of ideas, concepts, and theories in specific areas which are currently available to implement the marketing program. This bridges the gap in the marketing courses which follow the lecture method where time usually permits only the building of a framework for marketing thought. The symposium format is an aid for marketing courses which use the case method and are more concerned with problem solving than exploring emerging knowledge.

2. To give the student an insight into the dynamic character of the marketing discipline by an awareness of the changes which are taking place.

3. To personally involve the student in the marketing process.

4. To further innovation and experimentation in the teaching of marketing.

In the book, the editors have commented on the rapidity of changing events and technology. It is the opinion of the editors that marketing must keep pace with other changes in our society. The symposium format is a vehicle for student expression and contribution which is relevant to current needs.

Contents

I

Introduction:

A View of the Future, Marketing in the 1970's - A Symposium

One of the most significant advances in the 1960's was communication. For example, television via space satellites made it possible for events to be viewed instantly, not only in the United States, but all over the world. The *Journal of Marketing* recognized that marketing changes which previously extended over many years, now are telescoped into much shorter periods. As a prelude to the 1970's, the *Journal of Marketing* arranged for a symposium which would direct its attention to forecasting some of the remarkable marketing changes expected. The articles in this section constitute the symposium proceedings. This symposium acts as a broad framework for discussion of the articles which appear in the subsequent sections of the book. All the articles following the introductory group are more concerned with strategies and ideas which could be used currently to implement the marketing program, but they are also indicative of future developments. It would seem logical to the editors that a meaningful dialogue could develop between instructor and student if the discussions were to be arranged in a symposium format.

Marketing managers will face new kinds of problems during the coming decade as industry and company structures become more complex, and as environmental pressures increase. The author explores some of the anticipated trends of the 1970s and their effects on marketing organization and methods.

1

what's ahead for marketing managers?

robert d. buzzell

How will the problems and practices of marketing managers change during the 1970s? The only certain prediction is that there *will* be change, reflecting shifts in industry and company structures and in the social and economic environments within which marketing executives must function. I shall first look at these two areas and then discuss several trends and their likely effects on the practice of marketing management in the next decade.

INDUSTRY AND COMPANY STRUCTURES

The economies of the United States, Canada, and Western Europe will increasingly be dominated by large, highly diversified, multinational corporations operating at all levels of manufacturing and distribution. The marketing problems of these corporations will differ from those of traditional companies that operate on a more limited scale within a narrower range of products, markets, and production stages.

Reprinted from the *Journal of Marketing*, published by the American Marketing Association, Volume 34, No. 1 (January 1970), pp. 3-6.

Marketing executives will thus be faced with new challenges and pressures within their industry and company structures, resulting from increasing corporate size, greater diversification, and expanded internationalism.

Increasing Size

The continuing trend toward bigness in American industry has been measured, discussed, lauded, and lamented since the depression-ridden 1930s. The only constant factor in the controversy over increasing dominance of large corporations has been the trend toward bigness itself, which has continued unabated.

Statistics can be cited to show the increased importance of large firms in the American economy. For example, by 1966 the companies included in the *"Fortune* 500" — the 500 largest U.S. industrial firms — accounted for almost two-thirds of our total national employment.[1] These firms employed 9.3 million persons in 1961, for an average of 18,500 each. By 1966, employment had increased 40% to 13.1 million, and the average per company had grown to 26,150 employees.

The relationship between the nature of marketing management and company size is not well enough understood. It is clear, however, that increasing size does bring new problems and calls for new approaches. It seems virtually certain that many companies will enter new stages of their growth cycles during the 1970s, and will have to reconsider established marketing methods.

Greater Diversification

Both a cause and an effect of greater size is the continuing diversification of products and services within large corporations. The so-called "pure conglomerates" represent, perhaps, a special case. But even in more traditional firms such as Armour, General Mills, and R. J. Reynolds, the extent of product and service diversification has increased markedly during the 1960s and will probably continue to do so in the next decade.

A good example of the diversification trend is Beatrice Foods. Traditionally a dairy products producer, this firm acquired 100 other companies between the mid-1950s and mid-1960s. It presently distributes a wide range of industrial and consumer products including camping trailers, lubricants, and barbecue grills, as well as its many kinds of food products.[2]

Diversification is also changing the retailing landscape, and major companies which once specialized in food or general merchandise distribution seem likely to evolve into "retail conglomerates." These distributors are also increasingly involved in control or ownership of manufacturing facilities. Thus the once sharply drawn distinction between "manufacturer marketing" and "distributor marketing," is becoming less and less meaningful.

International Expansion

Increasing emphasis on international marketing activities is, in effect, another kind of "diversification." Throughout the 1950s and 1960s, companies based in North America have dramatically increased their foreign operations by establishing subsidiaries, building plants, and by undertaking more aggressive marketing efforts, especially in Western Europe. For some companies, sales and profits in foreign markets now exceed those earned domestically.

During the 1970s, expansion of international operations will probably continue at a somewhat lower rate of increase than in the preceding decade. More important, management approaches to foreign markets will mature. U.S. companies, particularly, have often regarded overseas markets as a strange kind of novelty, and some have committed egregious blunders through their marketing policies. Like tourists who have already visited Paris several times, they will now start to feel and display a greater savoir faire.

ENVIRONMENTAL PRESSURES

As industry and company structures change during the 1970s, managers will also be faced with new pressures from the social and economic environments. Since some of these developments are discussed in this section of the *Journal of Marketing*, I shall briefly mention three kinds of environmental changes that are of great importance to marketing organization and management.

First, technological change will almost certainly continue at a rate equal to or greater than that of the period 1950 to 1969. In many areas, new combinations of previously unrelated materials and processes will be developed. Traditional boundaries between areas of technology will become less meaningful.

Second, there will be an acute shortage of qualified managers. Simple projection of population figures in different age groups indicates that in 1975 there will be a decrease in the absolute number of men between 30 and 45 years of age of about 7% from the 1965 figure. The decline will obviously be much greater in relation to the increasing scale of business activity.

Third, there will be continued improvement in computer efficiency and in the quality of computer-based models and systems. To date, progress in the latter area has been discouragingly slow, but some basic problems have been solved, and a good foundation has been laid for future development.

EFFECTS ON MARKETING

The following predictions of the effects of structural and environmental challenges and pressures on marketing management and organization in the

1970s cover only several of what seem the most likely trends. These trends are based on conditions and changes evident in the late 1960s. Although the list is surely imcomplete and probably somewhat conservative, perhaps at least it will stimulate discussion and encourage the flexibility of thinking which is the only real means of dealing with change.

1. The trend toward decentralization of authority within large firms will continue, and probably accelerate. With occasional interruptions, this trend has been going on since the late 1940s. It is a direct consequence of increasing company size and diversity.

A substantial number of companies will discover what Du Pont, General Electric, and others already know: that top managers of large, diversified firms simply cannot acquire sufficient knowledge or maintain enough contact to participate effectively in all major decisions, for all products and markets. A good example is the Pillsbury Company, which has been decentralizing its management structure since the mid–1960s. In 1969, Pillsbury designated each of its product divisions as a separate "company," reflecting the substantial autonomy granted division managers.

During the 1950s and 1960s, the primary basis for decentralization has been products; product divisions, product groups, and product managers have all gained in importance. In the next decade, more emphasis is expected to be placed on markets as a basis for company organization. Ames had noted that differences in the needs, buying practices, locations and other attributes of industries and other customer groupings are often more significant than those among a company's products.[3] This is likely to become true in more and more cases, particularly where changes in technology obscure traditional product boundaries.

The values and limitations of the "market manager" form of organization are not yet well understood. Although they will be discovered primarily by trial and error, more intensive studies of the companies that have already tried this approach will also isolate the issues involved.

2. A critical shortage of qualified marketing management talent will develop. Indeed, many executives feel that such a crisis already exists. The decline in males aged 35 to 49, coupled with the demands created by newer types of company activities – such as urban development – will surely create a "talent squeeze" for most or all of the traditional management fields.

Beyond this, marketing may have special problems attracting the more competent younger men, because marketing careers seem inconsistent with the social goals and ideals advocated by the "Protest Generation." (To be sure, the most vocal critics of business are today's college students, who will not be 35 until after 1980. The substance of their ideas also has a powerful effect on their older brothers and sisters.)

How can business alleviate the shortage of marketing managers? Improved and accelerated management development is one obvious answer. Massive amounts are already being spent on university programs, short courses, and other educational efforts. Yet very little is known about what kinds of results can be achieved by various kinds of programs under different conditions. There is a clear need for research in this area.

Another avenue for expanding the supply of younger executives may be greater utilization of women. Already, of course, many women are engaged in marketing jobs, notably in advertising and retailing. During the 1970s, manufacturers and consulting firms may also give greater consideration to female candidates than in the past.

3. Top-level management will rely increasingly on formal corporate planning systems. Formal planning systems, usually computer-based, are used most extensively by large, diversified, multinational firms, such as General Electric, IBM, and the major oil companies. Utilization of formal planning, including quantitative estimation and measurement of key marketing variables and results, is not a substitute for decentralized management. Rather, it is a logical corollary.

As such, top management delegates wide-ranging authority to division, product, and market managers; however, it must retain control over the goals of each unit, and must have some means of measuring performance. The more diverse and scattered a company's operations, the less headquarters executives can rely on personal experience and direct contact — and the more it is forced to employ formal systems.

The development and use of formal planning systems may alter traditional approaches to marketing management. For one thing, most of these systems are designed to enable decision makers to estimate the "total effects" of an action. Traditionally, many marketing decisions have been made on the basis of "direct effects" — for example, sales force programs are appraised in terms of predicted or actual sales volume and selling costs, without full and explicit consideration of manufacturing costs, physical distribution costs, employment effects, and so on.

During the next decade, more and more firms will try to implement what is termed the total system viewpoint, and some will become reasonably skilled in doing so. It is not clear how this will affect traditional marketing practices, but it seems likely that changes will occur.

4. Some companies will have to modify their selling methods to meet the needs of large diversified, multinational customers, both manufacturers and distributors. The increasing size and diversity of both marketers and customer firms will greatly aggravate problems of duplication in sales contacts and intra-company competition. Often the various product divisions of large diversified firms have separate sales forces calling on the same customers. As these divisions themselves diverisfy their product lines, they become more and more competitive with each other. During the 1970s, corporate executives in many firms will be confronted with the problem of balancing economy and coordination of sales activities with the advantages of specialization and divisional autonomy.

At the same time, there is increasing interest among industrial buyers in "procurement systems" in which individual products and transactions are related to a broader context of supply needs and costs. Some companies have recently modified their organizational structures in order to offer coordinated "packages" of goods and services to system-minded customers. Others can be expected to follow suit in the decade to come.

5. There will be extensive experimentation in the definition of a proper role for corporate marketing units. Among large, diversified companies there appears to be considerable uncertainty about the nature and extent of authority that should be assigned to corporate marketing executives in relation to divisions or other "operating" units. For example, among 76 divisionalized companies covered by a National Industrial Conference Board study, 24 had *no* marketing units whatsoever at the corporate level and 12 had only small, specialized staff units. In the other 40 companies the functions of corporate marketing ranged from more extensive staff activities to direct line authority.[4]

Some of this variation is no doubt natural and proper, but the comments of executives in some companies reflect feelings of uncertainty about the role of corporate marketing. Should it be an internal consulting group? A firefighting squad? A training school? A watchdog, advising top corporate management? Whatever its role, what methods should be employed to achieve it?

During the 1970s, various approaches to corporate marketing coordination will be tried. This trial-and-error process might be facilitated by careful study of the experiences of selected companies which have already tested different organizational arrangements.

NOTES

1. *The Fortune Directory* (New York: Time, Inc., August 1962, October 1966, and June 1968).

2. "Beatrice Foods Savors a Zestier Cupboard," *Business Week* (December 16, 1967), pp. 122, 126, and 128.

3. Charles B. Ames, "Payoff from Product Management," *Harvard Business Review*, Vol. 41 (November-December, 1963), pp. 141-152.

4. Harold Steiglitz and Allen R. Janger, *Top Management Organization in Divisionalized Companies*, National Industrial Conference Board, Studies in Personnel Policy No. 195, New York, 1965.

Massive changes are taking place among firms in the distributive industries. These changes are as much qualitative as quantitative and defy objective appraisal on the basis of conventional data sources. The author identifies six major interrelated changes and comments about their managerial and research implications.

2

changes in distributive institutions

william r. davidson

The purpose of this article is to indicate briefly the major changes to be expected in the distribution industries during the first half of the 1970s. Some of the major implications of these changes from the standpoint of business strategy and research will be identified. The distributive structure of the economy is defined to include retailing, service, and wholesaling establishments, plus the distribution activities of manufacturers and other form-utility producers as well as the product-acquisition activities of consumers. It is important to consider both the manufacturer and the consumer as active participants in the distribution process, in an era characterized by increasing vertical integration and enlarged willingness to shift marketing functions among or between the traditional channel of distribution levels.

Reprinted from the *Journal of Marketing*, published by the American Marketing Association, Volume 34, No. 1 (January 1970), pp. 7-10.

CHANGES IN THE DISTRIBUTIVE STRUCTURE

It is not possible to deal with all anticipated changes in a comprehensive manner or to support points of view with documentation within the scope of this article. Consequently, attention is focused upon a few major interrelated institutional changes. The discussion will be somewhat oversimplified for purposes of emphasizing the major thrusts within a complex and dynamic distribution environment. Moreover, attention is restricted primarily to the distributive structure for consumer goods, although many of the changes here discussed have a counterpart in industrial marketing.

The following changes were selected for discussion:

1. Rapid growth of vertical marketing systems.
2. Intensification of intertype competition.
3. Increasing polarity of retail trade.
4. Acceleration of institutional life cycles.
5. The emergence of the "free-form" corporation as a major competitive reality in distribution.
6. The expansion of nonstore retailing.

Each of these changes represents a trend the direction of which is already evident. These trends are expected to accelerate and intensify in the early 1970s. The major impact of these trends will be upon the range of strategies which can be successfully implemented by firms within the distributive structure.

GROWTH OF VERTICAL MARKETING SYSTEMS

Conventional marketing systems are being rapidly displaced by *vertically organized marketing systems* as the dominant distribution mechanism in the economy. Conventional channels are those fragmented networks in which loosely aligned and relatively autonomous manufacturers, wholesalers, and retailers have customarily bargained aggressively with each other, established trade relationships on an individual transaction basis, severed business relationships arbitrarily with impunity, and otherwise behaved independently.

Vertical marketing systems, by way of contrast, consist of networks of horizontally coordinated and vertically aligned establishments which are managed as a system. Establishments at each level operate at an optimum scale so that marketing functions within the system are performed at the most advantageous level or position.

The recent rapid and expected continued growth of vertical marketing systems is evident by the performance of three major types of distributive systems with high vertical programming potential — corporate, contractual, and administered systems.

Corporate systems may be regarded as roughly synonymous with integrated chain store systems, although the impetus for vertical programming may come from companies primarily regarded as retailers (e.g., Sears, Roebuck & Company), or manufacturers (e.g., company-owned stores in the self supply network of Firestone Tire & Rubber Company), or wholesalers, some of whom have company-owned stores and are integrated into manufacturing. Chains of 11 or more store units, which accounted for a relatively stable one-fifth of total retail sales between 1929 and 1958, exhibited a renaissance of growth in the 1960s and now account for some 30% of all retailing, with a continuously accelerating growth rate evident.

Contractual systems include three sub-types — wholesaler-sponsored voluntary chains, retailer-cooperative organizations, and franchising organizations. Each sub-type involves voluntary but contractual integration of retail store or service units with other supply units at an antecedent channel level. There are no official data on the aggregate importance of such systems. A recent trade-by-trade analysis by the author and his associates suggests that 35 to 40% of all retail trade is accounted for by some form of voluntary chain, cooperative, or franchising organization. This includes old organizational forms such as automobile dealer franchises and the I.G.A. type of food store voluntary, and very new organizations such as Ethan Allen furniture franchise stores of the Baumritter Corporation. Other new forms are the various convenience food stores and fast food franchise operations.

Contractual systems, like chain store organizations, are not new. However, their recent and expected future rapid growth rate *plus* the increasing sophistication of vertical programming are of major interest. Once characterized primarily by goals of economy in the form of buying power and low operating expense ratios, such operations have moved into an era of complete management systems, achieving high market impact through the rationalization and clarification of the total firm product-service offer.

The third type of vertical system, *administered*, pertains to a line or classification of merchandise rather than to a complete store operation. While historically many examples of close store-vendor relationships existed, there is current intensification of such relationships by means of vendor-developed *comprehensive programs* for distribution through the entire channel. Of interest are retail merchandising programs developed by O. M. Scott and Sons Company in lawn products, by Villager in young women's apparel, by Magnavox Company in the home entertainment field, and by Kraftco Corp. in the supermarket dairy case. There are no data of any overall significance for administered systems of this type. However, proprietary studies conducted by the author and his associates for a group of leading firms in the general merchandising field clearly indicate that such vertically coordinated programs are growing rapidly.

INTENSIFICATION OF INTERTYPE COMPETITION

All channel levels are characterized by increasing competition of an intertype character. A phenomenon known in the early 1950s as *scrambled merchandising* has surpassed all early expectations predicted for it. Owing to increased fragmentation or segmentation of the consumer market, a wide variety of establishment types find it increasingly feasible to abandon "line of trade" conventions and to offer a variety of products that may be purchased by consumers to which that type of firm has market access. It is estimated that as many as 450,000 retail establishments (about one-fourth of all retail stores) are involved to some degree in selling tires, batteries, or other automotive parts, supplies, or accessories. As many as 200,000 outlets are believed to be involved to some degree in marketing housewares.

This accelerated trend means that wholesale distributors and manufacturers who wish to achieve a significant total market share will find it increasingly necessary to develop multiple marketing programs designed to meet the economic goals and operating characteristics of specific outlet types. It also demonstrates the diminishing analytical significance of conventional Census of Business classifications (e.g., drugstores, hardware stores, and jewelry stores).

INCREASED POLARITY OF RETAIL TRADE

Retail trade is becoming increasingly polarized at two extremes. On the one hand are mass-merchandising operations that have successfully implemented supermarket approaches. This group includes the general merchandise types of discount or promotional department stores, and also the more specialized establishments with a large mass appeal. Examples are the 70,000 square foot stores of Central Hardware Company of St. Louis, the home modernization stores of the Wickes Corporation and Lowe's Companies, Inc., and the large mass appeal drug store such as Super X, a relatively new division of The Kroger Company. Super X has developed into the third largest U.S. drug chain since its first store opening in 1961. At the other pole are highly specialized boutique types of stores which carry a deep assortment of a very specialized line, often limited to a concept or a "look," as opposed to commodity types. Illustrative examples are Villager specialty shops which feature only a well-coordinated assortment of classic sportswear items, and the Ethan Allen stores of Baumritter which sell only Early American style furniture and coordinated furnishings. Such shops tend to be strong on services and are often distinguished by the provision of consumption advice as opposed to conventional selling approaches.

At both poles, establishments tend to be organized into vertical marketing systems upon the achievement of scale. Between the poles are conventional and often nonprogrammed single-line stores of the family apparel, hardware, drug, and jewelry types. For these stores and their supply systems, the polarization is suggestive of increased obsolescence and profit difficulties in the 1970s.

ACCELERATION OF INSTITUTIONAL LIFE CYCLES

Institutions, like products, may be regarded as having life cycles which consist of stages such as inception, rapid early growth, maturity, and decline. The time required to reach a mature stage is constantly diminishing. Conventional department stores, as an institutional type, achieved a mature position over the span of about three-quarters of a century. The more standardized variety store reached maturity within half a century. Supermarkets achieved the same within little more than a quarter of a century. Fast food service chains and franchising organizations will have achieved maturity in little more than one decade.

Further acceleration of institutional life cycles is to be expected. There will be an attendant massive impact upon existing institutional forms. The reasons include a variety of total vertical marketing systems models, a growing number of entrepreneurs and managers with interorganizational administrative skills, and a stock market that will instantly fund on a large scale any promising new concept.

THE "FREE-FORM" CORPORATION IN DISTRIBUTION

Distribution industries, once characterized by institutions which specialized by channel level and by kind of business classifications, are feeling the accelerated impact of the emergence of the free-form distribution corporation as a major competitive reality. Free-form corporations are in part a response to other changes previously discussed, especially intertype competition and the polarity of trade, and in part a perceived opportunity to redefine business puspose so as to better utilize corporate resources and distinctive competences.

The J. C. Penny Company, Inc. is now an example of a free-form corporation. Ten to fifteen years ago, Penney's was a chain of small town, limited service, general merchandise stores. It has now evolved to an aggressive free-form operation consisting of full-scale urban Penney department stores, Penney auto and truck service centers, Treasure Island discount stores, the Thrifty Drug Company chain, a large catalog sales division, a financial subsidiary for accounts receivable funding, a life insurance marketing program and European stores through an equity interest in Sarma S.A., a Belgian company with 100 stores and 270 franchised units. Another outstanding and prophetic example is the Dayton-Hudson Corporation formed in 1969 by the merger of two of the best known department store companies (Dayton's of Minneapolis and Hudson's of Detroit). This corporation also operates Diamonds department stores (Phoenix);

Lipman's department stores (Portland, Ore.); Target Stores, Inc., a prominent general merchandise discount chain; Lechmere's, a Boston area hard lines mass merchandiser; two chains of specialty book stores; several jewelry store operations; and real estate subsidiaries engaged in shopping centers and other land development activities.

The number of corporations with a newfound willingness to go anywhere and do anything in distribution will have increasing competitive impact. This development is likely to enlarge markedly concentration ratios at all levels of distribution. Moreover, such corporate approaches are often perceived as strategic ways of avoiding the decline phase of the institutional life cycle.

GROWTH OF NONSTORE RETAILING

In an increasingly affluent society which is ever more oriented to education, leisure, and recreation, it may be expected that functions performed by consumers in the product acquisition process will be somewhat reshuffled with important benefits accruing to various forms of nonstore retailing and the distribution networks that supply nonstore operations. Many housewives will have a lower relative preference for "shopping," especially for routine categories of consumption, than for other demands upon or optional uses of time.

This trend is expected to benefit at-home selling, illustrated by the growth of Avon Products, Inc., with 1968 sales of $558.6 million, an increase of 59% since 1965. Catalogue selling is also expected to expand. Penney's adventuresome entry into this field and the expanded use of seasonal catalogues by all manner of regular store retailers illustrate the growth of catalogue selling. Marketing through the mail is presumably increasing as illustrated by single-item and short catalogue promotions. Examples are product selling promotions by major oil companies and banks to credit card customers, credit card companies, magazines, and other firms not basically in the business of operating stores. The consumer's desire for time and place utility is increasing the range of products available through vending machines as well as the number and types of vending locations. The development of electronic devices is making new approaches possible to at-home shopping for staples which can be supplied by routinized order processing and delivery from central distribution warehouses.

Many new concepts involving nonconventional forms are expected to emerge partly as the contribution of entrepreneurs and also as a new dimension of the mature corporation which has been reprogrammed for project management approaches under the free-form pattern.

RESEARCH IMPLICATIONS

None of the major trends selected for emphasis in the preceding sections is readily traceable through Census of Business benchmark data, other conventional wholesale trade series, or annual statistical series of trade associations. Hence, one research problem of considerable magnitude is merely one of measurement. Beyond that, there are research challenges of managerial significance to ascertain improved methods of managing interorganizational relationships, to devise sophisticated management systems which will provide information that will help managers understand and optimize total system relationships, and to explore ways in which product life cycle concepts can be better applied to institutions. In the realm of social concern, it is essential to study more comprehensively the impact of these developments upon consumer choice, the state of competition, and the need for modifications in public policy, especially antitrust.

Among the methodologies that are expected to receive major emphasis in the pursuit of these research objectives are (1) empirical economic studies of competitive conditions and market performance; (2) computer simulation models to evaluate total systems performance under varying conditions; (3) behavioral analyses of concepts of power and conflict in channel relationships; and (4) the utilization of laboratory methods in the refinement of such behavioral concepts, with a view to better understanding their utilization in total system marketing.

Several recent developments in marketing infor-mation systems and analytical marketing models are described. These developments in combination with others reported in this Journal of Marketing symposium will cast the future marketing executive in the role of a market engineer. He will have a heavier involve-ment in planning rather than doing, and in profit maximization rather than sales maximiza-tion.

the future of
the computer in
marketing

philip kotler

Executives who spend their days firing up a sales force, planning advertising campaigns, servicing and placating dealers, and trying to out-maneuver competitors believe that much of marketing defies classification and analysis. This is one reason the subjects of mathematics and the computer continue to have an alien ring in the ears of many marketing executives. Many managers have developed a natural suspicion about statements that mathematics and the scientific method might make a significant contribution to the understanding and solution of marketing problems. In fact, there is no question that many facets of the marketing process will not submit to scientific tidiness, particularly facets that rely heavily on creativity, human relations, and the like. But there are other facets of marketing that have responded well to systematic observation, analysis, and procedures. These marketing elements offer a golden opportunity for the

Reprinted from the *Journal of Marketing*, published by the American Marketing Association, Volume 34, No. 1 (January 1970), pp. 11-14.

marketing executive willing to adopt an innovative attitude toward the new knowledge.

Although mathematical models and computers are relative late comers in marketing, they have already paid off in such areas as new product development and strategy, advertising media selection, and product pricing.[1] A growing number of marketing executives are testifying to the various benefits of formal models and computers. In a private speech one executive in an automobile company said the new models have been instrumental in increasing marketing's self-respect and the respect shown by other company departments toward marketing. "Formerly, finance and production would go into the board meeting armed with their carefully documented plans spelled out in dollars and cents. Marketing would go into the same meeting with a lot of vague assertions, guesses, and hot air. We've spent the last couple of years learning and using decision theory, regression analysis, and simulation in our marketing work and now at the board meetings, our estimates and plans command considerable confidence."

TRENDS AND MAJOR DEVELOPMENTS

The character of future marketing management is already suggested by today's practices in some of the larger, market-oriented U.S. companies. Discussions with marketing executives in a number of these companies confirm that a major revolution is taking place in the information and analytical capabilities of marketing management. Here the more striking developments that are occurring in the areas of information technology and analytical tools will be highlighted.

Information Technology

Marketing executives derive their information about the marketplace through marketing intelligence, formal marketing research, and company accounting information. The alert marketing executive recognizes that each of these areas has a potentiality for considerable improvement. *Marketing intelligence activity* describes the continuous efforts of executives to keep informed about current developments among customers, dealers, competitors, and the marketing environment. Three key trends in the area of marketing intelligence are:

1. Companies are giving better training and motivation to their salesmen regarding their role and responsibility as "information officers" of the firm.

2. Some companies are assigning full-time personnel to the task of gathering marketing intelligence through field work and through continuous scanning of published information.

3. Companies are seeking to build central information files on dealers,

customers, and competitors so that their executives will have "fingertip" information.

One large company recently appointed an ex-military intelligence officer to take over, design, and manage a marketing intelligence service for the executives of the company.

Marketing research connotes more formal, project-oriented research that usually begins with a company problem or opportunity and ends with a management report. Three important trends in marketing research are:

1. Executives are increasingly recognizing that good marketing research is more than fact gathering. Much more effort is being put into defining the real problem and the managers' decision alternatives as a basis for collecting action-relevant information.

2. Market experimentation is becoming an increasingly significant information gathering technique, particularly for learning the response of sales to different types and levels of marketing inputs. A vice-president of a large company told the author he expects that marketing experiments will be budgeted into marketing plans as a routine matter in the seventies. "Some small part of every budget should always be assigned to finding out how to improve the spending of the big part."

3. Marketing executives are increasingly asked to quantify their feelings about sizes of markets, effects of marketing expenditures, and the probabilities surrounding critical marketing events. Their subjective estimates are essential inputs for the more advanced marketing models. The challenge to quantify sharpens the quality of marketing discussion and analysis.

The *company accounting system* serves the purpose of generating summaries of current sales and costs. Companies are investing heavily in improving their internal reporting systems. The following developments should be of great interest to marketers.

- There is an increased interest in storing sales and marketing cost on a disaggregative basis to permit executives to retrieve special configurations of information. In one company an executive can retrieve current and past sales and inventory figures for any brand and package size for each of 400 distributors. Or he can request the computer to list all distributors whose sales fall below a certain figure. In another company, marketing researchers can seek to measure the effects of specific marketing inputs on specific sales results by geographical area.

- Companies are attempting to reduce the length of time it takes for executives to learn of latest sales. The fast changing marketing scene means that line executives should be informed continuously of important sales developments. A few consumer goods companies are now able to provide executives with data on shipments that took place yesterday. Grocery goods companies are trying to figure out how they can learn of retail shelf-sales movement as it takes place.

Some companies in the airline and motel industries have managed to develop *real time* information, i.e., they know sales and product availabilities as of the latest second.

- Companies are finding new uses for their computer as a sales tool in the servicing of customer needs. Salesmen in one large paper company can dial the company computer while in a customer's office and learn in a matter of seconds whether a certain grade of paper is in stock and could be shipped to the customer to meet a target date. A large fertilizer company helps farmers decide on next year's best crops — and fertilizer — through a specially designed computer program. Several insurance companies use the computer to prepare long-range insurance programs for clients.

Analytical Models and Tools

The future marketing executive increasingly will rely on sophisticated tools and models to help analyze his information. His familiarity with the new tools will come about through MBA programs, executive development seminars, and exposure to computer *time sharing.* Computer time share will probably be the most potent force in dramatizing the new tools to marketing executives. Time sharing refers to a setup where several remote teletype terminals are linked to a central computer and an executive can sit down at any one, dial the computer center number, type in his user number, and have access to all the power of the computer. An increasing number of computer programs will be available on a conversational basis, that is, the typewriter will type out a description of the requested program and then instruct the executive as to how he should type in his data. After the computer has received the data, it types back a solution in a matter of seconds.

The potentialities of this tool can be dramatized by realizing that each of the following programs is already available in one or another company today for their marketing executives to use.

- A new product manager can sit down at a terminal, dial a new product computer program called SPRINTER I, and supply various estimates as they are called for by the computer, including the estimated size of the target group, recent product trial rates and repeat purchase rates, the promotional budget, size of investment, target rate of return, product price, and gross profit margin. The computer will digest this information and print out a monthly forecast for the next few years of the total number of buyers, company market share, period profits, and discounted cumulative profits. The new product manager can alter various input estimates and readily ascertain the effect of the altered data on sales and profits.[2]
- An advertising manager can dial a media selection computer program called MEDIAC, type in information on the size of his advertising budget, the number and size of important market segments, media exposure and cost data, ad size and color data, sales seasonality, and other information, and the computer will return a media schedule that is calculated to achieve maximum exposure and sales impact in the customer segments.[3]

● A sales manager can dial a sales redistricting program, type in data on the workload and/or sales potential of various counties, their distances from each other, and the number of sales territories he wants to create. The computer will digest this information and assign various counties to make up new sales territories in such a way that (a) the sales territories are approximately equal in workload and/or sales potential and (b) they are compact in shape, thus cutting down travel costs.[4]

● A marketing executive can dial a dealer site location program, type in a proposed location and size for a new dealership in a large city, and receive a forecast of sales and market share for the new dealership, and the loss of sales to other dealerships, including his own.[5]

● A salesman can dial a sales prospect evaluation program, type in information about a list of prospects, including the estimated value of their annual business, the maximum probability of conversion, the estimated number of years they will remain customers, etc., and receive back a table suggesting the optimal number of calls to make on each prospect and how the prospects rank in order of attractiveness.[6]

● The marketing controller can dial a dealer size evaluation program, type in data on annual sales of each dealer, servicing costs, and the behavior of unit production costs with scale of production. The computer program will suggest the minimum size dealer to retain.[7]

These computer programs represent only the beginning of marketing models tailored to the problems and needs of various industries and executives. They utilize a variety of mathematical and heuristical techniques, the basic principles of which can be conveyed to the executive-user. In fact, most of these models are formal codifications of how the executives tend to think about these problems, with the additional advantages offered by the computer of logical analysis, computational power, and sensitivity testing.

The two major modeling techniques that will be standard equipment of marketing executives in the seventies are *decision theory* and *simulation*. Decision theory is an organized approach for evaluating alternative strategies in the presence of risk or uncertainty. It calls for clarifying the (a) decision alternatives, (b) uncertain events, (c) their probabilities, and (d) the payoffs of every possible outcome. The decision maker can proceed to derive an expected payoff for each course of action and act accordingly. Decision theory has been applied by marketing executives to dozens of real marketing problems, and most of its users testify to its value as a way of organizing their attack on a problem.[8]

The other technique, *simulation*, describes models which are developed to imitate the essential behavior of a process or system. A simulation model is usually complex and probabilistic, and its properties are comprehended only by running it under different conditions and by studying the output. It is hoped that experimentation on the simulation model will yield insight and meaningful forecasts of the behavior of the real system. One of the most exciting applications of the idea of simulation is in the creation of complex computer models that imitate the behavior of real markets and which can be used by the firm to test and plan marketing strategies. Computer models of markets have already been developed in such industries as fertilizers,[9] copying machines,[10] drugs,[11] and frozen orange juice[12] and they are under development in a number of other industries.

In addition to these modeling techniques, the marketing executive will also have access on a time-sharing basis to various statistical tools for analyzing complex relationships in multivariate data; for example, regression and correlation analysis, discriminant analysis, factor analysis, cluster analysis, and multidimensional scaling. All told, the marketing executive of the future is headed toward a *brave new world* of instant information and sophisticated marketing decision models. These developments will lean the future marketing executive toward a more analytical frame of mind with a heavier emphasis on planning rather than doing, and profits rather than sales. If at the same time, he maintains a creative and innovative temperament and a people-empathy, he cannot help but be extremely effective in the marketplace.

NOTES

1. See Philip Kotler, "Operations Research in Marketing," *Harvard Business Review*, Vol. 45 (January-February, 1967), pp. 30 ff.

2. Glen L. Urban, "SPRINTER mod 1: A Basic New Product Analysis Model," Alfred P. Sloan School of Management Working Paper No. 397-69 (Massachusetts Institute of Technology, 1969).

3. See J. D. C. Little and L. M. Lodish, "A Media Planning Calculus," *Operations Research*, Vol. 17 (January-February, 1969), pp. 1-35.

4. See Sidney W. Hess, *Realignment of Sales and Service Districts*, Working Paper (Philadelphia, Pa.: Management Science Center, Wharton School, University of Pennsylvania, July, 1968).

5. T.E. Hlavac, Jr., and J. D. C. Little, "A Geographic Model of an Automobile Market," Alfred P. Sloan School of Management Working Paper No. 186-66 (Massachusetts Institute of Technology, 1966).

6. Private program by the author.

7. Same reference as footnote 6.

8. See Wroe Alderson and Paul E. Green, *Planning and Problem Solving in Marketing* (Homewood, Illinois: Richard D. Irwin, Inc., 1964).

9. George B. Hegeman, "Dynamic Simulation for Market Planning," *Chemical and Engineering News*, Vol. 43 (January 4, 1965), pp. 64-71.

10. Seymour M. Zivan, "Planning, Using a Corporate Model," paper presented at the American Meeting of The Institute of Management Sciences, Boston, Mass., April 5, 1967.

11. Henry J. Claycamp and Arnold E. Amstutz, "Simulation Techniques in the Analyses of Marketing Strategy," in *Applications of the Sciences in Marketing Management*, Frank M. Bass, et al., eds. (New York: John Wiley & Sons, Inc., 1968), pp. 113-150.

12. Stanley Buchin, "A Model of the Florida Orange Industry for Minute Maid Planning," Case A 1-270 (Boston, Mass.: Harvard Business School, 1968).

Progress in measurement theory and techniques of data analysis can be useful to both the management scientist and behavioralist. Recent developments in multidimensional scaling and nonmetric methods in analyzing associative data are discussed. The author further speculates that such techniques will lead ultimately to more realistic prescriptive models and more rigorous formulations of buyer behavior.

measurement and data analysis

paul e. green

To assert that "the use of quantitative methods in marketing is already large and continues to grow" is no longer newsworthy. Less than a decade ago, however, such a statement may have raised a few eyebrows. Somewhat less obvious are the changes that are currently taking place in the *kinds* of techniques bearing the quantitative label. A number of researchers who have long been interested in marketing models are now taking a hard look at the realism of these models and the problems associated with estimating values of the models' parameters.

Similarly, researchers interested in buyer attitudes and choice making are becoming increasingly aware of the need to develop operational measures of those aspects of human behavior deemed relevant to product purchase and consumption. In short, both prescriptive model builders and behavioralists are recognizing the need for better measures and better ways of analyzing the increasing quantities of data being generated by corporate research groups and commercial houses engaged in the data supply business.

A major factor contributing to the increased generation of data is, of course,

Reprinted from the *Journal of Marketing*, published by the American Marketing Association, Volume 34, No. 1 (January 1970), pp. 15-17.

the computer. It is only fitting, then, that the computer share in the task of making some sense out of the morass of output which it can so blithely generate. Fortunately, the techniques to be discussed in this note are congenial with − one might even say wedded to − the capabilities of modern computers.

My concern here is with measurement theory and techniques of data analysis. The major unifying descriptor characterizing recent developments in both fields is *multidimensional*. In measurement and scaling theory current research emphasis is on multidimensional models of human perception and evaluation. In the field of data analysis current developments have emphasized multivariate approaches to pattern identification and data reduction.

MULTIDIMENSIONAL SCALING

One of the more provocative recent developments in scaling methods involves the depiction of respondents' similarities and preference judgments as points in a geometric space. Recent versions of these models require only rank order data, yet they are capable of generating spatial configurations of stimulus objects − brands, suppliers of services, advertisements, "ideal" products, sales personnel images − whose interpoint relationships are metrically scaled. A number of applications of these techniques are being reported by academicians,[1] corporate researchers[2] and consultants.[3]

It would seem that these techniques, originally developed by psychometricians, may be useful in market segmentation analysis,[4] new product development,[5] and attitude measurement generally. Not surprisingly, implementation of these algorithms requires the capabilities of high speed computers. The lesson to be learned from the newer approaches is that one need *not* have "strongly scaled" input data to obtain interval or ratio scaled output. The implications of this viewpoint can be widespread since it is evident that much of the data collected on buyer attitudes can safely be assumed to be only ordinal scaled.

Multidimensional scaling using ordinal methods is less than a decade old; the first operational procedure appeared in 1962.[6] However, since that time a wide variety of computer algorithms have appeared which offer a significant degree of refinement relative to the original technique. In addition, a number of pilot studies have been completed utilizing these techniques. For example, many consulting firms and advertising agencies are starting to offer such services and the field (unfortunately) is even starting to take on a fad-like appearance.[7]

An associated area of research concerns evaluation functions − the ways that people, managers, or consumers choose among multi-objective alternatives. Virtually all decisions involve alternatives whose outcomes are multi-attribute; for example, a management policy may be "good" with respect to short-term profits, "fair" with regard to increased market share, "poor" with regard to enhancing distributor, relations, and so on. Often we attempt to develop some general measure of effectiveness in dealing with problems of this type. Such portmanteau measures are often quite unrealistic representations of how managers (or customers) effect "trade-offs" among multi-objective alternatives. Not surprisingly, many of the techniques that are relevant for the multidimensional scaling of perceptions are appropriate here as well. Progress in understanding this class of problems should lead to more realistic prescriptive models.

Other potential applications of multidimensional scaling — product life cycle analysis, brand switching phenomena, communication nets, to name a few — appear in the offing. The value of this methodology, if it makes good on its promise, is the quantification of phenomena heretofore thought to be too "qualitative" or "intangible" to measure.

MULTIVARIATE ANALYSIS

Closely allied, at least structurally, to the methodology of multidimensional scaling are techniques used in the analysis of multivariate statistical data; for example, factor analysis, discriminant analysis, and canonical correlation. It is, therefore, not surprising that analogs to these better known techniques — analogs which need only rank order input data — are being developed by many of the same psychometricians who are contributing to algorithm development in multidimensional scaling. It would be my guess that future developments in this area will be so extensive that a whole new branch of nonparametric statistics — corresponding to nonparametric procedures in univariate statistics — will be developed to cope with multivariate rank order data.

Marketing researchers have already embraced metric procedures for analyzing multivariate data with much enthusiasm. Since much of the marketing data are multivariate, and weakly scaled at that, it seems reasonable to suppose that nonmetric discriminant analysis, multiple regression, analysis of variance, and the like, will find increasing application.

Another area of fairly recent development is cluster analysis, that is, various methods for grouping multivariate profiles (e.g., households' vectors of socioeconomic scores) into more or less homogeneous groups. In these methods "homogeneity" must be defined in terms of the data itself rather than some outside criterion. Dozens of clustering programs have been developed and the field appears, if anything, to be suffering from a proliferation of methods and the lack of a firm theoretical base. Still there is some reason to believe that the currently large array of ad hoc clustering procedures will be replaced by a smaller number of algorithms expressly designed to handle data of specified form. To assert that clustering problems will be "solved" over the next five years seems highly optimistic; a more defensible view is to suppose that current problems in clustering will be reduced to a few prototypical cases, with special algorithms for each.

In short, it seems likely that users of multivariate methods will come to appreciate the *formal* unity of many approaches which appear to be described as separate techniques.[8] Already some investigators are combining "reduced space" approaches, using metric or nonmetric factor analytic models with clustering procedures.[9] Such tandem, and complementary, strategies of data analysis seem both reasonable and fruitful for grasping the salient features of data structures.

FUTURE DEVELOPMENTS

It seems very likely to me that recent progress in the development of scaling techniques and multivariate procedures will continue, both at the methodological and applied levels. Moreover, there is reason to suppose that current methods, dealing typically with two-way data matrices, will be extended to multiway matrices. And the current emphasis on linear models will be generalized to handle a wide variety of functional forms not even restricted to monotonic functions.

The diffusion of these techniques will, of course, be aided by the continued spread of computers. Indeed, it does not seem far-fetched to suppose that large, interactive "data analyzers" with visual display and hard copy, auxiliary output will be developed and made available on a real-time basis to marketing technicians and managers alike. The analyst will be able to try a number of different ways of summarizing his data and looking for significant patterns without the long delays associated with batch processing procedures.

What might be the "corporate obstacles" to such rapid diffusion? Somewhat ironically, I am afraid there may not be *enough* obstacles. The increasing proliferation of computer programs and the desire to try "new things" may lead to more abuses of these developments than could have possibly been committed before the computer. The availability of "canned" programs (as a seeming substitute for conceptional understanding of the methodology) will unfailingly provoke misapplications on the part of those too impatient to invest the time to understand the assumption base and rationale of the "black box."

Despite all this — or perhaps because of it — I feel sanguine about the future value of this methodology in marketing analysis. Overzealous application is bound to occur, but a kind of "residual" knowledge still seems to fall out and accumulate. The limitations of current methods are many and serious, but the core ideas embedded in the procedures appear both exciting and, in some cases, profound.

I started this note by suggesting that emphasis on measurement and data analysis seems necessary toward developing richer prescriptive models and testable behavioral theory. The major value of the techniques described here may just be that — providing an improved measurement base for the construction of better policy models for marketing management and a deeper understanding of buyer behavior.

NOTES

1. L. A. Neidell and R. D. Teach, "Preference and Perceptual Mapping of a Convenience Good," in *Marketing's Involvement in Society and the Economy*, Philip R. McDonald, ed. (Chicago, Ill.: American Marketing Association, Fall, 1969); and P. E. Green and F. J. Carmone, "Multidimensional Scaling: An Introduction and Comparison of Nonmetric Unfolding Techniques," *Journal of Marketing Research*, Vol. 6 (August, 1969), pp. 330-41.

2. D.H. Doechlert, "Similarity and Preference Mapping: A Color Example," in *Marketing and the New Science of Planning*, Robert L. King ed. (Chicago, Ill.; American Marketing Association, 1968), pp. 250-8; and Marshall Greenberg, "A Variety of Approaches to Nonmetric Multidimensional Scaling," paper presented at the 16th International Meeting of the Institute of Management Sciences, New York, March, 1969.

3. V. J. Stefflre, "Market Structure Studies: New Products for Old Markets and New Markets (Foreign) for Old Products," in Proceedings of the Purdue Symposium: *Application of the Sciences in Marketing Management*, Purdue University, July 12-15, 1966; and R. M. Johnson, "Marketing Segmentation – A Comparison of Techniques," paper presented at the 16th International Meeting of the Institute of Management Sciences, New York, March, 1969.

4. P. E. Green and F. J. Carmone, *Multidimensional Scaling and Related Techniques in Marketing Analysis* (Boston: Allyn and Bacon, Inc., 1970).

5. N. L. Barnett, "Beyond Market Segmentation," *Harvard Business Review*, Vol. 47 (January-February 1969), pp. 152-66.

6. R. N. Shepard, "The Analysis of Proximities: Multidimensional Scaling with an Unknown Distance Function," Part One, *Psychometrika*, Vol. 27 (June, 1962), pp. 125-39.

7. K. A. Longman, "Marketing Science?" *Management Science*, Vol. 15 (February, 1969), pp. B-331-33.

8. R. P. McDonald, "A Unified Treatment of the Weighting Problem," *Psychometrika*, Vol. 33, (September, 1968), pp. 351-81.

9. See R.N. Shepard, "Some Principles and Prospects for the Spatial Representation of Behavioral Science Data," paper presented at the Irvine Conference on Nonmetric Scaling Methods, June 1969; also, P. E. Green and F. J. Carmone, "The Performance Structure of the Computer Market," *Economic and Business Bulletin*, Vol. 21 (Fall, 1968), pp. 1-11.

The author offers his views regarding consumer behavior research, the progress in this field, and the impact of developments on market researchers, marketing executives, company presidents, public policy makers, and basic researchers. In the author's opinion, the integration of these developments represents a major breakthrough in marketing with important implications for the 1970s.

5

buyer behavior and related technological advances

john a. howard

"How much more will I sell if I double my advertising?" the manager asks. "How should I analyze these facts?" the market researcher wonders. "Is the concept of a marketing information system a sensible one?" many people are asking. "How do I explain to this Congressional committee that advertising will not change basic eating habits?" a company president contemplates. "Should the government provide consumer information programs?" a Congressman poses to his colleagues. "What is the process by which a buyer's attitude toward the brand causes him to buy or not to buy the brand?" a university researcher muses. The solution to these and many other important marketing problems are greatly influenced by the state of our knowledge of buyer behavior.

The decade of the 1960s has been a time of rapid growth in consumer behavior research and practice. Drawing on the theoretical contributions and empirical evidence of behavioral scientists in other fields of endeavor as well as

Reprinted from the *Journal of Marketing*, published by the American Marketing Association, Volume 34, No. 1 (January 1970), pp. 18-21.

their own creative work, marketing scholars such as Bass, Bauer, Ferber, Frank, Green, Kassarjian, Kuehn, Massy, Myers, Nicosia, and Pessemier have made major contributions to our knowledge of the processes of consumer behavior.[1] Much of this work has already resulted in substantial improvements in marketing operations.

The quantity of facts and propositions on the buying behavior of consumers accumulated by companies and researchers is enormous. However, many of these bits of information or propositions stand alone and are used in the context of a specific decision situation. What is lacking in this approach is the leverage to be gained from a comprehensive structure which makes possible substantial predictions about consumer behavior. The need for such a structure to guide research and to improve marketing practice is obvious. It is this author's opinion that efforts in the next decade will be directed at the empirical validation and continuing refinement of such a theory.

Based upon the splendid work of the men cited above, a comprehensive theory of buyer behavior has been developed at the Columbia Business School.[2] This theory integrates relevant behavioral propositions from learning theory, cognitive theory, and exploratory behavior theory, with other ideas from the behavioral sciences and systems analysis. The theory posits the nature, relationships, operating characteristics, and flows that exist in the consumer decision-making process. Given a knowledge of exogenous variables, the theory relates outputs (behavior) to inputs (internal and external stimuli) through hypothetical constructs which describe the processes internal to the consumer.

Developments such as those noted result in an operational technology which will have major impact on the science and practice of marketing. This technology represents a systems view of the market, a view which distinguishes between the controllable and uncontrollable that play upon the buyer, and which brings relevant factors into a quantitative, coherent, unified, operational picture.

The immediate importance of this technology is confined to the narrow topic of buyer behavior and to the interests of the market researcher. It has also far-reaching implications for the marketing manager, developer of marketing information system, company president, public policy maker, and university researcher.

FOR COMPANY MARKET RESEARCHERS

Market researchers will collect less data but will derive more information from it. In applying these ideas they will contribute to the technology and to fitting the theory to their particular markets.

First, the question of which facts to collect will be more systematically decided; i.e., those facts specified by the theory. The researcher can be more discriminating instead of collecting facts which he hopes will be useful.

Second, collecting facts from the same person at two or more points in time — a panel — will be more common. Panels have rarely been efficiently used.[3]

Third, more systematic data storage procedures will be adopted. Casual observation indicates that research departments' ways of storing facts have been a serious handicap to the extensive analysis essential for adequate diagnoses. There will be, for example, greater accessibility to "marginals" which are both important in themselves and an essential link between the questionnaire and the analyses that follow.

Fourth, statistical techniques which incorporate causality and its increased explanatory power will be more widely applied. Multi-equation models will enable us to deal rigorously with the complexity that characterizes consumer behavior in response to marketing effort.[4] From each period's data, lagged correlation can obtain more specific information about the nature of the relations[5] so that in the next period the multi-equation model can be more precisely specified to the particular market. In this way, the researcher can increase the precision of his methods from period to period. A goal of this technological development will be to get the "noise" level down; i.e., to reduce the unexplained variance in the dependent variable. Experience indicates that the crucially important variables of advertising, price, and selling effort are most subject to the "noise" problem, which limits linking them directly or indirectly to purchasing behavior. This linking is essential if real progress is to be made. The theory is deliberately designed to focus upon the marketing or controllable variables.

Finally, in every analysis there is the task of interpretation and logical extension of the conclusions beyond the data. Systematic diagnosis is currently so severely handicapped that it is almost never done. Even if diagnosis were so highly valued that effort was assigned to it in the face of horrendous time pressures, the appropriate data are not identified, the constructs are not validated, and they are treated piecemeal instead of as parts of a system. If appropriate data were identified, adequate means of collection would not be employed because of the exaggerated fear of contamination. If appropriate data were collected, they would be stored in such a way as to render them inaccessible for further use. Assuming these data were readily accessible, current techniques of analysis would not be up to these demands. Finally, even if all prior conditions were not met, diagnosis would probably be stopped because by and large we have not had the necessary theory nor developed the practical skills to use it. This description is a bit harsh but not much.

FOR MARKETING MANAGERS

"Marketing manager" refers to anyone who is concerned not only with marketing, but also with the total marketing picture irrespective of his level in the corporate hierarchy. The technology will yield the marketing manager more information with less data because the system is more efficient. The systems view will lay before him a quantitative review of the consequences of his marketing alternatives.

This integrated, causal picture of the influences affecting the buyer will provide a powerful lever to the marketing manager's understanding of the market by giving him concepts which cut through the maze of complexity and which will encourage sharp diagnoses of marketing failures and successes. These diagnoses will be adding to his comprehension of the market, enable the marketing manager to build a marketing philosophy which aids imaginative innovation and prevents him from being misled by minor aberrations of the market. More logical and elaborate control — performance measures — will be built into his marketing procedures. His observations of and conclusions about the meaning of these measures will enormously strengthen the more systematic diagnoses that follow.

Also, the premises underlying his strategy will be more explicit and articulated. These will not only guide him but also will facilitate *communication*. In relations with superiors, such as in defending his marketing plan and its supporting budget, he will be better able to secure approval because management will be in a better position to comprehend and appreciate his arguments. For the same reason his relations with his peers will improve. His directions to his subordinates will be more explicit, better understood, and therefore better executed. Some of the differences in views about the probable effectiveness of different plans will diminish. The better communication will improve relations with the market researcher. Thus, the manager can assume leadership in identifying and designing the necessary studies instead of passively reacting to proposals from the market research department. The manager can usually better perform this role than the researcher because he is more aware of the appropriate corporate goals and of broad market issues.

A variety of operations research and management science techniques lie fallow because of the lack of behavioral input. The technology will provide this input for some of these techniques which will simplify the manager's decision making and planning. In fact, with the behavioral relations better understood, simpler optimizing techniques will suffice.

FOR MARKETING INFORMATION SYSTEMS

The new technology will facilitate the development of a marketing information system. Such a system typically implies a commitment to collect facts on the same variables for several periods of time. The theory will assist this task (1) by specifying the facts, and (2) by suggesting ways of collecting facts. Moreover, the statistical techniques could form an essential part of such a system.

The comments made here, however, provide no answer to the central question of whether the facts or derived information will "fit the manager's head." An important but subtle phenomenon is that each experienced executive has a "model" of his market which is not only unarticulated but usually totally subconscious. Yet his "model" strongly shapes which facts he considers relevant and how he interprets them. Until we have a better understanding of what these "models" are and how the manager processes his information, our capacity to build useful information systems will be limited. Some evidence suggests that in a given type of decision situation, managers use very similar information processing approaches[6], but more conclusive evidence is needed.

FOR COMPANY PRESIDENTS

The technology has implications both internally and externally for the president. Internally, the concepts will make it easier for him to communicate with his marketing personnel and because of the better communication his respect for them will be enhanced.

Equally, if not more important in this day of consumerism, company presidents will be better equipped to explain and often justify their practices to the public and to government agencies. In a recent Congressional hearing, the presidents of two large companies were asked by the chairman why they did not use their advertising funds to change the basic eating habits of the poverty stricken. The hearing transcript indicates that the presidents did not answer the question. These very able men knew intuitively that such an approach was impractical, but they lacked the concepts to adequately articulate their experientially-derived beliefs to those less versed in their particular domain of expertise. This is a problem that all experts face, but those in a theory-based field can usually perform far more effectively.

FOR PUBLIC POLICY MAKERS

Consumer interests have become a politically relevant issue, and the many able Congressmen who are directing their energies to formulating and passing appropriate legislation will find this technology useful in developing a multi-faceted, rational consumer policy. Concepts they need for comprehending the buyer will enable them to communicate more easily with the scientists in the field, with the philosophically-oriented individuals who relate the scientists' facts to social values, and with the special interest groups. The same technology but with a somewhat different orientation in study design and interpretation can provide specific data to guide their decisions. One of the questions is what kind of evidence will be accepted because there has been a growing tendency to accept statistical inference as evidence.

FOR UNIVERSITY RESEARCHERS

In a splendid recent review of a definitive book in market segmentation, Ferber states: "It (the book) suggests in analyzing consumer purchase behavior we are still at the stage where the principal difficulty is not how to answer the questions but rather how to formulate the questions and obtain meaningful data."[7] The new technology implies that we are now ready to move beyond this stage.

One of the major tasks is to acquire a fuller understanding of the relations among the variables in the system. O'Brien[8] and others have shown that this can be done. Some of the relations are not only nonlinear but nonmonotonic over the relevant range. Hence, some of the relations may be too subtle for field research and the laboratory will play an essential role. The new technology too will be facilitated because testing ideas that are part of a system instead of an isolated hypothesis gives leverage in the development of new knowledge: control is easier to build in and interpretation is much more productive.

Another area of research will be directed toward reducing the high level of "noise" found in the research to date so as to improve prediction. Research on the relations among the variables will help by making it possible to specify the system more precisely. The timing of changes in the variables deserves particular attention. Much of the research, however, will be methodological. For example, more refined measuring instruments and better ways of analyzing data to determine causality are essential.

CONCLUSION

Large accretions of knowledge — often breakthroughs — seem to occur when different and often apparently unrelated strands of development begin to merge. The new technology represents one such merger, in fact, a set of two mergers. First, there is the merger in psychology. Cognitive, learning and motivation theories have begun to come together. Second, two types of research in marketing that were largely separate in the period 1955 to 1965 — the quantitative and behavioral approaches to buyer behavior — have since joined into a single stream.

Another but different kind of merger appears imminent — the manager and the market. Management science and operations research have largely been concerned with normative models. However, these models made no pretense of representing the manager's thought processes. They were substitutes for these processes. One is beginning to observe that some of the highly competent people associated with this management science-operations research point of view are attempting to build formal models that are integrated into a manager's thinking processes, which currently seem rather idiosyncratic.[9] This view will merge rapidly with the new technology, and a most exciting period in marketing should be the consequence. The new technology can replace many of the subjective estimates with objective data. Thus, because a manager's underlying premises will be more accurate, his decision process will be more systematic.

Finally, and for the sake of perspective, we must remember that ultimately, as in all good science, the product of this merger will also carry the seeds of its own destruction and yield to still better structures than we are now capable of envisioning.

NOTES

1. The list is too extensive to document here; see J. A. Howard and J. N. Sheth, *The Theory of Buyer Behavior* (New York: John Wiley & Sons, Inc., 1969), pp. 421-429.

2. Same reference as note 1, 458. pp.

3. Winston L. Ring, "Adjustment for Measurement Effects in Panel Data From Test Markets," paper presented at 1968 Fall Conference, Denver, Colorado.

4. J. U. Farley and W. L. Ring, "An Empirical Test of the Howard-Sheth Model of Buyer Behavior," to appear in the proceedings of the Third Annual Conference on Buyer Behavior, Columbia University, May, 1969.

5. T. V. O'Brien, "Information Sensitivity and the Sequence of Psychological States in the Brand Choice Process," unpublished doctoral dissertation, Columbia University, 1969.

6. J.A. Howard and W.M. Morgenroth, "Information Processing Model of Executive Decision," *Management Science*, Vol. 31 (March, 1968), pp. 416-428, at pp. 425 and 426.

7. Robert Ferber in a review of William F. Massy, Ronald E. Frank, and Thomas M. Lodahl, *Purchasing Behavior and Personal Attributes, Journal of Economic Literature*, Vol. 7 (June, 1969), pp. 483-485, at p. 485.

8. T. V. O'Brien, same reference as note 5.

9. John D. C. Little, "Models and Managers: The Concept of a Decision Calculus," paper delivered before the symposium "Behavioral and Management Science in Marketing," University of Chicago, June 29 to July 1, 1969.

6

Trends expected to dominate industrial market-ing during the 1970s are discussed. These are: (1) increased marketing involvement in providing direction to R&D and acquisitions, (2) more formal marketing planning, (3) emphasis on systems, (4) better direction of line marketing activities, and (5) new directions in marketing research.

industrial marketing - trends and challenges

elmer p. lotshaw

A frequent, though not universal, characteristic of the industrial field is the dual problem of gaining acceptance of the marketing concept and its effective implementation. Peter Drucker's general description of the problem is partic-ularly relevant to the industrial marketing situation."Most businessmen," according to Drucker, "when they speak of 'Marketing' mean nothing more sophisticated than the systematic and purposeful organization of all the work that has to be done to sell a product, to deliver it to the customer, and to get paid for it."[1]

There are at least two reasons for the prevalence of this narrow view of marketing in the industrial field. First, the education and experience of

Reprinted from the *Journal of Marketing*, published by the American Marketing Association, Volume 34, No. 1 (January 1970), pp. 22-24.

management in industrial firms emphasizes technical and production considerations which result in a strong product orientation. In addition, much of the information industrial marketing managers have to work with is classified on the basis of product, process, or material rather than markets. Second, demand for industrial goods and services is derived demand, whereby creating a customer often involves satisfying the needs of direct *and* indirect customers. Thus, the distance between the industrial marketer and those who are the ultimate arbiters of his fate is often so great that relevant needs and competition are obscured. The ability to take effective action on indirect customers is further restrained by the conflicting interests of direct customers.

While these features may lead to the conclusion that industrial marketing has not progressed to the same extent as consumer marketing, there exists much further evidence to the contrary. There are few industrial executives who do not profess the importance of customer orientation and, while this does not guarantee either its understanding or implementation, it is a necessary first step. The greater use of product and market managers, establishment of new product and new venture organizations, and the more extensive use of marketing research are all further evidence of moves in this direction.

In this article the expected trends in industrial marketing will be developed and the necessary support from research and management will be outlined if the full potential of the constructive developments are to be realized.

EMERGING TRENDS IN INDUSTRIAL MARKETING

The 1970s promise to be a period of rapid economic growth and turbulent social change. Although this is hardly news, environmental conditions affect not only industrial markets and competition, but also the very conception and practice of industrial marketing. Four developments, which have significant current momentum, appear of particular importance and provide the basis for expected trends in industrial marketing. They are the significant changes in the pattern of final demands, the rapid pace of technological change, the increasing size and complexity of the industrial firm and its customers, and the growing impact of the computer and management sciences.

Five emerging trends seem to exist in industrial marketing practice within the broader context of environmental change. Some imply radical departures from present practices while others do not. However, all are related to the environmental setting of the 1970s. These emerging trends are (1) increased marketing involvement in providing direction to R&D and acquisitions; (2) increased use of formal marketing planning; (3) emphasis on systems in all aspects of marketing; (4) more effective coordination, direction, and control over line marketing activities; and (5) new directions in marketing research.

Marketing Involvement in R&D and Acquisitions

As the pace of change quickens, industrial firms increasingly look to R&D and acquisitions for growth and diversification. In theory, marketing plays a vital role in matters of diversification and expansion, but in practice there is often a striking lack of customer orientation in such matters.

The direction of R&D effort is presently dominated by those interested primarily in technology and engineering, with marketing playing an after-the-fact role of seeking markets for what laboratories create. Donald Schoen describes it as a rigid division of labor between those concerned with the need (i.e., marketing) and those concerned with technology.[2] The same applies to acquisitions where financial and legal considerations are often foremost, and matters of customer orientation are an afterthought.

Even where the importance of a customer orientation is recognized, its implementation is frequently deficient. Industrial marketing personnel who have worked principally with established products, are often ill-suited to work in this field. Also, those with the necessary talent and interest find limited assistance in the established theory and practice of marketing as it relates to R&D and acquisitions.

Considerable progress has been made in recent years in providing more and better marketing guidance and support in new product planning and development and in strategic planning activities. There is also the recognition that innovative new products are fragile commodities which seldom thrive, and much less prosper, within existing organizational structures. As a result, there has been increased experimentation with organizational forms that are more conducive to new ventures.[3]

Marketing research is also being called upon to play a more imaginative and constructive role in providing direction to R&D and acquisition activities. Rather than simply serving as "fact finders," market researchers are being called upon to devise means of discerning and interpreting trends. Symptomatic of this is the growing interest in the projection of economic trends and forecasting technology.

Increase in Formal Marketing Planning

The emphasis on marketing planning for industrial products appears destined to increase in the future, although it is currently not well established.[4] This will be due to the increase in size and complexity of large industrial organizations, and also because of the increased sophistication of the tools available to the market planner. More information, improved forecasting methods, and advances in decision theory and simulation techniques are but a few of the developments contributing to more effective planning of marketing activities.

If the businessman has lacked a customer orientation because of a narrow viewpoint of marketing, those responsible for marketing can be accused of contributing to this deficiency through their emphasis on volume rather than profit, and the lack of precision in setting marketing objectives. The expansion of formal marketing planning as a part of total business planning promises to assist in the correction of these deficiencies. The profit implications of marketing actions can be seen, and planning procedures provide a means of developing and implementing the precise objectives which are required in today's increasingly complex markets. Because of the proliferation of alternative products and services resulting from the rapid pace of technological change, the industrial firm can no longer be "all things to all people" but rather must increasingly focus on particular market segments in which the firm can achieve a competitive advantage.

There are many examples of this in the container and packaging fields as the result of development of new, and improvement of existing, materials. At one time soft drinks were packaged exclusively in glass, but now the market is shared with steel and aluminum cans. Paper cups and tubs that once were the only means of packaging a wide range of dairy products now find active competition from a variety of plastic materials.

Emphasis on Systems

There is a growing recognition in industrial marketing of the value of viewing marketing as a system, or, more properly, as a set of subsystems, and of the applicability of systems analysis to marketing problems. This is manifest among practitioners by emphasis on such things as "systems selling" and "marketing information systems," and the investigation of the applications of systems analysis to a wide range of problems by students of marketing.

While there have been some notable applications of systems analysis to industrial marketing, they have been isolated and sporadic.[5] The reasons for this include not only the frequent preference of marketing management for acting on the basis of inspiration rather than systematic analysis, but also data limitations and the problems of translating sophisticated models into operationally useful tools.

Despite these difficulties, it is reasonable to expect the emphasis on systems and systems analysis in industrial marketing to grow in the future for two reasons. First, the more promising and complex types of systems analysis will benefit from the increased availability of computer facilities. Second, the growing complexities of industrial markets due to technological change, and increasing competition from new product development and diversification, will provide an incentive to employ the techniques of systems analysis.

Coordination, Direction, and Control of Line Marketing Activities

More effective coordination, direction and control of line marketing activities – advertising, promotion, and sales – will be possible through greatly expanded market and sales analysis and the application of the behavioral sciences to industrial buying behavior.

Before the advent of the computer, a substantial gap existed between the conceptually possible and the operationally practical in both market and sales analysis. Timely information was difficult and costly to obtain, and analytical techniques had to be simple and straightforward. Sophisticated techniques can now be employed to forecast market potential and to distribute it on a geographical basis. In addition, company sales data can be quickly broken down by combinations of region and customer. As a result of these improved procedures, programs keyed to specific market objectives can become something more than pious assertions for annual sales meetings.

There has recently been a growing interest in gaining a better understanding of industrial buying influences and behavior, resulting not only from a growing appreciation of its complexity, but also from the realization of the promise it offers for the development of more purposeful marketing strategies.[6] While progress in this area is slow, evidence of the application of behavioral sciences to industrial marketing is beginning to appear.[7]

Marketing Research

Several trends are under way in industrial marketing research. There is the growing trend to think of marketing research in terms of marketing information and as part of a marketing information system. A complete system would involve information from company records (the traditional domain of sales analysis) and information about external conditions obtained through continuous marketing intelligence and special purpose project research. The approaches and obstacles to conception and development of a marketing intelligence system for an industrial firm have been described by Richard Pinkerton.[8] Traditional marketing research has focused on project research but is now being called upon to fulfill the broader function.[9]

Second, the analytical techniques employed in industrial marketing research are becoming progressively more complex and computer based. In the past, forecasting techniques were rudimentary, but now the application of econometric methods is gaining acceptance. The combination of econometric models of the economy and input-output analyses holds the promise of providing not only improved industry forecasts, but also a clearer understanding of the way in which changes in final demand and technology affect particular industries.

Third, the behavioral sciences will play an expanded role in marketing research. Historically, industrial marketing research has drawn more heavily on economics than on the behavioral sciences. While this emphasis will probably remain, the industrial researcher will find increasing application of the behavioral sciences to such things as the study of industrial buying behavior. There is also evidence of greater use of consumer research among industrial firms, particularly where the consumer is an important and influential indirect customer.

THE CHALLENGE TO RESEARCH AND MANAGEMENT

The promise offered by constructive developments now under way, and which are expected to dominate the 1970s, is by no means assured realization. Success depends upon the continuing contributions of research into industrial marketing and industrial marketing management. The plea for marketing R&D made by Theodore Levitt a number of years ago is as pertinent now as it was in 1962.[10] There is evidence of more work being done in corporations, universities, and by large independent research organizations, but the effort is still limited when compared to the needs of the field. Part of the problem is the lack of professional identity on the part of many in industrial marketing. This identity is a requisite for generating the sustained interest and support necessary to advance the science and practice of industrial marketing. This is where those with established professional interests — those in the academic world and in research — have a special responsibility. With conscious effort on their part, management support and interest will develop more quickly.

NOTES

1. Peter F. Drucker, *The Age of Discontinuity* (New York: Harper & Row, Publishers, 1968), p. 52.

2. Donald R. Schoen, "Managing Technological Innovation," *Harvard Business Review*, Vol. 47 (May-June, 1969), p. 164.

3. Donald A. Künstler, "Corporate New Product Venture Groups: The Need, the Responsibility, the Organization, the Leadership," in *Marketing and the New Science of Planning*, Robert L. King, ed. (Chicago, Ill.: American Marketing Association, 1968), pp. 449-454.

4. B. Charles Ames, "Marketing Planning for Industrial Products," *Harvard Business Review*, Vol. 46 (September-October, 1968), pp. 100-111.

5. Lee Adler, "Systems Approach to Marketing," *Harvard Business Review*, Vol. 45 (May-June, 1967), pp. 105-118.

6. Frederick E. Webster, Jr., "Industrial Buying Behavior: A State-of-the-Art Appraisal," in *Marketing in a Changing World,* Bernard A. Morin, ed. (Chicago, Ill.: American Marketing Association, June, 1969).

7. J. W. Thompson and W. W. Evans, "Behavioral Approach to Industrial Selling," *Harvard Business Review*, Vol. 47 (March-April, 1969), pp. 137-151.

8. Richard L. Pinkerton, "How to Develop a Marketing Information System," *Industrial Marketing*, Vol. 54 (April, 1969), pp. 41-44, and subsequent May, June, and July issues.

9. D. Cox and R. Good, "How to Build a Marketing Information System," *Harvard Business Review*, Vol. 45 (May-June, 1967), pp. 145-154.

10. Theodore Levitt, *Innovation in Marketing* (New York, McGraw-Hill Book Company, Inc., 1962).

7

*The impact of marketing on society is
increasing as marketing becomes broader in
function and scope. The social responsibilities
of marketing practitioners and educators are
also expanding. These responsibilities and
related dangers and opportunities for service to
society during the next decade are discussed in
this article.*

the growing
responsibilities of
marketing

robert j. lavidge

Marketing is being widely criticized for its failure to contribute more to the solution of social as well as economic problems. This is a new phenomenon. Until recently, the expectation that marketing should, or could, contribute to society in a significant way was held by few.

AREAS OF GROWING RESPONSIBILITY

As a result of changes in both marketing and its environment, it is likely that marketing people will have an expanding opportunity, *and responsibility*, to serve society during the 1970s. Examples relate to:

1. Consumerism.
2. The struggle of the poor for subsistence.

Reprinted from the *Journal of Marketing*, published by the American Marketing Association, Volume 34, No. 1 (January 1970), pp. 25-28.

3. The marketing of social and cultural services.
4. The day-to-day functioning of the economy.
5. The use and pollution of society's resources.

Efficiency and Social Justice

Marketing has a key role to play in the drive for increased efficiency within our economy. It also has an opportunity to play a significant role in the drive for social justice which is replacing the drive for security or affluence among many members of our society. There is a need for more vigorous action in both of these areas, efficiency and social justice. There also is a need, which is likely to grow during the 1970s, for truly responsible marketing practitioners and educators to vigorously resist action proposed in the cause of either efficiency or social justice which is likely to damage the economy and to do more harm than good in the long run.

Consumerism

The "social concerns" of marketing men and women have been focused primarily on sins of commission — especially on fraudulent or deceptive advertising, packaging, pricing, and credit practices. Although some progress is being made, marketing leaders must do a more effective job during the next decade, of identifying and reducing these practices. Moreover, history suggests that standards will be raised. Some practices which today are generally considered acceptable will gradually be viewed as unethical, then immoral, and will eventually be made illegal. Rather than resisting such changes, marketing leaders have a responsibility to provide intelligent guidance in bringing them about. But that is not enough.

"Consumerism" related to sins of omission, as well as those of commission, will continue to grow during the 1970s. There will be further expansion in the demand for more useful information to help consumers decide what to buy. Both consumers and marketers will increasingly be concerned with warranties and guaranties, with the handling of consumer complaints, and with product performance testing. Marketing men and women also have a responsibility to provide intelligent *leadership* in this movement rather than to stand aside, to cast themselves in the role of obstructionists, or to go to the other extreme and lend support to actions in the name of social justice which are well-intentioned but reflect a lack of understanding of marketing.

The Struggle for Subsistence

For much of the United States' population the struggle for material subsistence no longer provides direction. But the subsistence struggle will continue during the

1970s throughout most of the world. Socially concerned marketing men and women will not be content with their role in satisfying other needs while a large share of the world's population struggles with hunger and starvation. With vastly improved communications and increased education, we will become increasingly conscious of the unsatisfied needs of people in the economically underdeveloped nations of the world and in the poverty areas of the United States. Growing recognition of these unsatisfied needs will continue to provide ammunition to those who think of marketing activities primarily in terms of stimulating selfish desires rather than satisfying both physical and psychological needs. Marketing people must work simultaneously in cultures of affluence and of poverty during the 1970s. The dual culture problem will pose difficulties because actions appropriate for one culture could be very inappropriate for the other.

More than a decade ago, Peter Drucker noted marketing's opportunity in connection with the ". . . race between the promise of economic development and the threat of international world-wide class war. The economic development is the opportunity of this age. The class war is the danger. . . . And whether we shall realize the opportunity or succumb to danger will largely decide not only the economic future of this world — it may largely decide its spiritual, its intellectual, its political and its social future. Marketing is central in this new situation. For marketing is one of our most potent levers to convert the danger into the opportunity."[1]

Walt Rostow, while serving as chairman of the Policy Planning Council of the Department of State, told the members of the American Marketing Association: "I can tell you — without flattery — that I believe the skills this organization commands and represents are going to prove critical in the generation ahead to the development of countries and regions which contain a clear majority of the world's population."[2] The opportunity and the challenge about which Drucker and Rostow spoke remain to be met in the 1970s.

Social and Cultural Services

The coming decade also will witness an expansion of the role of marketing in connection with ". . . markets based on social concern, markets of the mind, and markets concerned with the development of people to the fullest extent of their capabilities."[3] Kotler and Levy have pointed out that the work of marketing people is contributing to the enrichment of human life through improved marketing of educational, health and religious services, better utilization of natural resources, and enjoyment of the fine arts.[4] Marketing people are helping the institutions which provide such social and cultural services to improve the tailoring of their services to their "customers" and to improve the "distribution," "pricing," and "promotion" of them.

The Day-to-day Functioning of the Economy

During the coming decade, marketing people will be responsible for helping bring material rewards to more members of society. Ethical, creative, efficient day-to-day marketing activities help the economy function more effectively to serve mankind. And, as William Lazer noted in a recent *Journal of Marketing* article, ". . . it is clear that when abundance prevails individuals and nations can afford to, and do, exercise increasing social concern."[5] It is when basic needs are met that men can turn attention to other needs and values, to the higher aspirations of mankind.[6] Nevertheless, it is likely that marketing people will find themselves increasingly under fire and working in what seems to be a hostile environment during the coming decade. There are likely to be continued increases in the importance of noneconomic values with growing resistance to competitive activity and resultant attacks on marketing. This may be intensified during the latter part of the decade by movement toward the checkless, cashless society. This could result in changes affecting marketing institutions which make the distribution revolution of the 1950s and '60s seem like a period of relative stability. The resultant dislocations may lead to attacks on marketing from within, as well as outside, the marketing community.

Marketing leaders will have to respond to broader attacks on marketing, as well as to issues related to consumerism. The marketing leaders who truly serve society will be those who search for, seize, and act on opportunities for improvement rather than merely defend themselves or take popular actions in the name of social justice regardless of their impact on society.

The Use and Pollution of Society's Resources

During the 1970s, marketing men and women will become increasingly concerned with the pollution of our air, water, and land (by others as well as by business firms). With greater emphasis on business ecology, there will be expanding opportunities for marketing people to assist in the adoption and use of new techniques for preserving and improving the environment.

Marketing teachers and practitioners have a responsibility to play a role in discouraging activities which are generally agreed to be harmful to society. During the next decade, marketing leaders also will be much more concerned with the impact of their actions and inactions on society in connection with a host of goods and services which cannot be clearly labeled either good or bad. The automobile, for example, has contributed enormously to economic development and to the enrichment of human life during the past half-century. But this contribution has not been without cost. The automobile is a major factor in the pollution of our air. It contributes to a staggering number of accidental deaths and injuries, and its land utilization cost has reached significant levels in many urban areas. Marketing people will become increasingly involved in questions of the type to which this inevitably leads. In evaluating the opportunities for new products and services, for example, the role of marketing people heretofore has focused largely on the question: Can it be sold? During the 1970s there will be increasing attention to: *Should* it be sold? Is it worth its cost to society?

THE CHANGING NATURE OF MARKETING

The areas in which marketing people can, and must, be of service to society have broadened. In addition, marketing's functions have been broadened. Marketing no longer can be defined adequately in terms of the activities involved in buying, selling, and transporting goods and services. The role of marketing in determining what goods and services will be offered now is also widely, although not universally, accepted. In addition, the coordinating and integrating roles of marketing are being given more attention. Increasingly, we are recognizing that the organization — business, educational, governmental, religious, or other — functions to serve people, its "customers." This, of course, is the essence of the "customer concept" (a term I prefer to "marketing concept").

Planning and the Systems Approach

The next decade is likely to witness a significant increase in the use of marketing planning, with emphasis on integrating coordinated marketing activities into the total fabric of the organization. There will be greater use of the systems approach, with planning based on the "customer concept" to solve both business and nonbusiness problems and to take advantage of opportunities for improvement. This offers much that is good. Marketing people must be prepared to play a central role in this important advance. But in doing so, they must be alert to the danger of introducing rigidities which strangle our economy in the interest of efficiency. The type of problem which can be created was illustrated by J. B. McKitterick in "Planning the Existential Society."[7] He cited the person who chose the right course in school in order to gain admission to the right college where he could study the right subjects and move on to the right graduate school in order to work in the right career — only to discover that it really wasn't the right career for him. This, of course, is an argument for liberal education. It also illustrates the danger of commitment to a plan or a system which does not provide for revision of goals and the roads to them in the light of changing objectives and changing environmental factors. This is a danger to which marketing leaders must be alert in the '70s as planning based on the customer concept is adopted more widely by both business and nonbusiness organizations.

Moreover, marketers must avoid letting their desire for more and better information on which to base their plans blind them to the dangers to society which lie in the *improper* use of data banks and new surveillance techniques. Marketing men and women have a clear responsibility to provide leadership in avoiding the threats that George Orwell envisioned in 1984,[8] as well as in making proper use of such tools.

CONCLUSIONS

Marketing practitioners and marketing educators who are sincerely concerned about the impact of their actions and inactions on society will have no shortage of challenges during the 1970s. Facing the kinds of changes which can be anticipated plus those we do not now foresee, marketing people will have an opportunity to make a significant contribution to society in their day-to-day activities — influencing decisions about what goods and services are offered, as well as helping bring them efficiently to their end users in a climate which is increasingly hostile to competitive activity and to many of the functions of marketing. At the same time, socially concerned marketing men and women will strive during the '70s: (1) to reduce marketing abuses and upgrade standards; (2) to help mitigate and ultimately eliminate the effects of poverty; (3) to aid in improving the marketing of social and cultural services; (4) to reduce the pollution of our environment; and (5) to develop international marketing institutions which will contribute to improved utilization and distribution of the world's resources and, hopefully, as a result, to world peace. In all these efforts, the truly responsible marketing leader will vigorously resist actions which would damage the economy that serves society imperfectly but increasingly well — whether those actions are proposed in the interests of profits, efficiency, or social justice.

It has been said that the "... social responsibilities of businessmen arise from the amount of social power they have. The idea that responsibility and power go hand-in-hand appears to be as old as civilization itself."[9] As it matures, as it broadens in function and scope, marketing will become increasingly relevant during the 1970s to the fulfillment of man. And as the impact of marketing on society increases, so does the social responsibility of marketing people.

NOTES

1. Peter F. Drucker, "Marketing and Economic Development," *Journal of Marketing*, Vol. XXII (January, 1958), pp. 252-259, at p. 254 and 255.

2. Walt W. Rostow, "The Concept of a National Market and its Economics Growth Implications," in *Marketing and Economic Development*, Peter D. Bennett, ed. (Chicago, Ill.: American Marketing Association, September, 1965), pp. 11-20, at p. 11.

3. William Lazer, "Marketing's Changing Social Relationships," *Journal of Marketing*, Vol. 33 (January, 1969), pp. 3-9, at p. 4

4. Philip Kotler and Sidney J. Levy, "Broadening the Concept of Marketing," *Journal of Marketing*, Vol. 33 (January, 1969), pp. 10-15, at p. 10

5. Same reference as footnote 3, at p. 6.

6. A. H. Maslow, *Motivation and Personality (New York: Harper and Row, 1954).*

7. J. B. McKitterick, "Planning the Existential Society," in *Marketing and the New Science of Planning*, Robert L. King, ed. (Chicago, Ill.: American Marketing Association, August, 1968), pp. 3-9, at p. 3.

8. George Orwell, *1984* (New York: Harcourt, Brace & World, Inc., 1949).

9. Keith Davis, "Understanding the Social Responsibility Puzzle," *Business Horizons*, Vol. 10 (Winter, 1967), pp. 45-50, at p. 48.

What forces are bringing about changes in marketing? What are the likely effects of these changes? A synthesis of the changes in store for marketing in the 1970s is provided in this capstone article of the special Journal of Marketing symposium.

8

the expanding role of marketing in the 1970's

robert ferber

The accelerated change projected for the 1970s will provide additional impetus to the changes taking place in the field of marketing. Integration and diversification are likely to be the key words in a world in which marketing will be assuming increasing importance. In summary, this is what the foregoing papers in this special *Journal of Marketing* symposium seem to be saying.

THE CAUSES OF CHANGE

The forces bringing about these changes in the marketing field are well summarized by Buzzell and Lotshaw for the business sector and by Lavidge for the public sector. On the business side, we have the increasing size and

Reprinted from the *Journal of Marketing*, published by the American Marketing Association, Volume 34, No. 1 (January 1970), pp. 29-30.

complexity of business firms, stimulated by the worldwide growth in population and in purchasing power. Reinforcing these forces is the growth in communications, notably television, and the virtually universal attempts to increase literacy – characteristics most conducive to the development of multinational corporations and to corporate growth.

Still another factor stimulating change is the increasing pressure under which business firms are operating to develop and expand their operations. Markets and sales are being recognized for the longer run to be more important than profit maximization. The result is that a growing emphasis is placed on how to expand existing markets and how to develop new ones. The competitive race is one in which corporations have to keep moving ahead to hold a present position. Market-oriented companies are the ones most likely to pull ahead in this race; hence the growing emphasis on marketing in corporate planning.

Accelerating technology acts both as a cause and as an effect of marketing change. Lotshaw noted that marketing's casual role is reflected in the manner in which technology has accelerated the development of new products and the demise of old ones. It is further reflected in the manner in which technology has helped bring about a largely service economy in this country. Technology has revolutionized marketing through the development of the computer which is leading to the development of much more sophisticated methods of marketing analysis. These impacts are described very well by Kotler and Green.

While marketing has been assuming a more crucial role in determining the success of the business enterprise, it has also been coming to the fore in matters of public policy. This is due in part to the increasingly serious nature of domestic problems which, as Lavidge notes, are closely related to marketing. This is also due in part to the growing recognition that many of the social and public policy problems of our, and other, societies are especially amenable to solution through the use of marketing techniques.

Business leaders are becoming increasingly concerned with this problem. They recognize that civil riots and disruption of everyday activities can result in additional expenses and losses for their own operations. It is, therefore, not surprising that marketing and business executives are giving more attention to applying the methods they use in solving their marketing problems to those of improving the social welfare.

THE EFFECTS OF CHANGE

The foregoing trends suggest that marketing activities in the 1970s are likely to become both more integrated and more diversified when combined with the recent developments in the field of marketing itself (such as those relating to use of computers, systems analysis, and development of more formal models of decision making). Initially, these trends seem contradictory, but this apparent contradiction disappears when we consider what is meant by these terms.

Integration

Marketing will become more integrated in at least three ways. First, marketing functions will become more integrated with each other and with the other functions of the business enterprise. Thus, research is likely to be more closely tied with current operations as well as with accounting as part of an information system for the firm. The growth of vertical marketing structures, as explained by Davidson, will contribute to integration as will the increasing popularity of the systems approach to the analysis of marketing and business problems. Lotshaw notes that dealing with one type of marketing problem in large business enterprises frequently involves consideration of other marketing and business functions. This type of functional interaction serves to further stimulate the development of a more integrated approach to the analysis of marketing problems.

A second form of integration is that of marketing theory with practice. This is best illustrated in the article by Howard, which offers the promise of a comprehensive theory to interrelate the various aspects of buyer behavior. This theory will provide an operational model for evaluating the effects of changes in particular types of business policy on buyer behavior. Theories of this type will be increasingly sought and utilized in the coming decade.

Green discusses a similar approach. He stresses the growing emphasis upon obtaining more realistic models of marketing behavior and of obtaining operational measures for use in conjunction with these models. The growing power of the computer, and especially of time sharing systems, as described by Kotler, indicates that decision-making models formerly considered impractical because of their complexity will be made operational in the 1970s. As Green so aptly stresses, people are becoming increasingly aware that the world is multidimensional, and marketing is no exception.

A third facet of integration relates to the more unified approach likely to be taken in the 1970s toward the solution of marketing problems. To say as in the past that there are behavioralists and that there are quantitative people in marketing is no longer meaningful. Behavioral and quantitative approaches complement each other. Neither is likely to be of much use by itself. The solution of marketing problems in the 1970s will increasingly be attained through an integrated framework, probably through the use of more complex and much more realistic models of human behavior.

Much the same is true in the field of corporate organization, as noted by Buzzell. The increasing complexity of the modern corporation means that the different parts of the corporation will have to be linked with each other for maximum efficiency in more formal planning systems. Such systems will have to incorporate not only all the usual functions of marketing but many other functions as well.

Diversification

Diversification also will characterize marketing in at least three ways in the 1970s. One way will be through the growing decentralization of corporate operations. Decentralization as a change factor is noted by Buzzell for corporate management and by Davidson for the field of distribution. Greater responsibility will be delegated to individual units. At the same time these units will comprise part of a larger system in accordance with a carefully worked out model, or plan, designed for linking the operations of these different units.

Market segmentation represents still another form of diversification. Numerous studies have indicated that the customers for a particular product can be segmented into groups with different desires. As a result, a promising avenue for future growth is to determine the preferences for variants of a product by different groups and to develop new forms of the product to meet these needs.

Specification of market segments and development of appropriate product lines present unusual opportunities for corporate growth. This is true not only for a very wealthy country such as the United States but also for less developed countries. In developing countries, cultural differences rather than occupational or educational differences seem to become paramount. The delineation of such market segments and their incorporation in marketing strategy will be one of the major tasks of marketing in the 1970s.

Third, but by no means last, will be the diversification of marketing activities to the social and the public policy fields. As Lavidge points out, marketing has a major role to play in the enrichment of human life. This is particularly the case in an economy such as ours where production capabilities are virtually unlimited. The major problem in our society is how to design and distribute goods and services to meet the needs of the people, and how to help people obtain the means to acquire these goods and services. With government having become the biggest business of all, it is virtually a truism that the marketing techniques that have proven so successful in the business sector are equally applicable to solving many of the problems of society.

All things considered, the overall picture is for marketing to expand its scope of operations and to further develop its present procedures and techniques. Increased use will be made of the sophisticated tools and technology now available and still to come. It is clear that both in the public and private sectors, marketing will play an increasingly important role in the 1970s. As marketing analysts and executives, we will have to expand and broaden our horizons to make full use of these opportunities.

II

Consumers:

As Individuals
and in Groups

Final consumers are the subject of this section. Which type of utilities do they want, and how and why do they behave as they do in response to promotional effort? The analytical tools necessary to answer these questions derive principally from the behavioral sciences. Initially, each of the behavioral sciences was considered to be a discrete function of the marketing process. At present, however, they are becoming more integrated, more interrelated, and more fully coordinated into a single body of investigative knowledge which focuses on people.

Whereas psychologists analyze the reactions of individuals to various stimuli, sociologists examine group situations, physical anthropologists deal in body measurements, and cultural anthropologists probe taboos and prohibitions; it is the interrelation of people as individuals and as members of the various group within different cultures that is important to the marketer. Since the marketer makes use of the other disciplines, the tools of each discipline give him added insight into his own field.

The selected readings which follow illustrate the contributions of different behavioral sciences to marketing. They demonstrate interrelationships and show how individual theories are connected to other theories. For example, motivation research, one of marketing's tools, is often performed by clinical psychologists, yet it has been argued that it is within the realm of applied cultural anthropology.

Like marketing theories, consumer variables generally cannot be held constant; people often cannot or will not give truthful answers. Seldom, as in pupillometrics, can reactions be measured with laboratory precision. The selections here represent some of the more valuable efforts to observe trends and patterns as they have developed and have become integrated with the various behavioral areas.

Psychological classifications have the bonus of increasing our understanding of the market situation. And they directly identify needs, that a particular brand or product could be geared to satisfy.

9

psychological classification

j. a. lunn

INTRODUCTION – THE NEED FOR NEW CLASSIFICATIONS

In both marketing and advertising strategy, there is a growing emphasis on the need for market segmentation. Researchers are not merely being asked such questions as, "How many people bought our product last week?" or "What do people think of our product vis-á-vis competitors'?"

Increasingly, they are also being asked, "What *kind* of people are our heavy buyers, how do they differ from light buyers, from nonbuyers?" or "Who are the best prospects?"

The assumption made is that people are not all equally likely to buy a given brand or product. Needs and circumstances differ, and, with them, so do purchasing patterns. Granted this assumption, it may be unwise to aim a product at the total population. The initial success of a new launch or the continuing success of a long-established brand, may hinge upon the precise identification of the best *target subgroup* – a group of people whose needs and circumstances predispose them towards purchase of the product.

Reported from *Commentary*: the Journal of the British Market Research Society, July 1966, pp. 161-73, by permission of the publisher.

For instance, it might be important to identify our target group for product testing, so that their preferences are not swamped by the irrelevant, possibly misleading, preferences of people for whom this kind of product has little appeal. The same considerations apply throughout the research process, for example in brand-image research, copy testing, and media allocation.

This growing wish to focus attention on specific population subgroups has led to a critical re-examination of market research tools for this purpose — that is upon the standard repertoire of consumer classifications. For years we have analyzed our data by such characteristics as age, social class, region, household size. These so-called demographic variables have an obvious value. They identify important differences in peoples' circumstances, which are often reflected in their buying behavior. For example, larger households often buy more and different kinds of products than smaller households; sheer size of disposable income obviously sets certain constraints on purchasing.

However, it is becoming increasingly realized that demographic classifications alone are inadequate for segmentation. Some of their limitations may be summarized as follows:

1. People from different demographic groups often show similar purchasing behavior;

2. People from the same demographic groups — people with similar incomes, household sizes, and the like — often show very different purchasing behavior;

3. Even where demographic classifications are closely related to buying, they may tell only one part of the story. Jaguar cars may be bought mainly by ABs But only by a small proportion of ABs. We may still wish to know what distinguishes the ABs who buy Jaguars from those ABs who do not;

4. Sometimes, a demographic variable is an indirect representation of an underlying need. For example, older people might be more prone to buy our product because they tend to be more obsessional, and the product appeals to more obsessional people. But there may be younger people — although proportionally fewer of them — who are just as obsessional, and who also buy the product. In such cases it would be preferable to classify directly by "obsessionalism" than indirectly by age.

PSYCHOLOGICAL CLASSIFICATION BY PERSONALITY TESTS

Consequently, a demand has arisen for new forms of classification, both to provide a sharper description of present and potential buyers and at the same time, to increase our understanding of the market situation. And considerable interest has been taken in the possibilities of classification by psychological characteristics.

A number of published attempts have been made to examine these possibilities. Probably the best known in the U.K. is *The Londoner.* [1] These studies have taken advantage of the progress made in both academic and applied fields of psychology in the investigation of personality.

This progress is broadly of two kinds. Firstly, much work has been done in mapping out the basic structure of personality; that is, in mapping out the main predispositions that people have to consistently think, feel, and behave in certain ways. Here the psychologist is attempting to do systematically what all of us do habitually in everyday life, when we categorize our friends, acquaintances, or casual encounters — "She is rather a feckless woman," "He is a rather dominant individual," and so forth.

Secondly, psychologists have devoted considerable attention to devising measuring instruments for these personality characteristics. Just as there are tests for measuring intelligence, likewise there are personality tests, which enable one to assess the extent to which a person is dominant or submissive, anxious or relatively stable, and so on. Many of these personality tests have been successful for specific practical purposes: for example, in helping clinical psychologists in the diagnosis of the mentally ill, in helping industrial psychologists to identify the kind of people who are likely to be successful in a given job.[2]

To put it briefly, the approach adopted in *The Londoner* and similar studies has been to take over a number of these personality tests and to relate peoples' scores on them to their behavior as consumers, and, in some studies, to their reading and viewing habits as well.

The results have been largely disappointing. Personality tests have shown much less correlation with consumer behavior than was hoped for. Little has been added to the picture provided by demographic variables.

Does this mean that the search for psychological classifications is a dead end? Not at all. But it does suggest the need for a rather different approach.

In these studies, as far as I know, the psychological tests were adopted without any hypothesis as to their relevance to consumer behavior. They were simply tried out. So perhaps it is not so surprising that they did not work, especially when it is considered that they were designed for use in totally different contexts (for example, clinical psychology), and often developed on highly literate sections of the population. Moreover, the personality characteristics in question have usually been of a very general nature, applying to a wide span of human behavior.

This raises a general point that has a particular application to consumer classification. Market research has borrowed methods and findings from a number of disciplines, psychology included. And fruitfully. But it is dangerous to assume that we can always borrow. Our particular problems often require special tools.

The implication of this is that we should not necessarily rely upon classifications that have been successful in other fields. We should be prepared to develop our own. And I should now like to discuss briefly some current development work.

AN ALTERNATIVE APPROACH – ATTITUDE CLASSIFICATIONS

Our basic approach is not to try to fit the consumer to a predetermined set of classifications; it is rather to derive new classifications from a study of the consumer. We have not ruled out the possibility that, for some product fields, very general personality characteristics may be important. But they must be shown to be important. And we expect that the most valuable characteristics will be found close to the context of product usage and purchase – for example, in terms of basic attitudes to such tasks as cooking, housework, and shopping.

We have been encouraged in this approach by the increasingly successful application of psychological methods to consumer research. Firstly, there has been the undoubted success of many exploratory motivation-research studies, using group discussions, extended interviews, and projective tests, in throwing light upon fundamental attitudes critical to consumer choice. Secondly, the development of techniques such as attitude scaling makes it possible to measure with some precision the extent to which people hold these attitudes.

In seeking new classifications we have drawn upon both the former "motivational" techniques and the latter "psychometric" ones.

How does this approach work out in practice? Let me illustrate how we developed new classifications for a product field I will call S (Fig. 1). In this study we used what might be called the criterion group approach – that is, we began by identifying groups with known different purchasing patterns, and then sought the psychological characteristics that differentiated between them. This, we felt, would give us the maximum chance of finding relevant classifications.

The first step was to conduct one hundred short interviews, in order to identify people with different purchasing patterns for product S: that is, to establish the criterion groups we want to distinguish between.

In stage II we conducted extended interviews with thirty of these people, who could be broadly categorized as heavy, medium, and light buyers of S. The psychologists conducting the interviews thoroughly explored a wide spectrum of the respondents' attitudes, ranging from relatively detailed opinions about the product in question, to their self-image as cook, housewife, and mother. As a result, we obtained fairly comprehensive portraits of each respondent.

The verbatim transcripts of the interviews were searched for evidence of psychological – or any other – characteristics that appeared to differentiate the three groups of buyers.

Our next task (*stages III, IV, and V*) was to develop measuring instruments for each of the characteristics thought to be important.

TO DEVELOP PSYCHOLOGICAL CLASSIFICATIONS FOR PRODUCT 'S'

Stage I   100 SHORT INTERVIEWS
                            to establish use and purchase of 'S'

Stage II   30 EXTENDED INTERVIEWS

10 HIGH   *10 MEDIUM*   *10 LOW*
BUYERS   +   *BUYERS*   +   *BUYERS*
OF 'S'   *OF 'S'*   *OF 'S'*

                    to derive distinguishing psychological characteristics

Stage III   SELECTION OF STATEMENTS FOR ATTITUDE SCALES
                    for measurement of these characteristics

Stage IV   SCALE DEVELOPMENT SURVEY
                                 (300 interviews)

Stage V   ATTITUDE SCALING

Stage VI   SCALE VALIDATION SURVEY
                                 (1000 interviews)

Figure 1. Stages of research

Now, there are several ways in which this could be approached, each with their respective advantages and disadvantages. For market research purposes, we clearly require a technique which, while sound and reliable, is at the same time quick and easy to administer by normal market research interviewers, and is not threatening or annoying to respondents. What we require, if at all possible, is something short that can be added to routine survey questionnaires.

Probably the best approach for our purposes is to develop short sets of statements that express the attitude in question, and to ask respondents to agree or disagree with these statements: that is, to develop "attitude tests."

At stage III, firstly, we attempted to clarify our ideas about psychological characteristics that appeared to be important. Then, for each characteristic, we drew up a set of statements: where appropriate, we selected phrases and expressions used by housewives in the extended interviews (*stage II*).

At stage IV, a questionnaire was given to a representative sample of 300 housewives who indicated their agreement or disagreement to the total set of statements. A five-point measure of agreement was used, ranging from strongly agree to strongly disagree.

At stage V, we built our measuring instruments.

Firstly, we factor analyzed all responses to all statements. This process explored the main ways in which the statements grouped together: it enabled us to check our original hypothesis about the attitude dimensions we were trying to measure.[3] For a comprehensive account of factor analysis, see Harman.[4]

Secondly, we applied scaling techniques to each set of statements thought to express a separate attitude dimension, to establish whether or not these statements were all measuring one and only one dimension. Details of these techniques are beyond the scope of this paper. Briefly, we conducted principal component analyses on the matrix of intercorrelations between the statements in each set using the ratio of the first two latent roots as our criterion of scalability; we also tried to obtain cumulative scales, using the Guttman scalogram method. (A useful short description of some scaling techniques is given in a Market Research Society publication.[5] There is, in fact, scope for empirical work to determine which of several possible techniques are most suitable for market research problems and conditions).

Finally came *stage VI* where, in a separate survey, we examined the usefulness of the developed scales, by relating scores on them to different patterns of buying and usage.

Before leaving this account of methodology, I should make two points:

a. This research method will obviously be modified to suit each particular problem, for example, we may select our criterion group sample at *stage I* according to their *manner of usage*, or their brand buying. Or we may require two or more scale-development stages before we are satisfied with the attitude tests, and possibly more than one stage of explanatory interviewing.

b. Where possible we replicate our findings; that is, using additional samples, we check both on the uni-dimensionality of the scales, and on their correlations with consumer behavior.

RESULTS

What kind of results are we obtaining? I shall briefly discuss some of these under two headings, firstly, the new classifications themselves, and secondly, their relationships with consumer behavior.

The New Classifications Themselves

We have developed a number of new attitude classifications. Some of these have been very specific, and mainly applicable to the product field in question. Others, however, have been of a more general nature, clearly applicable to a much wider span of consumer behavior. These latter we regard as the first steps towards our final objective; namely, the establishment of a small repertoire of consumer personality scales, each of proven value to several product fields.

I shall now outline some of these more general dimensions under three headings.

a. Firstly, the area of *economy*. Despite a certain amount of initial scepticism we have found it possible to develop measures reflecting a concern with economy that applies to a wide range of purchases. This does appear to be a general housewife characteristic. What we have found, however, is that there are at least two distinct facets between which it is important to distinguish. Firstly, there is what we call "economy-mindedness" − the tendency to buy cheap rather than expensive goods, to keep within a strict housekeeping limit, to deny oneself luxuries. This is quite different from what we call "bargain-seeking," which reflects the satisfaction of saving a few pennies by shopping carefully and comparing prices, and the relish of hunting for bargains. One way of putting the distinction is that whereas the economy-minded housewife abhors extravagance, the bargain-conscious woman may welcome it: but she looks for the cheapest shop to be extravagant in.

We have checked on this distinction a number of times, and found the two scales to have a quite distinct pattern of correlates. For example, the more *economy-minded* housewives tend to come from the lower social classes, but not from any particular family-size group. However, the more *bargain-seeking* housewives are found amongst all social classes, but tend to come from larger households. The two scales also identify separate patterns of consumer behavior.

b. Another area is that of *experimentalism*, which may be defined as a willingness to and relish in buying new and different things. This again appears to be a very general characteristic. It does, however, have two quite distinct opposites. On the one hand are the rigid people who have an almost compulsive need to do and buy the same kind of things: on the other hand are the people who are afraid to buy something new or different, unless, say, it has been strongly recommended, and who are anxious in case a purchase turns out to be a mistake.

c. A third and quite different area is *conservatism*. Here we mean the people who have relatively old-fashioned tastes and habits. For example, in housework they relish doing things by hand, and enjoy cleaning and polishing the hard way; they abhor quick, easy methods and labor-saving devices: in cooking, they prefer the traditional methods and recipes.

Some general points about these classifications. So, in the areas I have quoted, we have one scale for conservatism, a choice of two for economy, and of three for experimentalism. We prefer to have one scale only for each area. We wish to avoid accumulating a plethora of different scales. But more than one may be necessary where there are differences of meaning, which relate to different aspects of consumer behavior. Our approach is to begin with relatively specific scales that discriminate sharply with a narrow range of behavior, and, by experience, to reduce these to a smaller subset of more general but equally predictive scales.

Each scale consists of a set of statements. The number of statements required is largely a function of the average level of correlations between them. For each scale, we try to obtain between six and ten well-correlated items. To measure the attitude on a particular occasion we may use a subset of these items, depending on how much precision we require from our measurement.

Our interpretations of the scales are based largely on the statements that comprise them. But we do not rely entirely on this "face validity." We also see with what other attitudes and with what aspects of behavior the scale is correlated. And from our use of a scale over a number of studies, we hope to accumulate a rich collection of ways in which high-scale scorers differ from low-scale scorers.

This extra information also helps us to give clearer descriptions to copy writers about the nature of the target group at which they are aiming.

How Do the New Classifications Relate to Consumer Behavior?

Our first results have been very encouraging. We are identifying pronounced differences in patterns of usage and purchase for both products and brands.

I have only space for a few illustrations, and have chosen examples for scales mentioned in the previous section. I am unable in this paper to specify product fields.

Example 1 – conservatism. The *conservatism* scale was tried in a field where there are two distinct types of product: *A* requires considerable effort in its usage, whereas *B* is very much a labor-saving product.

Analyses by demographic breakdowns had shown no significant discrimination between regular buyers of the two products: analysis by conservatism showed quite marked discrimination (Fig. 2).

Example 2 – experimentalism. My second example is from a product field of fairly recent origin, but in which a high proportion of housewives purchase. There is a slight tendency for buying to vary with age and social class. But much sharper relationships were found between heaviness of buying and each of four psychological classifications. The most pronounced of these was experimentalism.

Analysis by product *type* proved even more illuminating. In Fig. 3, type *A* is a fairly recent launch, type *B* one of the earliest launches. It can be seen that *A* is achieving its sales chiefly to keen experimentalists. However, a disinclination to be experimental is no longer a barrier to buying *B*.

Incidentally, some analyses currently being performed are confirming the general value of the experimentalism scale. High experimentalists show much more brand-switching and, correspondingly, less brand-loyalty over a range of product fields. Moreover, there are indications that this scale may help to identify "new product buyers" or even "innovators,"[6] groups whose possible existence has intrigued market researchers for some time. (See, for instance, the paper given by John Clemens at the 1963 M.R.S. Annual Conference.[7])

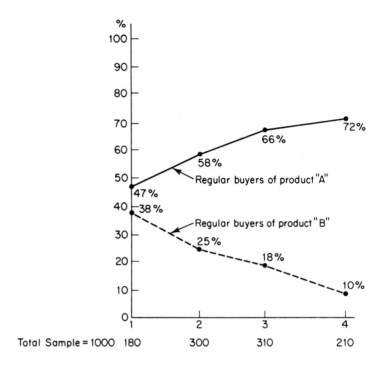

Figure 2. Score on conservatism scale

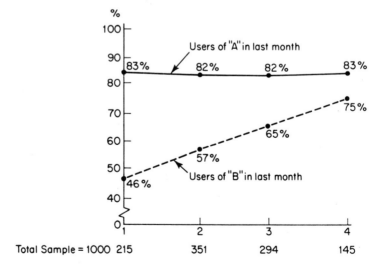

Figure 3. Score on experimentalism scale

Example 3 – "economy." The first two examples showed simple relationships between a single scale on the one hand and a measure of consumer behavior on the other. Clearly, the situation is more complex than this. And to give a more precise and, therefore, valuable picture, we need to interrelate those classifications, psychological, demographic, or whatever, that are important for the aspect of consumer behavior under study.

The techniques for doing this are beyond the scope of this paper. Suffice it to say that markets are not necessarily homogeneous: the variables critical to buying do not necessarily apply right across the market. It may be that the market is rather composed of a set of subgroups, each comprising a separate set of variables.

We are currently examining possible segmentation techniques which would reveal anew such heterogeneity. The example shown in Fig. 4 is for a product field where demographic variables do in fact correlate highly with purchasing.

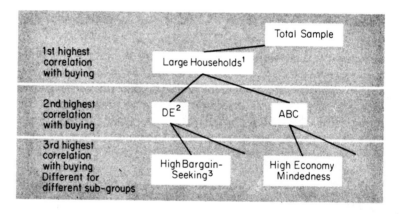

Figure 4. Segmentation of market into sub-groups in terms of correlation with heaviness of buying

In this case all variables were dichotomised, and their correlations with heaviness of buying examined in a series of stages. The highest single correlation was household size, large households being the heaviest buyers. *Within large households,* the next test correlate was social class, proportionally more *DE*s than *ABC*s being heavy buyers.

At a *third level of segmentation*, the highest correlate differed, according to the subgroup. Amongst *DE* large households, the highest correlation with buying was *bargain-seeking consciousness*, among *ABC* large households, it was *economy-mindedness*.

The increasing precision gained from this kind of analysis can be seen from the following measures:

Proportion of heavy buyers among subgroup

Large households	41%
DE large households	54%
High bargain-seeking *DE* large households	73%

VALUE FOR MARKETING AND ADVERTISING

The kind of classifications I have discussed are quantitative: they enable us to divide people into groups in terms of their different positions along the dimensions concerned. And to a large extent they can be used throughout the market research process in the same way as demographic classifications.

Assume we have shown, or have reason to believe, that experimentalism is a key variable for our brand: our target group lies mainly among high experimentalists. We might select our sample for product testing and copy testing chiefly from among the high-priority group: we might use experi-mentalism as a breakdown in usership and brand-image studies: and, if high experimentalists are shown to have particular viewing or reading habits, we might give media instructions accordingly.

Moreover, being expressed in terms of motivations, psychological classifica-tions increase our understanding of the market and suggest marketing action. Take the example shown in Fig. 2. Here, it seems that there are two distinct submarkets separately catered for by product types *A* and *B*. If our brand was an *A* type, we would focus attention upon the more conservative groups and stress one set of product benefits; if it was a *B* type, we would focus attention upon the least conservative groups and stress a quite different set of benefits. (There might, of course, be benfits common to the two types.)

At the same time, we might obtain leads for pack design; or even for a new or modified product to satisfy needs not at present fully catered for. We might also obtain leads for distribution, if we discovered that our target group say high conservatives favored a particular type of outlet, say counter-service stores.

This greater understanding of the consumer not only helps marketing decisions: it also helps advertising men, and in broadly two ways.

Firstly, we are able to provide copywriters with rich and detailed portraits of the kind of people on whom they should focus their advertising − and of the most persuasive copy themes, either to reinforce existing buyers or to win over fresh buyers.

Secondly, where psychological target groups can be shown to have particular viewing, reading, even travelling patterns, there may be an opportunity for more efficient media allocation.

CONCLUSIONS

The search for psychological classifications is a logical extension of our interest in, say, demographic classifications: we are looking for ways of pin-pointing crucial target subgroups.

Psychological classifications have the bonus of increasing our understanding of the market situation. And they directly identify needs, that a particular brand or product could be geared to satisfy.

It is more fruitful to develop our own classifications based upon an understanding of the consumer, rather than look for pre-existing classifications developed in other contexts.

It may be preferable to begin with relatively specific dimensions of proven discriminatory power in particular product fields. In time we may be able to reduce these to a smaller number of "consumer personality traits," more general dimensions, which are reflected in many aspects of consumer behavior.

I do not wish to imply that psychological classifications represent the only way ahead. Nor that the approach I have outlined is the best or the only one. But it is, I believe, a valuable approach that is already starting to pay dividends.

NOTES

1. Associated-Rediffusion, *The Londoner*, 1961.
2. There are in fact, a number of ways of trying to measure personality. A valuable critical survey can be found in P. E. Vernon, *Personality Assessment: A Critical Survey* (London: Methuen, 1964). It should be remembered that Vernon is here discussing personality measurement from the standpoint of placing *individuals*, whereas in market research our concern is to make comparison between *groups*. And under conditions more difficult than the psychologist encounters in other fields.
3. Sometimes two attitude dimensions thought to be separate, merge into a common dimension, or one hypothesized dimension may be shown to contain two clearly distinct dimensions. An example of the latter was for the "economy" area, further described below, where "economy-mindedness" and "bargain consciousness" emerged (from a common set of statements) as two clear groupings.
4. H. Harman, *Modern Factor Analysis* (Chicago: University of Chicago Press, 1960).
5. The British Market Research Society, "Attitude Scaling," *Publication* # 4 (London: The Oakland Press, 1960).
6. The assumption is sometimes made that it is important, when launching a new product, to ensure that it appeals to a group of "innovators," at once experimental and

influential whose acceptance of the product will do much to ensure its success. And that, consequently, we should focus upon them in all the research stages preparatory to the launch of a new brand or product. There may be a lot in this. But there are a number of other considerations. For instance, unless the product also satisfies some specific additional need, psychological or physical, the innovators, while happy to give it a trial will quickly transfer their allegiance elsewhere. Indeed, there may be a group of extreme experimentalists — "try anything onceers" — whose purchasing is so fickle and changeable that their opinions should be isolated in new product research in order to be ignored: at least in the field of frequently purchased consumer expendables.

7. J. Clemens, "New Product Buyers," in *New Development in Research* (London: The British Market Research Society, 1963).

A new device that measures changes in pupil diameter while subjects view advertisements, packages, etc., offers promise of becoming a powerful tool for studying the interest-arousing qualities of stimuli. Encouraging evidence of the reliability and validity of this device has been found in a series of studies – two of which are described in this article.

10

some applications of pupil measurement

herbert e. krugman*

In 1960, Hess and Polt [1] reported finding a relationship between pupil dilation and the interest value of visual stimuli. Since then, over seventy studies utilizing measurement of changes in pupil diameter have been conducted by Marplan personnel on problems involving the evaluation of advertising materials, packages and products. These studies have led to a growing conviction that in many areas of human behavior one might make better predictions of behavior from pupil responses than from verbal or opinion data. The purpose of this report is to provide a brief review of the concepts involved, method of measurement, measurement goals, problems of data collection, two recently completed validation studies, and some objectives for the future.

*Dr. Krugman is a vice president and a director of research at Marplan, a research division of the Interpublic Group of Companies, Inc.

The basic design for the equipment and data handling procedures were developed by Dr. Eckhard Hess and Mr. James Polt, both of the University of Chicago, under a grant from Marplan.

Grateful appreciation is extended to the management, and particularly to Mr. Just Lunning, President of Georg Jensen, Inc., for providing the opportunity to collect and report the sterling silver data presented in this article.

Reprinted from the *Journal of Marketing Research*, published by the American Marketing Association, Volume 1, No. 4 (November 1964) pp. 15-19.

CONCEPT

Hess and Polt reported that "Increases in the size of the pupil of the eye have been found to accompany the viewing of emotionally toned or interesting visual stimuli." A technique for recording such changes was developed so that the factor of adjustment to light was eliminated as a measurement problem. While the pupil is capable of changes from about 2 to 8 mm. in response to light, or an areal increase of 16 fold, the variation in pupil diameters involved in studies of interest is usually well within ± 10 percent and often within ± 2 percent.

The "plus or minus" quality referred to here is an operational function of the method of measurement (to be described). However, it does raise the question of what kinds of stimuli create measurable dilations and what kinds create measurable contractions.

Apparently there are two broad categories of affect-arousing or interest-producing stimuli that create dilations. The first category involves pleasant stimuli; the second involves stimuli that evoke fear, anxiety or shock. Contractions, on the other hand, are associated with stimuli that lack the power to interest or arouse the viewer. While stimuli that evoke fear, anxiety or shock are usually absent in commercial objects and symbols, the meaning of stimuli must be considered before one can infer that a dilation indicates pleasurably toned interest.[1] Airline, insurance, and drug advertising, for example, might be ruled ineligible for measurement of pupil response because a dilation might represent anxiety rather than pleasurably toned interest. In the case of such questionable stimuli one might have to consider the circumstances, inquire of the respondents, and exercise a degree of judgment before deciding that dilation represented a favorable response. While such problems are in fact quite rare in the commercial environment, their possibility must be noted.

METHOD

To conduct pupil dilation studies in the manner developed by Hess and Polt, three work stages are required.[2] First, the material to be tested is prepared in 35 mm. slide form and each stimulus slide is matched for reflected illumination with a neutral control slide containing nothing but the numbers one through five. Each study usually accommodates ten stimuli, or a total of ten pairs of stimulus and control slides.

In preparing stimulus slides it may be necessary to reduce light/dark contrasts within a picture. Modification of the stimulus to reduce light/dark contrasts may diminish somewhat the aesthetic value of pictures, but this has not yet seemed to present a problem.

The subject looks at each slide for ten seconds while his left eye is photographed at the rate of two photographs per second. While looking at each control slide, the pupil diameter is primarily a function of the light value of the slide.[3] As the matched (for light value) stimulus slide comes on, the pupil diameter may increase (as a function of greater interest) or it may decrease (as a function of lesser interest). It is this increase or decrease which is measured for each pair of control and stimulus slides.

The films are developed and each negative is projected onto a special scoring table large enough for the pupil to be measured with a ruler. The basic measure is the percent increase or decrease in the average pupil diameter for the twenty photographs taken while viewing a stimulus slide, in comparison with the average pupil diameter for the twenty photographs taken while viewing the control slide.

MEASUREMENT GOALS

Early studies were concerned primarily with measuring the pleasurably toned interest or "appeal" of individual ads, packages or product designs.[4] To this was added before-and-after measurement in which responses to a photo of the product were measured twice. Between exposures to the photo of the product, different respondents were exposed to different information (*i.e.,* different ads, paragraphs of copy, *etc.*) to see which information was more persuasive or which added more appeal to the product (which, along with awareness, is the goal of advertising).[5]

Television commercials have also been inserted as "in-between" stimuli for before-and-after studies. In this indirect manner, animate stimuli were evaluated for the first time. Equipment has since been developed to take direct measures of response to animate stimuli, so that pre-testing of television commercials, television programs and motion pictures can be considered as possible applications of pupil research.

DATA COLLECTION

Conventional measures usually require the subject, as he views stimuli, (1) to decide whether he likes or dislikes the stimuli, (2) to decide how he will tell this, and (3) to tell it. These three operations or units of response are absent in pupil measurement. Pupil measurement therefore circumvents language and translation problems in cross-cultural opinion and attitude surveys.

Subjects who participate in pupil measurement studies look at slides with the assumption that questions will be asked when the slides have all been shown. To fulfill this expectation, and also to interrelate pupil with verbal data, an interview is always conducted. The camera is quiet though visible and few subjects comment about it. Those who ask are answered frankly.

VALIDATION

A number of studies suggested the usefulness of pupil measurement as a predictor of behavior. In the case of products, pupil response was found to be related to sales data for watches, while in the case of ads, pupil response was found to be related to (split-run) coupons returns.[6] These studies, however, were confined to pairs of stimuli. To evaluate the extent of the relationship, or to determine whether pupil response was perhaps more predictive of sales than were other measures, it became desirable to compare an array of pupil responses and an array of verbal responses (*e.g.,* ratings) from the same subjects against a similar array of sales data. Two such studies were conducted and are reported here. They involved greeting cards and sterling silver patterns.

Greeting Cards

Ten humorous greeting cards (four friendship and six birthday) were chosen by a cooperating manufacturer to represent wide ranges in sales performance. Each card was photographed with the first and third slides of the four-sided (foldover) card showing on the slide. This eliminated the surprise element of "turning the page" and, in one card, of a mechanical pop-out device. More recently developed equipment permits a film presentation of realistic card handling and card opening.

Camera equipment was installed in a rented store in the Roosevelt Field Shopping Center (Garden City, Long Island) during January 1964, and twenty-three male and twenty-six female subjects were recruited from among passing shoppers.[7] Immediately after pupil measurement, interview data were obtained on order of recall, and then with the actual cards shown, on "card liked best" and "card liked least." The data were given to the manufacturer who then provided rank order information on sales. Results are shown in Table 1.

Although the pupil response correlated approximately + .4 for both sets of cards, because of the small number of cases neither correlation is statistically significant. The correlation of pupil response with sales rank would possibly have been higher if the testing procedure had not required removal of the pop-out spring from "Hi!" before photographing.

It may also be worth noting that, in the case of the larger group (birthday cards), the correlation between pupil response and sales was numerically larger than that between verbal rank and sales, but also that pupil response was *negatively* correlated with verbal rank (R = − .60).[8]

Sterling Silver Patterns

A cooperating retailer (Georg Jensen, Inc.) selected ten sterling silver patterns to represent a wide range in sales performance. These patterns are an exclusive line

Table 1
Comparison of Sales, Pupil Responses, and Verbal
Ratings for Greeting Cards

Title of Card		Pupil response		
	Sales rank	*Rank*	*Percent change*	*Verbal rank*
(Friendship)[a]				
Hi!	1	3	− .1	2
Awkward Age	2	1	+1.7	3
Dolce Vita	3	2	+1.0	1
You're Nice	4	4	− .2	4
(Birthday)[b]				
Old as Hills	1	1	+2.9	4
Elephant	2	6	− .1	2
Swiss Cheese	3	2	+2.7	5
Cane	4	4	+1.7	1
Witch	5	3	+1.8	6
Horn	6	5	+ .4	3

[a]Rank order coefficient: Sales rank with Pupil   rank = +.4
                           Sales rank with Verbal   rank = +.4
                           Neither value is significant.
[b]Rank order coefficient: Sales rank with Pupil   rank = +.37
                           Sales rank with Verbal   rank = +.09
                           Neither value is significant.

identified with the retailer. Each pattern was represented by a single place setting consisting of knife, fork, and spoon, and was photographed on a blue velvet background.

Camera equipment was installed in an alcove at the rear of Jensen's Fifth Avenue store during February 1964, and thirty-nine female subjects were recruited from among those shoppers entering the silverware section to examine this category of merchandise. Immediately after pupil measurement, respondents were shown the ten actual place settings and were asked to rank them in order of liking, *i.e.*, 1 high to 10 low. As it happened, the thirty-nine subjects included thirteen who reported that they were actually shopping for sterling and twenty-six who were only browsing. The data were given to the retailer who then provided retail sales data for the completed year of 1962. It must be noted, however, that these 1962 data represent a combination of sales of flatware (primarily) and serving pieces and are not available on a separate basis. However, to supplement these data, Table 2 includes some retailer comments which appear relevant.

Table 2
Comparison of Sales, Pupil Responses and Verbal
Ratings for Silverware

Pattern[c]	Sales[a] rank	Shoppers[b] Pupil rank	Percent change	Verbal rank	Browsers Pupil rank	Percent change	Verbal rank
Acorn	1	5	+ .5	8	1	+1.0	2
Acanthus	2	1	+2.3	6.5	3	+ .2	4.5
Cactus	3	7	- .9	3	6	- .1	3
Cypress	4	3	+1.7	4	5	0.0	7
Continental	5	2	+2.1	2	2	+ .6	4.5
Pyramid	6	10	-2.6	1	8	-1.4	1
Blossom	7	9	-2.2	10	10	-3.7	10
Caravel	8	4	+ .8	9	4	+ .1	9
Argo	9.5	6	- .1	6.5	7	- .9	8
Nordic	9.5	8	-1.4	5	9	-2.2	6

[a]The following rank-order correlation were obtained:
Sales rank with shoppers' pupil   rank = +.43
Sales rank with shoppers' verbal   rank = +.14
Sales rank with browsers' pupil   rank = +.66 (p = .05)
Sales rank with browsers' verbal   rank = +.60 (p = .05)

[b]The shoppers' percent change in pupil dilation was more favorable than the browsers', i.e., larger +% or smaller -%, for seven of the ten patterns, suggesting greater interest in silverware in general on the part of the shoppers. A one-tail test of this hypothesis shows that t = 1.84, df = 9, p = .05.

[c]Retailer's comments:

Acorn	"This gets the bulk of our advertising by far"
Acanthus	
Cactus	
Cypress	"Sells better out of town"
Continental	"Only pattern that doubled its volume in recent years — will be advertised next year"
Pyramid	"What the public thinks is tasteful but isn't"
Blossom	
Caravel	"A 'designer's design' — not expected to sell in the USA"
Argo	"Introduced in 1963 and not doing well"
Nordic	"Discontinued years ago — didn't sell"

For both the shoppers and the browsers, the correlation between sales history and pupil response was numerically larger than the correlation between sales and verbal ratings (the difference was not statistically significant, however).[9]

It is interesting to note that the pupil response and verbal rating differed sharply for "Pyramid," with the pupil response in "agreement" with sales.

"Pyramid" received the highest verbal rating from both shoppers and browsers, but ranked tenth and eighth, respectively, in pupil response. Apparently the public showed better taste than their verbal ratings would indicate.

Logically, we would expect that shoppers (who are actually planning to purchase silver) would be more "interested" in sterling than browsers. The results of the pupil response, i.e., shoppers having larger percent increases and small percent decreases in pupil size, support this expectation. This finding, which was statistically significant, adds suggestive, though not definitive, indication of validity.

RELIABILITY

The results of the studies reported in this paper, as well as the accumulating results from a variety of similar studies, encourage the belief that pupil response is a promising new tool for study of consumer behavior.

However, because the magnitude of changes in pupil diameter are relatively small, the question of reliability of measurement becomes important. For example, in view of the relatively small range of pupil response (from approximately -2 percent to $+3$ percent in the studies reported in this paper), are the responses to these stimuli really significantly different, or are they simply within the range of random fluctuation? Furthermore, is there any real agreement from subject to subject? We shall present what data are available bearing on these two questions.

SIGNIFICANCE OF STIMULUS EFFECTS

An analysis of variance was performed at the time the pupil response data were collected for the greeting cards. This analysis was designed to evaluate the effects attributable to sex stimuli, (the greeting cards), and interaction of sex and stimuli. The results are presented in Table 3.

Table 3
Analysis of Variance Summary

Source of variation	Sum of squares	d.f.	Mean square	F
Sex	17,987.72	1	17,987.72	2.78
Error 1	304,064.39	47	6,469.46	
Greeting cards	57,157.72	9	6,350.86	5.29[a]
Sex x cards	46,848.62	9	5,205.40	4.33[a]
Error II	508,264.86	423	1,201.57	

[a]p = .01

The results presented in Table 3 may interperted as follows:

1. On the whole, male and female subjects do not differ significantly in their pupil responses to greeting cards.
2. The various greeting cards do evoke significantly different pupil responses.
3. Male and female subjects *do* differ significantly in their pupil responses to certain greeting cards.

In other words, the differences in pupil response, though numerically small, are real.

INTERSUBJECT CONSISTENCY

In Tables 1 and 2, pupil responses were averaged for all subjects, then ranked for comparison with sales rank data. The question remains, to what extent do pupil response rankings agree from subject to subject? To answer this question, Kendall's coefficient of concordance (W) was computed with the results shown in Table 4.

Table 4
Intersubject Consistency

Stimulas	Shoppers	W	P
Greeting cards	Total (49)	.11	<.001
Sterling silver	Shoppers (13)	.19	<.01
Sterling silver	Browsers (26)	.11	<.005

For each of the groups, the odds are better than a thousand to one that the consistency of pupil response ranking was not due simply to chance. In short, the answer to the question is that pupil response rankings do agree significantly from subject to subject. Furthermore, in the case of the greeting card study, the average pupil response rank of cards for male subjects correlated $+ .77$ ($p = .01$) with the average pupil response rank of cards for female subjects. For shoppers and browsers in the sterling silver study, the correlation was $+ .81$ ($p = .01$).

THE FUTURE

In general, the results of our experience with measurement of pupil response indicate that this is a sensitive and reliable technique with considerable promise for study of the interest-arousing characteristics of visual stimuli. The impact of the environment is often difficult to determine from conscious impressions verbally reported. For a variety of reasons, people may not be practiced or competent to accurately verbalize their feeling in certain areas of living. Pupil measurement seems to provide a powerful new tool for the study of these areas.

REFERENCE

1. E. H. Hess and J. M. Polt, "Pupil Size as Related to Interest Value of Visual Stimuli," 132, *Science* (1960), 349-350.

NOTES

1. Presumably we are concerned here with the parasympathetic branch of the autonomic nervous system (vegetative functions) whereby the pupil may be dilated via inhibition (the lay term might be "relaxation") of that system and a weakening of control of the sphincter muscle in the iris; one would hope to eliminate the role of the sympathetic branch (fight, flight, *etc.*) whereby the pupil may be dilated via stimulation of the system and a contraction of the dilator muscle in the iris.

2. For further details of the method see E. H. Hess and J. M. Polt, "Pupil Size in Relation to Mental Activity During Simple Problem Solving," 143, *Science* (1964), 1190-1192.

3. The control slide probably has some interest in its own right or as a signal to anticipate something of interest. Contraction may involve disappointment. Rotation of stimuli is, therefore, quite important.

4. By-product data obtainable from pupil photographs include where subjects are looking during the period of exposure. Thus, dilation or contraction can be traced approximately to parts of a stimulus. In addition, a persistently ascending or descending response can be identified, if such occurs during the period of exposure.

5. This may circumvent the problem of an anxious response to airline, insurance, or drug *advertising, i.e.*, instead of measuring response to the ad itself the emphasis is on shifts in the non-anxious product appeal.

6. Conducted and to be published by F. J. Van Bortel of the Chicago office of Marplan.

7. Actually, a total of 57 subjects was tested, but records for eight had to be discarded because of incomplete or blurred photographic plates.

8. The agreement between sales and pupil response is relatively independent of the influence of verbal rating, as determined by the Kendall partial rank correlation coefficient. With verbal rating partialled out, the Kendall coefficient increased + .04, a negligible change. (See S. Siegel, *Nonparametric Statistics*, New York: McGraw-Hill, 1956, 223-229, for details of this test.)

9. A more precise test of interpretations of this order might be to compare the predictive power of pupil and verbal data against the later sales behavior of the same group, *i.e.*, even though it may be practical to use pupil data on small groups to predict something about larger groups, the interpretations underlying these predictions would in most cases require special testing.

*Many sociologists have made significant con-
tributions to marketing by their impact on the
general climate of ideas concerning the nature
of man and society and the relations of
economic institutions to society.*

11

contributions of
sociology to
marketing

christen t. jonassen

A sociologist is a social scientist who undertakes to isolate, define, and describe
human behavior in groups and social settings. He seeks to formulate valid laws
and generalizations about human nature, social interaction, social organization,
and culture.

Anyone who engages in such activities, seeks such ends, and who in the eyes
of other sociologists contributes to these functions is practicing sociology.
Therefore, a *sociological contribution* to marketing is anything done by a
recognized sociologist that leads to a better understanding of the nature,
functions, and processes of marketing.

In what areas and in what ways have sociologists developed materials
significant for marketing? And what impact has this knowledge had on
marketing, and through what channels has this impact been transmitted? This
article gives some of the answers.

Reprinted from the *Journal of Marketing*, published by the American Marketing
Association, Volume 24, No. 4 (October, 1959), pp. 29-35.

NATURE OF MARKETING

We have come a long way from the mechanistic, self-regulating approach of the *laissez-faire* economic theorists. They viewed the market in terms of an equilibrium of forces and general, universalistic, immutable, physical-like laws. The classical economist saw the consumer as an "economic man," a creature who exercised free individual choice in a market which seemed to operate in a cultural and social vacuum. This view looked on individual wants and desires as motivating forces, and on individuals as the acting agents.

Sociological influences are most apparent in the modern institutional approach, which sees economic processes as part of an organic whole of the total society. This approach means that marketing activities are not looked on as the individualistic acts of atomistic man, but rather as *functions* operating through various marketing structures which are part of the total social organization.

It views marketing processes as the *activities* of groups of people: buyers, sellers, and marketing functionaries, who are motivated by group pressures as well as individual predilections. It recognizes the influence of culture, custom, heritage, and mores in determing the final outcome.

Its emphasis throughout is not on the individual, but on the *group* . . . not on mechanistic, self-regulating, universalistic forces, but on particularistic *social* and cultural forces . . . not on "rational economic" man, but on men as members of *social* groups susceptible to irrationality and sentiment, as well as social values and pressures generated within such groups. Duddy and Revzan, for example, say that "what the producer is finally confronted with is the forecasting of human behavior," and that "in our modern dynamic society the individual, whether consciously or unconsciously, more often acts as a member of a group."[1]

Such terms as "institution," "group," "society," "mass," "culture," "structure," and "structure-function," are found in the institutional approach. These are terms constantly in use by sociologists, and they have had considerable influence on people in other disciplines. Fundamental changes in viewpoint about the nature of man and his marketing behavior have been due largely to the impact of sociological thought and research on economics, psychology, and marketing.

SOCIOLOGICAL CONTRIBUTIONS

Population Studies

The statement, "Markets are people with money to spend — and the desire to spend it"[2] points to two additional areas of sociological contribution: *population studies and consumer motivation.*

For a long time population studies have been a branch of sociology. In most universities the subject is taught in the department of sociology, and sociological journals contain numerous articles on this subject. Precise knowledge of population factors enables the marketing man to determine how many and what kinds of people there are and where they are. This enables him to predict future populations and thus gives him lead time which helps to adjust the distribution system to future requirements. This is an obvious necessity for a scientific approach to marketing.

Thompson and Whelpton,[3] Hauser, Ogburn, Margaret Hagood, Hawley, Kingsley Davis, Paul Hatt, Kiser, Duncan, Bogue, and Schmid are a few of the sociologists who have made contributions to our knowledge and understanding of populations, processes, and problems. Their publications in this area are so numerous that each would require a bibliography too long to cite here.

Consumer Motivation

In some of the early marketing texts motivation is discussed in terms of the now-discarded instinct theories, emphasizing the individual and largely ignoring the group. But marketing men today are aware that men to do not possess "instincts," and that if they have such desires or motives they are the products of group life. This evolution of thought owes much to sociological influences. Knowledge significant for understanding motivation has emerged from sociological research on class, voluntary association, leisure-time activities, and attitude measurement.

Numerous studies of social class — such as those of the Lynds,[4] Davis,[5] Dollard,[6] Hollingshead,[7] Warner,[8] and Kahl[9] — have focused attention on the implications of class and status, and have described differential motivational patterns and styles of life in different classes. Understanding of motivation is also aided by findings from research on participation in voluntary association such as that of Kamarovsky,[10] and by studies of leisure and recreation such as the one made by Alfred Clarke.[11]

Men like Bogardus[12] and many of the sociologists discussed below in the section on measurement and scaling were among the first to devise valid and reliable instruments and scales for the measurement of attitudes. Sociologists also have been a healthy counterbalance to the more extreme claims of Freudians and some of their anthropological followers. Rigorous research like that of Sewell, Mussen, and Harris[13] has shown that there is little evidence for many of the theoretical pronouncements regarding the effects of early child-rearing on the personality.

Human Ecology

Another area where sociologists have made a considerable contribution is in human ecology which analyzes the processes involved in the spatial and temporal adaptation and distribution of human beings and their institutions. Those aspects of marketing which can most directly profit from a knowledge of ecology are: transportation and storage, and the whole area concerned with market-area structures.

In all approaches to marketing, the *area* is an important variable and factor. Sociologists have been concerned with spatial systems for over forty years – in 1915 Galpin[14] brought out *The Social Anatomy of an Agricultural Community*, and in 1916 Robert E. Park[15] published his article "The City" in the *American Journal of Sociology*. Galpin's pioneering study introduced a technique of marketing research which has been widely used since, with certain modifications.

Since then the contributions of sociologists to the description, delineation, and analysis of the dynamics of spatial and temporal systems has been continuous and constitutes a vast amount of research too great to analyze here. There should be mentioned, however, the contributions of Odum and Moore,[16] Murkerjee,[17] and Mangus[18] to the study of regional systems; of R. D. McKenzie,[19] Hawley,[20] and Bogue[21] to the analysis of metropolitan community systems; of Park, Burgess, and McKenzie,[22] Schmid,[23] Firey,[24] Wirth,[25] Duncan and Reiss,[26] and Quinn[27] to the analysis of urban systems; and of Galpin,[28] Kolb and Polson,[29] and Brunner[30] to investigation of rural systems.

Most marketing people are familiar with Reilly's[31] law, and equations of retail gravitation. Those interested in the mathematical-model approach to spatial systems would be rewarded by a study of Stouffer's[32] theory of intervening opportunities, of Zipf's[33] equations and hypothesis on intercity movement of persons, and of Dodd's[34] equations describing message diffusion.

Collective Behavior

The realization of distribution specialists that they are dealing with interacting groups, masses, and publics, and the fact that our nation and the world are developing more characteristics of the mass society make the area which sociologists call "collective behavior" ever more important and relevant for marketing. The contributions of sociologists to this area of human behavior have been fairly continuous since Durkheim's[35] early work. Another pioneer in this area was LeBon.[36] Recent contributors are Albig,[37] LaPiere,[38] Lazarfeld,[39] Merton,[40] Raper,[41] Lee,[42] and Blumer.[43] *An Experiment in Mass Communication* by Otto Larsen and Melvin L. DeFleur[44] contributes to the understanding of the phenomena indicated by the title.

Measurement and Scaling

Another contribution to marketing research made by sociologists is in methodology, measurement, scaling, and prediction. Chapin,[45] Sletto,[46]

Bogardus,[47] and Guttman[48] have made basic contributions to scale construction; Burgess,[49] Hornell Hart,[50] Monachesi,[51] and Stuckert[52] to the science of prediction; Chapin[53] and McCormick[54] to the development of models and research design; Parten[55] to sampling; Sletto[56] to the use of control groups in social research; Bowers[57] to methods of studying paths of diffusion in the use of new products; Galpin[58] and Schmid[59] to techniques for mapping quantitative social data; Lazarsfeld[60] and Stouffer[61] to the use of quantitative methods in the study of many areas of human behavior; and Moreno[62] and Lundberg[63] to sociometry.

IMPACT OF SOCIOLOGISTS ON MARKETING

How much impact, if any, have sociological contributions had on marketing? This is difficult to determine. But inferences may be drawn from marketing literature, from an examination of activities of sociologists in the marketing field, and from a look at the structures and processes through which sociological knowledge diffuses into the marketing area.

Publications

Normally one should expect academic channels and textbooks to be an important means of diffusion, but they appear not to be in this instance. Writers of marketing textbooks, while showing evidence of some of the substance of sociology, rarely mention sociology or sociologists. It would require considerable research to determine definitively what emphasis if any is given to sociology in undergraduate courses; but if textbooks are a guide it would seem to be rather negligible. On the graduate level, however, there seems to be more attention given to this subject matter, *The Shopping Center Versus Downtown*,[64] for example, is being used in graduate marketing training programs of some universities.

In marketing and business publications, on the other hand, evidence of sociological influence is more evident. Bartels, for example, in an article in the *Journal of Marketing* in 1951 considers certain aspects of sociology, economics, and some other disciplines, to be part of the area of marketing.[65] *Business Week* of March 29, 1958, reporting on a marketing conference, featured the remarks of sociologist David Riesman.[66] *The Shopping Center Versus Downtown* mentioned above has been reviewed extensively by marketing and business publications. *Consumer Behavior*,[67] published in 1955, has an article by Nelson N. Foote on "The Autonomy of the Consumer," and another by Frederick L. Strodtback on "Recent Developments in Attitude Research." An article entitled "A Commercial Application of Guttman Attitude Scaling Techniques"[68] appeared in the *Journal of Marketing* in 1957.

Climate of Ideas

Much sociological influence on marketing, of course, is exerted indirectly through the medium of the general culture and climate of ideas. Another means is through the effect of sociology on other disciplines such as psychology and economics, which in turn produces similar reactions in marketing.

Sociological contributions to the general evolution of thought about the nature and dynamics of man as a consumer and of the market as a social institution and structure have already been discussed. But much sociological material reaches marketing men secondhand, very late, and sometimes in garbled fashion.

Participation of Sociologists in Marketing

Another path of diffusion of sociological knowledge is through direct participation of sociologists in the marketing process as researchers, consultants, and participants in marketing seminars and conventions. The participation of David Riesman in the *Life* sponsored regional round-table in Chicago has already been mentioned. Packard would have us believe that there may be sociologists behind the so-called "hidden pursuaders," and states that Likert and Stouffer participated in public-relations conference at Columbia University.[69] Some sociologists are now found in marketing-research organizations and on the staffs of advertising agencies.

Evidence of direct and indirect influence of sociologists is furnished by the results of some recent marketing research. For example, one of the most ambitious pieces of marketing research of recent years, the *Life Study of Consumer Expenditures*,[70] conducted by Alfred Politz Research, Inc., offers much internal evidence of sociological influence in research design, sampling, questionnaire construction, and selection of essential categories of analysis. The "wave" technique of intermittent interviewing of the same households, for example, is very similar to the technique developed by Lazersfeld in his study of voting behavior.

The study is not of individuals, but of groups, families, and households living in the United States. These families and households are studied by socio-economic states; education of head of family; stage of "life cycle"; age of household head; and by regions, urban, rural, and different-sized communities.

One category which appears in the *Life* research that is not common in previous marketing studies is "Household's Stage in the Life Cycle." The study credits the development of this concept to the Survey Research Center of the University of Michigan;[71] but the concept of stages in family life cycle has been common coin in sociology for a long time. In their *Systematic Source Book in Rural Sociology*,[72] Sorokin, Zimmerman, and Galpin discussed four stages of family life cycle as early as 1931; and E. L. Kirkpatrick in 1934 wrote an article entitled "The Life Cycle of the Farm Family in Relation to Its Standard of Living."[73] The concept appears in a book of Waller's[74] in 1938; and it is the organizing theme of Duvall's *Family Development.*[75] Thus, what appeared originally as a concept in sociological literature appears about a generation later in a marketing study as an important category in terms of which data are gathered and analyzed.

Similarly, the use of such categories as "metropolitan" and "non-metropolitan" owes much to McKenzie, whose writings on the metropolitan region appeared as early as 1924 and 1926, and whose *The Metropolitan Community* was published in 1933.[76] Bogue's *The Structure of the Metropolitan Community* appeared in 1949;[77] and this research monograph as well as the earlier work of McKenzie, Hawley, and other sociologists probably contributed heavily to the decision of the U.S. Bureau of the Census to order its data in terms of Standard Metropolitan Areas.

In Conclusion

Lack of space has made it necessary to omit names of other sociologists and also some relevant work of the sociologists who are mentioned. Many sociologists have made significant contributions to marketing by their impact on the general climate of ideas concerning the nature of man and society and the relations of economic institutions to society. They have also carried out important studies on population, communication, collective behavior, motivation, stratification, methodology, research design, measurement, prediction, human ecology, and the family. Sociological knowledge and methods have diffused into marketing through marketing publications, through participation of sociologists as consultants and researchers, and to a lesser extent through academic channels.

The participants in the *Life* marketing conferences mentioned earlier stressed the necessity of developing basic theories and facts to explain buying behavior. The present article has pointed to some aspects of sociological activity and to some materials that might aid in the solution of this problem.

NOTES

1. Edward A. Duddy and David A. Revzan, *Marketing* (New York: McGraw-Hill Book Co., Inc., 1953), pp. 124 and 125.

2. Duddy and Revzan, same reference, p. 8.

3. Warren S. Thompson and P. K. Whelpton, *Population Trends in the United States* (New York: McGraw-Hill Book Co., Inc. 1933); Warren S. Thompson, *Population Problems* (New York: McGraw-Hill Book Co., Inc., 1953).

4. Robert S. Lynd and Helen M. Lynd, *Middletown* (New York: Harcourt, Brace & Co., Inc., 1929); *Middletown in Transition* (New York: Harcourt, Brace & Co., Inc., 1937).

5. Allison Davis, Burleigh Gardner, and Mary Gardner, *Deep South* (Chicago: University of Chicago Press, 1941).

6. John Dollard, *Caste and Class in a Southern Town* (New Haven: Yale University Press, 1954).

7. August B. Hollingshead, *Elmtown's Youth* (New York: John Wiley and Sons, Inc., 1949).

8. Lloyd Warner and Paul S. Lunt, *The Social Life of a Modern Community* (New Haven: Yale University Press, 1941).

9. Joseph A. Kahl, *The American Class Structure* (New York: Rinehart and Co., Inc., 1953).

10. Mirra Kamarovsky, "The Voluntary Association of Urban Dwellers" *American Sociological Review*, Vol. 11 (December, 1946), pp. 686-699.

11. Alfred C. Clarke, "The Use of Leisure and Its Relation to Levels of Occupational Prestige," *American Sociological Review*, Vol. 21 (June, 1956), pp. 301-307.

12. Emory S. Bogardus, "Measuring Social Distance," *Journal of Applied Sociology*, Vol. 9 (March-April, 1925), pp. 299-308.

13. William H. Sewell, Paul H. Mussen, and Chester W. Harris, "Relationships Among Child Training Practices," *American Sociological Review*, Vol. 20 (April, 1955), pp. 137-148.

14. C. J. Galpin, *The Social Anatomy of an Agricultural Community* (Madison: Agricultural Experiment Station of the University of Wisconsin, May, 1951), Research Bulletin 34.

15. Robert E. Park, "The City," *American Journal of Sociology*, Vol. 20 (March, 1916), pp. 577-612.

16. Howard W. Odum and Harry E. Moore, *American Regionalism* (New York: Henry Holt and Company, 1938).

17. Radhakamal Mukerjee, "Social Ecology of River Valley," *Sociology and Social Research*, Vol. 12 (March, 1928), pp. 341-347.

18. A. R. Mangus, *Rural Regions of the United States* (Washington, D.C.: U.S. Government Printing Office, 1940).

19. Roderick D. McKenzie, *The Metropolitan Community* (New York: McGraw-Hill Book Company, Inc., 1933).

20. Amos H. Hawley, "An Ecological Study of Urban Service Institutions," *American Sociological Review*, Vol. 6 (October, 1941), pp. 629-639; also *Human Ecology* (New York: The Ronald Press Company, 1950).

21. Don J. Bogue, *The Structure of the Metropolitan Community: A Study of Dominance and Subdominance* (Ann Arbor: Horance H. Rackham School of Graduate Studies, University of Michigan, 1949); see also the numerous population studies by the same author published by the Scripps Foundation, Miami University, Oxford, Ohio.

22. R. E. Park, E. W. Burgess, and R. D. McKenzie, *The City* (Chicago: University of Chicago Press, 1925); E. W. Burgess, "The Growth of the City: An Introduction to a Research Project," *Publications of the American Sociological Society*, Vol. 18 (1924), pp. 85-97.

23. Calvin F. Schmid, *Social Saga of Two Cities* (Minneapolis: Minneapolis Council of Social Agencies, 1937), *Social Trends in Seattle* (Seattle: University of Washington Press, 1944).

24. Walter Firey, *Land Use in Central Boston* (Cambridge: Harvard University Press, 1947).

25. Louis Wirth, *The Ghetto* (Chicago: The University of Chicago Press) 1928; "Urbanism as a Way of Life," *American Journal of Sociology*, Vol. 44 (July, 1938), pp. 1-24.

26. Otis Dudley Duncan and Albert J. Reiss, Jr., *Social Characteristics of Urban and Rural Communities*, 1950 (New York: John Wiley and Sons, Inc., 1956).

27. James A. Quinn, *Human Ecology* (New York: Prentice-Hall, Inc., 1950).

28. Galpin, same reference as footnote 14.

29. J. H. Kolb and R. A. Polson, *Trends in Town-Country Relations*, Research Bulletin 117, Agricultural Experiment Station, University of Wisconsin, (September, 1933).

30. Edmund de S. Brunner, "Village Growth and Decline, 1930-1940," *Rural Sociology*, Vol. 9 (June, 1944), pp. 103-115; "Village Growth 1940-1950," *Rural Sociology*, Vol. 16 (June, 1951), pp. 111-118.

31. William J. Reilly, *The Law of Retail Gravitation* (New York: W. J. Reilly, Inc., 1931).

32. Samuel A. Stouffer, "Intervening Opportunities: A Theory Relating Mobility and Distance," *American Sociological Review*, Vol. 5 (December, 1940), pp. 845-867.

33. George Kingsley Zipf, "The Pl. P2/D Hypothesis: On the Intercity Movement of Persons," *Americans Sociological Review*, Vol. 11 (December, 1946), pp. 677-686.

34. Stuart Carter Dodd, "Diffusion Is Predictable: Testing Probability Models for Laws of Interaction," *American Sociological Review*, Vol. 20 (August, 1955), pp. 392-401.

35. Emile Durkheim, *Les Formes élémentaires de la vie religieuse, le système totémique en Australie* (Paris: F. Alcan, 1912). Translated by Joseph Ward Swain, *The Elementary Forms of Religious Life: A Study of Religious Sociology* (London: George Allen and Unwin, Ltd., 1915; also Glencoe, Ill.: The Free Press, 1947).

36. Gustave LeBon, *The Crowd* (London: Unwin, 1899).

37. William Albig, *Public Opinion* (New York: McGraw-Hill Book Co., Inc., 1939).

38. Richard T. LaPiere, *Collective Behavior* (New York: McGraw-Hill Book Co., Inc., 1938).

39. Paul F. Lazarsfeld, Bernard Berelson, and Hazel Gaudet, *The People's Choice* (New York: Duell, Sloan and Pearce, 1944).

40. Robert K. Merton, *Mass Persuasion: The Social Psychology of a War Bond Drive* (New York: Harper and Brothers, 1946).

41. Arthur F. Raper, *The Tragedy of Lynching* (Chapel Hill: University of North Carolina Press, 1933).

42. Alfred McClung Lee, *The Daily Newspaper in America* (New York: Macmillan, 1937).

43. Herbert Blumer, "Collective Behavior," Part IV of *An Outline of the Principles of Sociology*, Robert E. Park, Editor (New York: Barnes and Noble, 1939).

44. Otto Larsen and Melvin L. DeFleur, *An Experiment in Mass Communication* (New York: Harper and Brothers, 1958).

45. Stuart F. Chapin, "Preliminary Standardization of a Social Insight Scale," *American Sociological Review*, Vol. 7 (April, 1942), pp. 214-224.

46. Raymond F. Sletto and E. A. Rundquist, *Personality and the Depression* (Minneapolis: University of Minnesota Press, 1936); Sletto, *Construction of Personality Scales by the Criterion of Internal Consistency* (Hanover: The Sociological Press, 1937).

47. Bogardus, same reference as footnote 12.

48. Louis Guttman, "A Basis for Scaling Qualitative Data," *American Sociological Review*, Vol. 9 (April, 1944), pp. 139-150.

49. E. W. Burgess, "Factors Determining Success or Failure on Parole," in A. A. Bruce, E. W. Burgess, and A. T. Harno, *The Workings of the Indeterminate Sentence Law and the Parole System in Illinois* (Springfield: The State of Illinois, 1928).

50. Hornell Hart, "Predicting Parole Success," *Journal of the American Institute of Criminal Law and Criminology*, Vol. 14 (Nov., 1923), pp. 405-413.

51. Elio D. Monachesi, *Prediction Factors in Probation* (Hanover: The Sociological Press, 1932).

52. Robert Paton Stuckert, *A Configurational Approach to Social Predition*, unpublished Ph.D. Dissertation, The Ohio State University, 1956; "A Configurational Approach to Prediction," *Sociometry*, Vol. 21 (September, 1958), pp. 225-237.

53. S. F. Chapin, *Experimental Designs in Sociological Research* (New York: Harper and Brothers, 1947); *Design of Social Experiments* (New York: Harper and Brothers, 2nd ed., 1956).

54. Thomas C. McCormick, *Elementary Social Statistics* (New York: McGraw-Hill Book Co., Inc., 1941); Thomas C. McCormick and Roy G. Francis, *Methods of Research in the Behavioral Sciences* (New York: Harper and Brothers, 1958).

55. Mildred B. Parten, "Leadership Among Preschool Children," *Journal of Abnormal and Social Psychology*, Vol. 27 (January-March, 1933), pp. 430-440; *Surveys, Polls and Samples* (New York: Harper and Brothers, 1950).

56. Raymond F. Sletto, "Sibling Position and Juvenile Delinquency," *American Journal of Sociology*, Vol. 34 (March, 1934), pp. 657-669.

57. Raymond B. Bowers, "The Direction of Intra-Societal Diffusion," *American Sociological Review*, Vol. 2 (December, 1937), pp. 826-836.

58. Galpin, same reference as footnote 14.

59. Schmid, same reference as footnote 23; also *Handbook of Graphic Presentation* (New York: The Ronald Press Co., 1954).

60. Paul F. Lazarsfeld, *et al.*, *Mathematical Thinking in the Social Sciences* (Glencoe, Ill.: The Free Press, 1954).

61. Samuel A. Stouffer, *et al.*, *The American Soldier: Adjustment During Army Life*, Vol. 1 (Princeton: Princeton University Press, 1949).

62. J. L. Moreno, *Who Shall Survive?* (Washington, D.C.: Nervous and Mental Disease Publishing Co., 1934).

63. George A. Lundberg and Mary Steele, "Social Attraction Patterns in a Village," *Sociometry*, Vol. 1 (April, 1938), pp. 375-419.

64. Christen T. Jonassen, *The Shopping Center versus Downtown: A Motivation Research on Shopping Habits and Attitudes in Three Cities* (Columbus: The Ohio State University Bureau of Business Research, 1955); also published as *Shopper Attitudes*, Special Report 11-A (Washington, D.C.: Highway Research Board, National Research Council, 1955).

65. Robert Bartels, "Can Marketing Be A Science?" *The Journal of Marketing*, Vol. 15 (January, 1951), pp. 319-328 at p. 323.

66. "The Riddle of Consumer Behavior," *Business Week* (March 29, 1958), p. 95.

67. Committee for Research on Consumer Attitudes and Behavior, *Consumer Behavior*, Lincoln H. Clark, editor (New York: New York University Press, 1955).

68. Elizabeth A. Richards, "A Commercial Application of Guttman Attitude Scaling Techniques," *Journal of Marketing*, Vol. 22 (October, 1957), pp. 166-173.

69. Vance Packard, *The Hidden Persuaders* (New York; David McKay Co., 1957), pp. 220, 221.

70. Time, Inc., *Life Study of Consumer Expenditures*, 1957, Vol. 1.

71. Same reference p. 13.

72. Pitirim Sorokin, Carl C. Zimmerman, and C. J. Galpin, *Systematic Source Book in Rural Sociology* (Minneapolis: University of Minnesota Press, 1931), Vol. 2, p. 31.

73. E. L. Kirkpatrick, *et al.*, "The Life Cycle of the Farm Family in Relation to its Standard of Living," Research Bulletin No. 121 (Madison, Wisconsin: Agricultural Experiment Station, University of Wisconsin, 1934).

74. Willard Waller, *The Family: A Dynamic Interpretation* (New York: The Cordon Co., 1938).

75. Evelyn Millis Duvall, *Family Development* (New York: J. B. Lippincott Co., 1957).

76. McKenzie, same reference as footnote 19.

77. Bogue, same reference as footnote 21.

12

The kind of information which marketing-research studies seek on how people live and what products they use represent first-rate material for the cultural anthropologist.

anthropology's contribution to marketing

charles winick

The relative slowness of anthropologists and marketers in finding common ground is surprising.[1] Anthropologists have served as colonial administrators, in foreign-aid programs, and in other situations requiring a special sensitivity to foreign cultures. They have also developed sales-training procedures which involve the analysis of the rate of speech of salesmen with potential customers, through devices which measure the rate of interaction between people talking.[2] Another specialized industrial situation in which anthropologists have worked involves the application of their knowledge of the field of anthropometry or measurement of the body, in the design of products like chairs and knobs.[3]

Other anthropologists have worked in applied fields such as: reactions to disaster, the operation of internment and relocation centers, mental health, medical care, labor-management relations,[4] the culture of a factory,[5] community organization, social work,[6] military government, the cultural change associated with economic development,[7] contact between cultures, the nature of

Reprinted from the *Journal of Marketing*, published by the American Marketing Association, Volume 25, No. 5 (July, 1961), pp. 53-60.

small-town life, behavior in extreme situations, the study of culture at a distance,[8] the reconstruction of the themes of a culture, relations among minority groups, the social structure of a hospital,[9] American national character,[10] and television.[11]

Although anthropologists have published their findings on America in very accessible formats,[12] there has been little discussion of how their findings could be applied to marketing problems.[13] One advertising publication has published an article on the possibility of using anthropology in advertising.[14] The journal of applied anthropology, formerly called *Applied Anthropology* and now called *Human Organization*, almost never carries any material on marketing; and the national journal, *American Anthropologist*, also ignores the subject.

ANTHROPOLOGY, SOCIOLOGY, AND PSYCHOLOGY

Anthropology is usually defined as the study of man. Such a definition is so all-inclusive that the field is generally divided into four sub-fields: archeology, cultured anthropology, linguistics, and physical anthropology. Archeology is concerned with the historical reconstruction of cultures which no longer exist. Cultural anthropology examines all the behaviors of man which have been learned, including social, linguistic, technical and familiar behaviors; often it is defined as the study of man and his works. Linguistics is the comparative study of the structure, interrelationships, and development of languages. Physical anthropology is concerned with human biology and the development of the human organism, with special interest in race differences.

When anthropology is employed in marketing, it is usually cultural anthropology which is relevant. Cultural anthropology began with the study of primitive cultures, and its comparative analyses documented the different ways in which cultures have solved their problems of living.

Cultural anthropology has much in common with psychology and sociology. All three are concerned with the examination of man in his cultural setting. They differ in the emphases which they place on different elements of the relationship between a person and his environment. It can be said that all human behavior essentially is a function of the interrelations of personality, the social system, and culture.

Oversimplifying, psychology is concerned with personality, sociology addresses itself to the social system, and anthropology explores the culture. The interdisciplinary field of social psychology may draw on all three of these fields, and there are integrated social psychology texts which do so.[15]

A sharper focus on the differences among these three social sciences may be obtained by speculating on how each of the three might look at a family.

The psychologist would be interested in the personal adjustment and emotional health of each member of the family. He would want to examine their attitudes, mutual perceptions, and motivational systems. Their happiness or lack of it would interest him.

The sociologist would be concerned primarily with the dimensions of role and status within the family and with the number of different kinds of families. He would examine how the social structure created various kinds of internal arrangements which made it possible for the family to exist. He would be interested in the norms of behavior and the stresses and strains shown by the deviations from the norm and resulting from role conflict. He would study class membership as well as the rates of various kinds of behavior, such as the birth rate.

The cultural anthropologist would examine the technological level which the culture had reached and the interrelations of technology with culture. He would scrutinize the procedures for inheritance of property and how kinship was reckoned and described, and how the spouses got to know each other. He would study the family's food and housing. He would be interested in the language level and dialects and in who talked to whom. He would be concerned with how the age of different members of the family affected their behavior, and with trends in illnesses. He would study how the culture "rubbed off" on the family unit. The anthropologist thus does not have information which it would be impossible for the sociologist or psychologist to obtain, but he has a special sensitivity to certain facets of social life.

The sociologist and psychologist bring a powerful and varied arsenal of concepts and approaches to the study of social life. In what ways is the anthropologist able to contribute insights and experience toward the science of "marketology," and to what extent may they not be immediately accessible, for example, to the sociologist?[16] The anthropologist is especially trained to have empathy with groups other than his own and to "tune in" on their patterns of culture. Inasmuch as his training has exposed him to a wide variety of cultures, he can take a global view of a situation and see it in the context of a larger background. His training makes him sensitive to cross-cultural differences which may be of crucial importance in many different situations, because his entire training is geared toward awareness of such differences.

Anthropology has less of the factionalism which characterizes psychology and sociology. This is not to suggest that all is serene in anthropology or that it has never been troubled by theoretical or methodological issues. However, even though anthropologists may disagree on something like the exact value of the contribution of a particular anthropologist, they would generally agree on what the cultural anthropologist looks for, and there are standardized check lists on how to view a culture.[17] In contrast, a psychologist's allegiance to the Gestalt, behaviorist, psychoanalytic, learning-theory, or perception schools is likely to influence what he does with a given problem. A sociologist's commitment to the structure-function, historical, ecological, "middle range," environmental-determinism, or demographic schools would largely determine the emphases of his approach to a problem. Since such divergent schools are less likely to exist in cultural anthropology, it is probable that anthropological guidance on a given marketing problem would be relatively consistent.

WHAT THE ANTHROPOLOGIST KNOWS

The anthropologist is specifically trained to study national character, or the differences which distinguish our national group from another. He should be able to provide measures for distinguishing the subtle differences among a Swede, a Dane, and a Norwegian; or between a Frenchman and an Englishman; or a Brazilian and an Argentinian; or between a typical resident of Montreal and one of Toronto. The anthropologist is also a specialist in the study of subcultures. He would be able, in a city like New York, to differentiate the patterns of living of such disparate but rapidly homogenizing groups as Puerto Ricans, Negroes, Italo-Americans, Jews, Polish-Americans, and Irish-Americans. Because almost any large community consists of a variety of subcultures, this awareness of subcultural trends can be especially useful. A more subtle area of special interest to anthropologists is the silent language of gesture, posture, food and drink preferences, and other nonverbal cues to behavior.[18]

Related to this is the anthropologist's professional interest in languages and symbols. He might, for example, be especially concerned about why a particular shape has special significance as a symbol in a society, or how the structure of a language or a regional speech pattern was related to how people think.[19]

Another area of concern to the anthropologist, because of its symbolic meanings has to do with "rites de passage" or the central points in a person's life at which he may ritually be helped to go from one status to another, for example, birth, puberty, or marriage.[20]

Taboos represent a continuing area of interest to the anthropologist.[21] Every culture has taboos or prohibitions about various things, such as the use of a given color, or of a given phrase or symbol. The anthropologist is aware of the larger values of a culture, which represent the substratum of custom which is taken for granted and the violation of which represents a taboo.

The anthropologist's method is primarily the exposure of his highly developed sensitivity to the area in which he is working, via observation and extended interviews with informants. Projective tests have also been widely used in anthropological studies. The anthropologist can bring a wealth of insight to marketing situations.

USE OF ANTHROPOLOGY IN MARKETING

There are at least three kinds of situations in which the knowledge of the anthropologist has been employed in marketing: specific knowledge; awareness of themes of a culture; sensitivity to taboos.

Specific Knowledge

Here are a few cases in which the specific knowledge of an anthropologist was applied to marketing situations.

A manufacturer of central heating equipment was planning to introduce central heating to an area which previously had used other heating. Since people generally grow up to accept a certain approach to heating which they take for granted, introduction of the new central heating posed marketing problems in coping with deeply imbedded consumer resistance to what would be a major innovation. An anthropologist was able to draw on his knowledge of the folklore and symbolism of heat and fire in order to suggest methods of presenting the new system, so as to make it as consonant as possible with the connotations of heat, even though the nature of the heating method had changed radically. There was considerable consumer resistance to the central heating, but it decreased substantially after the first year.

In addition to a marketing problem, the introduction of central heating also posed problems of public policy which the manufacturer had to overcome before he could obtain approval for the introduction of the heating equipment. The area was one which suffered from a declining birth rate, and officials were concerned about the extent to which central heating might cause the birth rate to decline further, because of their belief that heated bedrooms would cause a decline in sexual activity and utilimately in births.

The anthropologist was able to point to some cultures in which the birth rate had declined and some in which it had not done so after the introduction of central heating. The anthropologist's data made it possible for the manufacturer of the central-heating equipment to discuss its probable effects realistically with the appropriate officials.

Another field in which the anthropologist has specific knowledge that other social scientists are not likely to have is that of clothing and fashion. The only empirical study of the fashion cycle in woman's clothing which has successfully been used for predictive purposes by clothing manufacturers was conducted by anthropologists.[22] In marketing situations, the anthropologist has often been able to combine his special knowledge of the needs of the body for clothing of various kinds at different ages, his sensitivity to what technology makes possible and his awareness of fashion.

For example, an anthropologist was consulted by a leading manufacturer of overalls for young children, a product which had remained unchanged for decades. He examined the product in the light of the special needs of children who wear overalls, the growing use of washing machines to launder the overalls, their relative frequency of laundering, and contemporary technology. He suggested that the overall straps have a series of sets of metal grippers instead of buttons, thus making it possible to use different sets of grippers as the child grew instead of tying or knotting the straps. Noting that the straps often fall off the shoulders when children played, he suggested that the shirts which children wore under the overalls have either a loop for the straps to pass through or a synthetic fastener which faced matching material on the strap, so that the shoulder of the shirt could be pressed against the strap and remain attached to it until shoulder strap and shirt were pulled apart.

He also recommended that the seams of the overalls, previously single stitched, be double stitched like those of men's shirts, which have to withstand frequent launderings. The double-stitched overalls would be less likely to come apart as a result of frequent launderings in a washing machine. These recommendations were adopted, and within a few years substantially changed and expanded the nature of the overall market for young children. The children's parents were more pleased with the overalls because they lasted longer and looked better on the children, and they were far more functional than before.

The special knowledge of the anthropologist has been called into play where there are special subcultural groups to which the marketer wishes to address himself. One beer manufacturer wished to extend his market share among Negroes in a large eastern city in the United States. He was advised about reaching this group by an anthropologist who was familiar with the special subculture of Negroes, and who pointed to the profound effects of Negroes' caste membership on their purchasing behavior. The ambiguity of their role has led many Negroes to be especially aware of articles that have status connotations and of whether a brand symbolizes racial progress. Examination of the manufacturer's marketing program by the anthropologist led to several recommendations for change. The manufacturer began to help in the support of several major social events related to the arts in Negro communities, and to stress that the beer was a national brand with quality-control procedures. He changed the content of his advertising in the direction of enhancing its status and quality connotations. These changes were all directed toward improving the status connotations of the beer to Negroes.

Guidance on related problems with respect to the Puerto Rican and Jewish markets has also been used constructively. Since 35 to 40 per cent of the population of the United States consists of minority subcultures, the anthropologist's contributions may be considerable.

Another situation had to do with the selection of specific symbols for various purposes. A major manufacturer of women's products was uncertain about whether to continue using the Fleur de Lis emblem on his package. Anthropological analysis of the symbol suggested that its association with French kings and other cultural connotations of maleness made it more masculine than feminine. The anthropologist's recommendations were confirmed by subsequent field testing.

In a related case, a manufacturer of women's cosmetics conducted an anthropological study of the comparative symbolism in our culture of women's eyes and mouth, which suggested that the eye tends to be experienced as a relatively protecting organ while the mouth tends to be experienced as more nurturing. This knowledge of the differences between the special meanings of eye and mouth could constructively be used in marketing the products, and especially in advertising. The advertising explicitly and implicitly mentioned the role of the eye in protection of the woman. It stressed the role of the mouth as the organ which both symbolically and literally gives love. This replaced the manufacturer's previous advertising, in which both eye and mouth were treated in the same way, as organs which could be made beautiful.

Awareness of Themes

The anthropologist has functioned in situations in which he can use his special understanding of themes of a culture, oftentimes taken for granted.

A major chain of candy shops was suffering a decline in sales. A marketing-research study had established that the brand was usually bought as a gift, either for others or as a gift for the purchaser. The chain was unable to develop any ways of using this finding that were not hackneyed. Anthropological guidance on the symbolism of gift-giving enabled the chain to develop merchandising, packaging, and advertising formats for the gift theme. Anthropological study of the connotations of the major holidays suggested themes for window displays, and advertising of the candy in conjunction with the holidays. The chain's marketing strategy was revised on the basis of the anthropological interpretation and clarification of the marketing-research study. Anthropologists are the only social scientists who have systematically studied gift-giving and gift-receiving.[23]

Another example of anthropological interpretation of a marketing-research study was provided by a shirt manufacturer. The study had established that women buy more than half of men's shirts in a particular price range. The anthropologist was able to interpret this finding in the light of several anthropological studies of the relations between husbands and wives in America. The manufacturer had been thinking of placing advertising for his men's shirts in selected women's magazines. The anthropologist was able to point to a number of studies of husband-wife relations which suggested growing resentment by men over the extent to which women had been borrowing and buying men's clothing, and which suggested that the proposed advertising campaign might not be propitious.

Another anthropologist's special sensitivity to the "rites de passage" helped a shoe manufacturer whose sales were declining because of aggressive foreign and domestic competition. The anthropologist was able to point to the extent to which shoes represent major symbols of our going from one stage of life to another, and to assist the manufacturer in developing methods for using the relationship between shoes and "rites de passage."[24]

A landmark along the road of an infant becoming a child usually is found between the ages of 4 and 6 when he can tie his own shoe laces. The manufacturer developed some pamphlets and other instructional material for parents on how to help children to learn to tie their shoe laces. Distribution by local retailers contributed toward making parents favorably aware of the brand's line for children in this age group.

The teenager signalizes her entrance into a new social world by her first high heels. Window displays and advertising which explicitly stressed the new social activities of the teenager wearing her high heels, and naming specific shoe models after teenage social events ("The Prom") contributed toward associating the manufacturer's name with the excitement of the new world symbolized by the high heels.

Older people see the wearing of special "old people's shoes" as the ultimate reminder that they are becoming old. The manufacturer was able to redesign his line for older people so that it retained its special health features but still looked as stylish as any adult shoe, and had no visible stigma of "old people's shoes."

Sensitivity to Taboos

Marketers may unwittingly violate a taboo, whether cultural, religious, or political, especially in selling overseas. Blue, for example, is the color for mourning in Iran and is not likely to be favorably received on a commercial product. Green is the nationalist color of Egypt and Syria and is frowned on for use in packages. Showing pairs of anything on the Gold Coast of Africa is disapproved. White is the color of mourning in Japan and, therefore, not likely to be popular on a product. Brown and gray are disapproved colors in Nicaragua. Purple is generally disapproved in most Latin American markets because of it association with death. Feet are regarded as despicable in Thailand, where any object and package showing feet is likely to be unfavorably received.

The anthropologist can cast light on taboos and on their opposite: favored colors and symbols. The reason for the people in a country or an area liking or not liking a particular color or symbol may be a function of political, nationalist, religious, cultural, or other reasons.

SOME APPLICATIONS IN CANADA

Canada represents a special opportunity for the application of anthropology in marketing situations. Twenty-nine per cent of the country's entire population is in French-speaking Quebec, and over half of this number know no English. Canada thus offers a changing kind of bilingual and culture contact situation with major cross-cultural differences for anthropological analysis.

Both the farm community and the industrial community of Quebec have been studied by anthropologists.[25] The re-evaluation of the nature of Quebec family and community life sparked by Dean Phillipe Garigue of the University of Montreal and a team at Laval University has led to renewed interest in Quebec on the part of anthropologists. Their studies have produced considerable information on styles of life in Quebec which should be translatable into marketing data on pricing policies, colors, package size, flavor and taste of various food items, texture of fabrics, automobile symbolism, product scents, and related subjects.

Specific Knowledge

Perhaps the most frequent occasion for the anthropologist to demonstrate specific knowledge in Canada has to do with language. One laundry-soap company had point-of-sale material on its soap describing it as extra strong and the best one to use on especially dirty parts of wash ("les parts de sale"). After sales of the soap had declined, an anthropologist who was called in by the company pointed out that the phrase is comparable to the American slang phrase "private parts." This kind of mistake might have been avoided if anthropological guidance had been available before sales declined.

Some products do not sell well in Quebec because the English name may be almost unpronounceable to a French speaker, or the name of the product may be meaningless even when translated idiomatically. Even the English spoken in Montreal differs somewhat from the English spoken in Toronto, creating potential hazards for the marketers who may not know, for example that a "tap" in a "flat" in Toronto is likely to be a "faucet" in a Montreal "apartment."

Awareness of Themes

A study done by an anthropologist for a food manufacturer demonstrated the relationship between the purchases of certain food items and the gradual decline of the wood-burning stove which used to be a staple of Quebec farm kitchens The wood stove would almost always have a stew pot ("pot au feu") simmering all day. Various ingredients were put into the pot to provide flavor. With the introduction of gas and electric kitchen ranges, it not only became relatively expensive to keep the stew pot going but the simmering could not be sustained because the pot would tend to boil rather than simmer.

This change was accompanied by some radical adjustments in food consumption which were of great relevance to food marketing. The manufacturer was able to begin distribution of canned soups and stews which soon found a very large market and rapidly replaced the "pot au feu."

Taboos

Alertness to taboos was illustrated by an anthropologist's suggestion to a manufacturer of canned fish for changing a series of advertisements which were appearing in Quebec magazines and newspapers. The same advertisement was run repeatedly. The advertisements showed a woman in shorts playing golf with her husband. The caption read that the woman would be able to be on the golf links all day and still prepare a delicious dinner that evening if she used the product. Every element in the advertisement represented a violation of some underlying theme of French Canadian life; the wife would not be likely to be playing golf with her husband, she would not wear shorts, and she would not be serving the particular kind of fish as a main course. In this case, the anthropologist was consulted *after* the series had been running for awhile.

THE MARKETER AS AN ANTHROPOLOGIST

A good case could be made for the thesis that marketing researchers do more anthropological research on modern cultures than do anthropologists. Marketing researchers are studying national character, subcultures, themes, and ways of life. The kind of information which marketing-research studies seek on how people live and what products they use represent first-rate material for the cultural anthropologist.

The questionnaire, panel, audit, sales analysis, and other methods of modern marketing differ in degree but not in kind from the trained observations of the anthropologist, but there is no reason why the two methods cannot complement each other. Greater communication between these two fields can and should lead to mutual enrichment of both.

NOTES

1. John Gillin, "The Application of Anthropological Knowledge to Modern Mass Society," *Human Organization*, Vol. 15 (Winter, 1957), pp. 24-30.

2. Eliot D. Chapple, "The Interaction Chronograph," *Personnel*, Vol. 25 (January, 1949), pp. 295-307.

3. Earnest A. Hooton, *A Survey In Seating* (Cambridge: Harvard Department of Anthropology, 1945).

4. Charles R. Walker, *The Man on the Assembly Line* (Cambridge: Harvard University Press, 1952).

5. Eliot Jaques, *The Changing Culture of A Factory* (New York: Dryden Press, 1953).

6. Franklin K. Patterson, Irving Lukoff, and Charles Winick, "Is Society the Patient," *Journal of Educational Sociology*, Vol. 30 (October, 1956), pp. 106-112.

7. Almost every issue of *Economic Development and Cultural Change* carries relevant articles.

8. Margaret Mead and Rhoda Metraux, *The Study of Culture At A Distance* (Chicago: University of Chicago Press, 1952).

9. Charles Winick, "The Hospital As A Social System," *New York State Nurse*, Vol. 26 (January, 1954), pp. 9-13.

10. David M. Potter, *People of Plenty* (Chicago: University of Chicago Press, 1954).

11. Charles Winick, *Taste and the Censor In Television* (New York: Fund For the Republic, 1959).

12. Margaret Lantis, editor, "The U.S.A. As Anthropologists See It," *American Anthropologist,* Vol. 57 (December, 1955), pp. 1,113-1,380.

13. Richard C. Sheldon, "How The Anthropologist Can Help The Marketing Practitioner" in W. David Robbins, editor, *Successful Marketing at Home and Abroad* (Chicago: American Marketing Association, 1958), pp. 209-304.

14. Alan S. Marcus, "How Agencies Can Use Anthropology in Advertising," *Advertising Agency*, Vol. 49 (September 14, 1956), pp. 87-91.

15. Steuart Henderson Britt, *Social Psychology of Modern Life* (New York: Rinehart & Company, 1949 revised edition). S. Stanfeld Sargent and Robert C. Williamson, *Social Psychology* (New York: The Ronald Press Company, 1958).

16. Robert Bartels, "Sociologist and Marketologists," *Journal of Marketing*, Vol. 24 (October, 1959), pp. 37-40; Christen T. Jonassen, "Contributions of Sociology to Marketing," *Journal of Marketing*, Vol. 24 (October, 1959), pp. 29-35.

17. Royal Anthropological Institute, *Notes and Queries on Anthropology* (London: The Institute, 1956).

18. Edward T. Hall, *The Silent Language* (New York: Doubleday & Co., 1959).

19. Benjamin Lee Whorf, *Collected Papers on Metalinguistics* (Washington: Department of State Foreign Service Institute, 1952).

20. Jan Wit, *Rites De Passage* (Amsterdam: De Windroos, 1959).

21. Franz Steiner, *Taboo* (London: Cohen and West, Ltd., 1957).

22. Jane Richardson and Alfred L. Kroeber, *Three Centuries of Women's Dress Fashions* (Berkeley: University of California Press, 1940).

23. Marcel Mauss, *The Gift* (London: Cohen & West, Ltd., 1954).

24. Charles Winick, "Status, Shoes, and the Life Cycle" *Boot and Shoe Recorder*, Vol. 156 (October 15, 1959), pp. 100-202.

25. Horace Miner, *St Denis* (Chicago, University of Chicago Press, 1939); Everett C. Hughes, *French Canada In Transition* (Chicago: University of Chicago Press, 1943).

The low income neighborhood, because of the differences in income and life style of its residents, creates a different marketing environment. This not only affects the requirements of various marketing functions but their interrelationships. The synergistic effects of various marketing programs to low income consumers calls not only for a different marketing mix but for a systems approach.

13

marketing to low income neighborhoods - a systems approach

kelvin a. wall

Because it is generally agreed that marketing in the low-income segment needs improving, we should first review current levels of performance and isolate these by functions. This process provides a clearer picture of the interrelationships of marketing functions as they affect low-income consumers.

Any analysis of this marketing problem is complicated by the fact that low-income family buying patterns tend, in general, to be determined by neighborhoods. These neighborhoods are composed of a "sizeable complement of individuals who differ in one way or another from the neighborhood norm. Nonetheless, even these people tend to conform to their own group behavior

Reprinted from Bernard A. Morin (ed.), *Marketing in a Changing World*, Proceedings of the National Conference of the American Marketing Association, published by the American Marketing Association, June 1969, pp. 24-27.

pattern."[1] Marketers should however, carefully appraise their tendency to draw conclusions from the characteristics of a single segment or neighborhood.

Before presenting reasons for developing a systems approach, let's first define the low-income market. My definition of low-income segment, purely on a dollar basis, has to be arbitrary, because of the differences in spending power at different cost of living levels in various parts of the country. Also, both the aspiration level and the life cycle are variables difficult to pinpoint.

LOW INCOME DEFINITIONS TODAY AND TOMORROW

For purposes of this study, we shall consider families earning $5,000 or less annually as components of the low-income segment. By this standard, over nineteen million families were low-income in 1960. This represented close to 41 percent of the total U.S. population at the time.[2] It is estimated that, by 1970, approximately seven million white families and two million black families will still be below the $5,000 income mark. This represents a substantial decrease from the nineteen million families in 1960. The median income by 1970 will be $9,600; however, the U.S. Bureau of Labor Statistics estimates a comfortable living cost of $9,200 for urban dwellers. A little less than half the population will fall below this mark, with 11.6 million white and 3.9 million Negro families below $7,000.

Marketing to low-income neighborhoods demands a consideration of center city populations statistics. By 1970, it is estimated that whites will show a decrease of two million, and the Negro, an increase of 3.3 million in these vital centers. Close to 58.9 million people will live in these areas, with the Negro representing 20 percent of the total.[3]

Much emphasis has been placed on the non-white urban poor in this country; yet, in 1960, 10.7 million white families in urban areas were in this category as compared with 5.5 million blacks.[4]

Of all white families earning over $5,000, the percentage of two wage earners per family ranged from a low of 44.3 percent for the $5,000-$7,000 group to a high of 75 percent for the $12,000-$25,000 group. Most of the ten million-plus white families earning under $5,000 have only one wage earner in their households. Even in the center city of these metro-markets, poor whites outnumber black by 1.2 million people. [5]

INFLUENCE OF LIFE STYLES ON MARKETING

When considering the low-income segment, there are a number of socio-economic characteristics, and life style factors which encourage a systems approach to marketing. Some of these are:

1. Increased center city low-income population.
2. Low-income groups have experienced a greater increase in income than their cost of living.
3. Their neighborhoods primarily consist of small outlets. Consumers purchase frequently and in smaller units.
4. Community organization exerts pressure for faster economic and social changes.
5. Life style of consumers is need-oriented, peer directed, income-limited, mobility-inhibited, and isolated from the rest of the city.
6. Low-income families are heavily concentrated by region and within the city.
7. Unique communications network exists within the community or neighborhood.

Now let's investigate some of the life style patterns of low-income consumers that are unique in either degree or kind. These patterns, when interrelated with consumer behavior, can be linked to a number of critical marketing functions, such as: distribution, merchandising activities, product mix, packaging mix, advertising programs, sales policies, and dealer relations activities. These various marketing functions tend to interrelate in response to the unique environment of the low-income neighborhood.

"The low-income consumer is a block dweller, who sees himself as part of his immediate environment and neighborhood, rather than a part of the city in general. His peer relationships are close in this limited environment, and as a consumer, he is strongly motivated to shop within these confines."[6] "The poor consumer is less psychologically mobile, less sctive, and more inhibited in his behavior than well-to-do customers. The stores he considers for possible purchases are always small. The poor people more often buy at the same store."[7] "A comparison of shopping habits of middle class and working class women shows . . . fewer lower class regularly shop in the central business district. The low-income white housewife shops in 'local' stores. The working man's wife or the low-income white wife most frequently prefers to shop in a local and known in store."[8] Because of this narrow territorial view, product availability is an important factor in the marketer's distribution system in low-income areas. Add to this the fact that low-income consumers make frequent shopping trips for smaller package sizes, and you can see the importance of delivery frequency or frequency of sales calls and other sales management policies. Along with product availability, the type of outlet that dominates low-income neighborhoods should also be considered.

REACTION TO COMPANY POSTURE

Community relations has only a minor influence on immediate sales in market segments other than low-incomes. However, such secondary issues as employment policies toward minority groups are particularly important to low-income Negroes, and consequently influence their purchasing behavior.

"A company which advertises in Negro media, contributes to the United Negro College Fund, and employs Negroes is perceived as being concerned with the welfare of Negroes, and therefore is entitled to special concern and patronage." Edward Wallerstein, of The Center For Research and Marketing, went on to state that "Negroes tend to believe that a company which advertises in Negro media will be fairer in terms of its employment practices than most companies . . . further, our respondents said that they would tend to switch to the products of the company which advertised in Negro media."[9] Because Negroes look more favorably on companies which advertise in Negro media and employ Negroes, the marketing man is operating in a climate of increasing intensity. As Thomas F. Pettigrew predicted in 1964, "Negro protests will continue to grow both in intensity and depth". It "will increasingly attract larger proportions of low-income Negroes and shift from status to economic goals". He further stated, "a more intensive use of local and national boycotts of consumer products will be made".[10] His statements clearly indicate the interrelationship between sound community relations efforts and employment practices and sound marketing programs as they effect low-income blacks.

Recent organized boycotts have intensified these attitudes. The physical isolation caused by segregation in housing, either by income or race, has compounded marketers' problems. Another factor is the low-income consumer's "lack of mobility, both physical and psychological".[11] Car ownership is low, and parking space is scarce. This means that besides the general tendency of low-income people to stay within their neighborhoods, there are fewer opportunities for them to travel outside this environment. Therefore, marketing performance in low-income areas must be measured by the success — or lack of it — of retailers in these neighborhoods.

MEETING THE ADVERTISING CHALLENGE

The problem of communicating to residents of these neighborhoods offers a challenge to a variety of marketing and marketing-related functions. Advertising strategy, both from a copy platform and media planning standpoint, is as affected as sales promotion and point-of-sale activities. One reason why this variety of selling activities needs to be tailored to low-income consumers is because of the uniqueness of their life style patterns, including their language and communications patterns and attitudes toward advertising.

The language of this group is *concrete*. They are "less verbally oriented than better educated groups, and their interpersonal exchanges involve smaller amounts of symbolic linguistic behavior."[12] Their day-to-day conversations are less abstract and have less conceptualization. They deal primarily with concrete objects and situations. The fact that they generalize less and are less reliant on the intellectual process, than on observations, often renders some sophisticated advertising and sales promotion efforts of major marketers ineffective.

To fully appreciate the burden that advertising communications must carry into low-income neighborhoods, one should remember that advertising must function as a persuasive vehicle that stimulates the desire to consume, as well as increasing their ability to consume. The educational function that advertising performs in this regard is important. Many low-income housewives, both white and black, look to advertising to fulfill an educational role. Nearly twelve million U.S. adults have less than a sixth grade education, with 2.7 million never having attended school at all. More than 23 million never completed grade school.[13]

Low-income consumers' preference for certain types of models also affects commercial communications. In the case of white blue-collar wives, "advertising which is people oriented is much more meaningful than . . . advertising that communicates a highly technical, impersonal or objective atmosphere".[14] A study conducted by Social Research asserts that "the safest route to high rewards from the Negro audience is to be found in advertisements which feature Negroes exclusively".[15] Naturally this preference should be considered when planning media, advertising, and sales promotions programs.

BRIDGING CULTURAL AND CREDIBILITY GAPS

Understanding the behavior patterns of residents of low-income neighborhoods requires a clear understanding of their attitudes toward the world outside their enviroment. They often consider it hostile, and think in terms of "we" and "them". "The lack of effective participation and integration of the poor in the major institutions of the large society is one of the critical characteristics of the culture of poverty."[16]

Although it is difficult, a marketer in a low-income area must translate his image from "them" to "we". "Supermarkets operating in disadvantaged areas do not enjoy the confidence of their customers . . . Negroes believe that they are treated as undesirables or untouchables . . . there is a definite credibility gap between what the food chain says they are doing for Ghetto residents and what these people think is being done". Both white and black Ghetto residents have more complaints about their local food stores — "prices are high, service is bad and unfriendly, stores are dirty, and lighting is inadequate".[17]

Both marketers and retailers are faced with a number of problems. In the case of the marketer, has he made certain that the items that appeal most to low-income consumers — the items that fit best into their life style — are available in the right package size? And is the product continuously available for a consumer who has a more frequent shopping pattern than the average?

The pre-conditioning done by the marketer effects the retailer and the consumer. The retailer who has the right variety of merchandise, meaning the merchandise most appropriate to the needs of the low-income community and most readily accepted by that market, will greatly improve his image. Since the food chain store has a poor image among this group, the responsibility of the marketer is more critical. Consequently, such functions as merchandising policies, distribution and sales activities, as well as community relations and public relations functions, are key factors.

BETTER RESEARCH IS SORELY NEEDED

The marketing executive who relies on information derived from his own life experiences is handicapped when faced with the problems of marketing to low-income groups, because their life style is quite different from his middle class one. Nor can he rely on usual sources to help him to narrow his informational gap. It is "acknowledged that most market research is now focused on middle and upper income people, but there is increasing awareness of the need to focus more marketing attention on those in low-income groups".[18] This executive discovers that A. C. Nielsen and other store audit services usually do not have a large enough sample in this segment to produce reliable data.

These combined factors clearly indicate the need for a systems approach to dealing with the low-income segment. For example, the system of small outlets, that is, outlets that have a physical space limitation, is interlocked with the fact that merchants usually running them have limited financial resources and management skills, Both their physical and financial limitations usually only allow these retailers to purchase limited quantities at a given time. If the manufacturer's delivery frequency cannot fit these limitations that the retailers operate under, product availability and dealer goodwill become critical problems accentuated by the low-income consumer's propensity to buy often and in smaller units. To attack the problem of product availability, it will be necessary to deal with several marketing functions, such as frequency of delivery, credit policies, and merchandising and display facilities. Changing a single marketing function probably would not be effective.

SUMMARY

A list of factors which influenced our conclusion that there is a need for a systems approach to improve the effectiveness of marketing programs directed at low-income neighborhoods would consist of the following:

1. Marketing administrators responsible for share of market in the major urban centers have to look at how their total system is working in this part of their sales environment.

2. While consumers in low-income neighborhoods are increasing their income more rapidly than their cost of living, there is still a lag in education and income. These two factors will influence a number of marketing functions differently than for other income groups.

3. Life style differences will tend to prevail and marketers will be forced to respond with a different marketing mix. Factors such as varying product or packaging mix policies will be required.

4. Finally, the concentration of low-income families in certain regions of the United States and within certain parts of the city will continue. Communications problems to this group, because of educational differences, will continue to be a challenge for progressive marketers.

Low-income neighborhoods will continue to be a problem to marketers who have not adjusted their total system to this segment's needs.

NOTES

1. Alvin Schwartz, "Study Reveals 'Neighborhood' Influence on Consumer Buying Habits," *Progressive Grocer*, April 1966, pp. 269-272, at p. 269.

2. *United States Census*, 1960.

3. "Changing American," *U.S. News and World Report*, June 2, 1969, p. 69.

4. "Forgotten Men: The Poor Whites," *U.S. News and World Report*, November 27, 1967, p. 76.

5. "Most U.S. Income Found Inadequate," *The New York Times*, November 18, 1968, p. 38.

6. (Unpublished Report), "The Low Income Study," 1969.

7. David Caplovitz, *The Poor Pay More*, New York, The Free Press, 1963, p. 49.

8. Lee Rainwater, Richard P. Coleman, Gerald Handel, *Workingman's Wife*, New York, Oceana Publishers, 1959, pp. 163, 164.

9. "Negro Boycott Could Have Serious Lasting Effects on Sales, Study Shows," *Advertising Age*, September 30, 1963, p. 38.

10. Thomas F. Pettigrew, *A Profile of the Negro American*, Princeton, D. Van Nostrand Co., 1964, pp. 197-199.

11. David Caplovitz, *The Poor Pay More*, New York, The Free Press, 1963, p. 49.

12. Lola M. Irelan, ed., *Low Income Life Style*, Washington, D.C., Health, Education and Welfare, August 1967, p. 72.

13. "The New Market," *Harvard Business Review*, May-June 1969, p. 61.

14. Lee Rainwater, Richard P. Coleman, Gerald Handel, *Workingman's Wife*, New York, Oceana Publishers, 1959, p. 153.

15. *Negro Media Usage and Response to Advertising*, Social Research, Inc., April 1969, Study No. 362/1, p. 4.

16. Oscar Lewis, "The Culture of Poverty," *Man Against Poverty: World War III*, Bernstein, Woock, ed., New York, Random House, 1968, p. 264.

17. "Poor Still Don't Trust Chains, *Chain Store Age*, February 1969, p. 63.

18. "Lavidge Says Market Researchers Must Focus on Minorities," *Advertising Age*, May 26, 1969, p. 45.

APPENDIX*

*This appendix was not with Kelvin A. Wall's article in Bernard A. Morin (ed.) Marketing in a Changing World.

A Systems View of Marketing in Low Income Neighborhoods

Sociological-Economic Characteristics	Marketing Implicati...	Marketing Function or Function Affecting Mktg.
Increase Center City Low-Income Population as Middle-Class Out-Migration Continues	Low income segment more important to most major consumer goods marketers and in city retailers.	Distribution/Physical Sales Coverage Advertising Coverage Product & Package Mix Package Size Mix Wholesaler/Jobbers
Greater Increase in Income of Low Income Group than Cost of Living	This part of the total market will exercise more influence because of increased income and rapid population growth. Competition for their dollars will intensify	New Products New Outlets Sales Coverage Distribution/Physical Product, Package, Package Size Mix Advertising Coverage
Neighborhoods Have Small Outlets Consumers Purchase Smaller Units	Maximizing sales or profits requires different marketing and sales strategy because of different outlet mix and purchasing patterns.	Distribution/Physical Sales Coverage Dealer Promotions Product, Package, Package Size Mix Sales Promotion Retail Store Audits
Community Organization Pressure for Social and Faster Economic Changes	Mass urban marketers, both retailers and manufacturers, will either respond to these pressures voluntarily or be forced to respond through direct economic action against them.	Product or Service Quality Existing Outlets New Outlets Employment Practices Personnel Training Advertising Content Advertising Media

Life Style
- Need-Orientated
- Peer-Orientated
- Mobile-Inhibited
- Income-Limited
- Isolated From Rest of City

Both retailers and other marketers faced with wider differences in consumer motivations and behavioral patterns between low income consumers than with any other combination of income groups.

Public Relations
Sales Promotion
Joint Ventures
New Distributors

New Products
Merchandising Policies
Outlets – Old and New
Copy Platforms
Sales Promotion
Fashion/Styling/Colors
Music
Advertising Media
Retail Store Audit
Market Research
Public Relations
Distribution

Low-Income Families Heavily Concentrated by Region and Within Cities
- density increase with low-income
- low-income white
- low-income Negroes (Both important factors)

The problems and the needs of low-income people are more similar than unique or distinct among sub groups. The amount of money they have to spend and their relationship with the total community are, in general, their two most important problems.

Sales Promotion
Point-of-Sales
Advertising Media
Copy Platform
Music
Package Size
Product Mix

Communications
- neighborhood outlet-part of communications network
- conversation topics limited
- how as important as what is said
- metaphoric and anecdotical
- peer group network

Conventional media can and do bring messages into the low-income areas. But, these are considered messages from the "outside" and the impact is questionable since their form and language is not their own.

New Media
New Copy
Sales Promotion
Point-of-Sales
Music
Public Relations
Outlets

Residential Patterns for Whites and Negroes

	Whites		Negroes	
	1960	1970 (est.)	1960	1970 (est.)
Central cities	48,800,000	46,800,000	9,800,000	12,100,000
Suburbs	55,700,000	74,400,000	2,900,000	4,400,000
Small towns and other nonfarm areas	42,500,000	49,400,000	4,600,000	5,100,000
Farms	11,800,000	7,800,000	1,510,000	1,100,000
TOTAL U. S.	158,810,000	178,400,000	18,900,000	22,800,000

Source: 1960, U. S. Census Bureau: 1970, projections by USN&WR Economic Unit, based on census data.

White Americans increased by 19.6 million, or 12.3% in the 1960s, while Negro Americans increased by 3.9 million, or 20.6%. Central cities lost an estimated 2 million whites and gained about 2.3 million Negroes.

Percentage Distribution of Population
by Income Groupings for Regions of the United States *

	Under $5,000		$5-8,000		$8-10,000		Over $10,000	
	% Households	% Inc.	% Households	% Inc.	% Households	% Inc.	% Households	% Inc.
New England	25.7	8.1	31.1	22.8	16.7	16.5	26.5	52.6
Mid Atlantic	28.7	8.5	28.3	20.8	15.5	15.4	27.4	55.3
E. North Central	27.8	7.8	26.7	19.6	16.5	16.3	29.0	56.3
W. North Central	37.1	11.7	26.1	21.8	14.3	16.3	22.4	50.2
South Atlan	41.3	13.7	25.2	21.6	12.3	14.6	21.2	50.1
E. South Central	49.3	18.0	23.5	23.3	10.8	14.9	16.2	43.8
W. South Central	45.4	15.9	24.8	22.8	11.7	14.9	18.1	46.4
Mountain	37.9	13.2	29.4	25.7	13.1	15.8	19.5	45.3
Pacific	31.3	8.9	26.2	19.7	15.1	15.5	27.4	55.9
Total	34.4	10.5	26.7	21.2	14.3	15.6	24.5	52.7

* Cash Income.

Source: *Sales Management Magazine*, June 1968, p. B

Income Trends for the United States

Yearly Income	White Families		Negro Families	
	1960	1970 (est.)	1960	1970 (est.)
Under $3,000	7,800,000	3,000,000	1,900,000	1,000,000
$3,000-$4,999	8,100,000	3,900,000	1,000,000	900,000
$5,000-$6,999	10,000,000	4,600,000	600,000	1,000,000
$7,000-$9,999	8,700,000	11,100,000	300,000	900,000
$10,000-$14,999	4,600,000	13,900,000	200,000	700,000
$15,000 plus	1,600,000	9,700,000	20,000	400,000
	Whites		Negroes	
Persons living in poverty*	27,500,000	13,600,000	10,500,000	6,400,000

Income gains are dramatic for both white and Negro families. Median income for Negro families has doubled since 1960, to an estimated $6,500 in 1970. Median income for white families rose 65 per cent, to $9,600.

*Single persons or members of families with incomes below officially designated "poverty" levels, set at $3,060 per year in 1960 and $3,358 in 1968 for a nonfarm family of four.

Source: 1960, U.S. Census Bureau; 1970, projections by USN&WR Economic Unit, based on census estimates through 1968.

II. CONSUMERS - SUGGESTED ADDITIONAL READINGS

Donald Auster, "Attitude Change and Cognitive Dissonance," *Journal of Marketing Research*, 2, November 1965, 401-405.

Raymond A. Bauer, "The Role of the Audience in the Communication Process: Summary," Stephen A. Greyser, ed., *Toward Scientific Management*, Chicago: American Marketing Association, 1963, 73-82.

Gerald D. Bell, "Self-Confidence and Persuasion in Car Buying," *Journal of Marketing Research*, 4, February 1967, 46-52.

Gerald D. Bell, "The Automobile Buyer After the Purchase," *Journal of Marketing*, 31, July 1967, 12-16.

Frances S. Bourne, "Different Kinds of Decisions and Reference Group Influence," Perry Bliss, ed., *Marketing and Behavioral Sciences*, Boston: Allyn and Bacon, Inc., 1963, 247-255.

Richard P. Coleman, "The Significance of Social Stratification in Selling," Martin L. Bell, ed., *Marketing: A Mature Discipline*, Chicago: American Marketing Association, 1960, 171-184.

Ross M. Cunningham, "Customer Loyalty to Store and Brand," *Harvard Business Review*, 39, November-December 1961, 127-137.

Ernest Dichter, "Can We Have Research Without Creativity," *Marketing Review*, 24, June 1969. (Publication of American Marketing Association, New York Chapter), 12-17.

Ira J. Dolich, "Congruence Relationship Between Self Images and Product Brands," *Journal of Marketing Research*, 6, February 1969, 80-84.

James F. Engel, "Are Automobile Purchasers Dissonant Consumers," *Journal of Marketing*, 27, April 1963, 55-58.

"Further Pursuit of the Dissonant Consumer: A Comment," *Journal of Marketing*, 29, April 1965, 33-34.

"The Psychological Consequences of a Major Decision," William S. Decker, ed., *Emerging Concepts in Marketing*, Chicago: American Marketing Association, 1962, 462-475.

Edward L. Grubb and Harrison L. Grathwohl, "Consumer Self Concept, Symbolism and Market Behavior: A Theoretical Approach," *Journal of Marketing*, 31, October 1967, 22-27.

Eckhard H. Hess, "Attitude and Pupil Size," *Scientific American*, 212, April 1967, 46-54.

Robert J. Holloway, "An Experiment on Consumer Dissonance," *Journal of Marketing*, 31, January 1967, 39-43.

Charles W. King, "Fashion Adoption: A Rebuttal to the 'Trickle Down' Theory," Stephen A. Greyser, ed., *Toward Scientific Management*, Chicago: American Marketing Association, 1963, 108-125.

Xavier Kohan, "A Physiological Measure of Commercial Effectiveness," *Journal of Advertising Research*, 8, December 1968, 46-48.

Herbert E. Krugman, "The Learning of Consumer Preferences," *Journal of Marketing*, 26, April 1962, 31-32.

William Lazer, "Life Style Concept and Marketing," Stephen A. Greyser, ed., *Toward Scientific Management*, Chicago: American Marketing Association, 1963, 130-139.

Leonard A. Losciuto and Robert Perloff, "Influence of Product Preference on Dissonance Reduction," *Journal of Marketing, Research,* 4, August 1967, 286-290.

Pierre D. Martineau, "The Social Class and Its Very Close Relationship to the Individual's Buying Behavior," Martin L. Bell, ed., *Marketing: A Mature Discipline*, Chicago: American Marketing Association, 1960, 185-192.

Fredrick E. May, "Buying Behavior: Some Research Findings," *Journal of Business*, 38, October 1965, 379-396.

Stuart U. Rich and Subhash C. Jain, "Social Class and Life Cycle as Predictors of Shopping Behavior," *Journal of Marketing Research*, 5, February 1968, 41-49.

Burt K. Scanlan, "Anthropology's Potential Role in Gauging Consumer Desires," *Business and Society*, Spring 1965, 28-32.

James E. Stafford, "Effect of Group Influences on Consumer Brand Preference," *Journal of Marketing Research*, 3, February 1966, 68-75.

Bruce C. Straits, "The Pursuit of the Dissonant Consumer," *Journal of Marketing*, 28, July 1964, 62-66.

F. J. Van Bortel, "Commercial Applications of Pupillometrics," Frank M. Bass, Charles W. King, and Edgar A. Pessemier, eds., *Applications of the Sciences in Marketing Management*, New York: John Wiley & Sons, Inc., 1968, 439-453.

William D. Wells and George Gubar, "Life Cycle Concept in Marketing Research," *Journal of Marketing Research*, 3, November 1966, 355-363.

Ralph Westfall, "Psychological Factors in Predicting Product Choice," *Journal of Marketing*, 26, April 1962, 34-40.

Walter A. Woods, "Psychological Dimensions of Consumer Decision," *Journal of Marketing*, 24, January 1960, 15-19.

III

Utilities:

Strategies For Their Organization, Creation, and Replacement

Viewing the marketer in his role as a creator of utilities lends a broader perspective to and emphasizes the primacy of his function.

A product or service has to be available *where* it is wanted (place utility), *when* it is wanted (time utility), and in such a fashion that a consumer can, with no misunderstanding, *acquire* it (possession utility). The creation of these utilities is clearly the function of marketing.

Marketing also directs the nature of the form utility which the product must have before it is produced. This responsibility of the marketer is not widely recognized. It is the marketer who must analyze just what specific utility the product or service is to provide and at which target consumers it is to be aimed. Marketers also have to decide whether to make clothes which will keep people warm or cool, or make them look beautiful; to supply food which will be nourishing or non-fattening, or to furnish automobiles which will provide reliable transportation or give people a feeling of power. Marketers must analyze the desires of people for products or services which cater to their needs to be loved, to feel young, to be distinctive, to be informed, to be entertained, to "do their own thing" and so on.

111

If marketers can rightly appraise some of these varied needs and suggest a form of product or service to meet them, then the actual production process may not prove to be very difficult. Time, place, and possession utilities will follow as a natural consequence of the correct appraisal. For the purpose of focus, we have included articles related to product utility only. Physical distribution is another source of utility creation.

In this section, these problems of appraisal are analyzed from various viewpoints. Some interesting ideas have been developed concerning products and how they have a life cycle not unlike a human life cycle. Maximizing the life of product utilities may be accomplished by understanding the product life cycle. Products pass through recognizable marketing stages. Predicting the shape and duration of each stage is the goal of efficient marketing management.

Product characteristics may be used to explain marketing department: policies, methods, and marketing mix. A broad spectrum of organizational structures is examined for their usefulness to effect fruitation of the intended utilities inherent in product innovations. For the purpose of spreading consumer acceptance of these utilities, the diffusion process is considered.

14

The purpose of this paper is to explain how one type of formal corporate organization structure works more efficiently than another type in the development of new products. That is, if a company has a full-time new product department, can their performance, in terms of new product marketing, be superior to a company with a part-time new product executive or one without any new product executive at all.

Included in this paper will be the results of research conducted among the 125 largest consumer package goods companies in the United States.

if you want new products you better organize to get them

robert a. grayson

Since the beginning of recorded history we have been able to trace the existence of bodies of people that have arranged themselves in a particular way — which we have come to call "Organizations". We are not sure that there were Stone Age Hadassahs or Garden Clubs complete with Presidents and Recording Secretaries but we do know that the Armies had hierarchical structures and that the civilizations along the Euphrates were not unlike those that exist today.

In its broadest sense we "organize" in order to increase efficiency. But what happens if we organize improperly? Might it not be said that we thereby guarantee inefficiency?

The purpose of the research done in support of this paper was to ascertain if there is one way of organizing for new product development which is more efficient, i.e., leads to greater productivity, than any other.

Reprinted from Bernard A. Morin (ed.), *Marketing in a Changing World*, Proceedings of the National Conference of the American Marketing Association, published by the American Marketing Association, June 1969, pp. 75-79.

First we shall examine some of the ways we can organize. Then we will examine some of the organization theories that might lead to the selection of the best system on a normative basis, and then to the research which was done among the 125 packaged goods manufacturers who do over $25 million dollars per year, and finally, the conclusions which the research indicated.

A successful new product program means that, against a pre-determined objective, a given quantity of new products are spewed forth by the organization. Some of these might be regarded as line extensions, brand extensions, products new to the company but developed first by competition, or truly unique products. Whichever definition is used depends upon the corporate predisposition.

A successful program may then be considered to be one that met the objectives established for it.

If we assume that "success" is the basic requirement of any new product program we should then examine two major ingredients of "success". These are 1) creativity and 2) output. One without the other could lead to a suboptimization of any new product program.

If we examine the six general types of new product organizations we can provide some generalizations regarding creativity, but there is no data to back up our opinion. This research was designed to measure output vis-á-vis type of organization. We suspect that there may very well be a trade-off between creativity and output but 1) this has not been proved and 2) most corporations cannot and do not knowingly make this trade-off because the truly creative new products may come only once every ten years, e.g. nylon, Xerox, Polaroid, etc.

In Figure 1, the new products are developed by the same brand manager who is working on going brands. The conclusion is that most emphasis would be oriented towards the existing market place and so he would be more concerned with line extensions. This is not really very creative but a necessary bit of pragmatism for today's marketing climate. Brand extensions also come from this source with some small increment in creativity such as using the Kraft name for jams and jellies. The innovation is not very exciting but it ultimately leads to good reading on the balance sheet. As long as the brand manager's products are not in a state of crisis some output with be forthcoming but heaven help us if the shares of the going brand are off. Goodbye new products.

In Figure 2 we see a popular adaptation of the system in Figure 1, but here we have interposed a group product manager so that one product manager works on going brands and another on new products. In this case the crises of the regular brand manager become those of the group product manager and the new products manager has to wait until the dust subsides to "get in his licks". It should be noted that the longer he has to wait to get his new products approved and moving, the more sure it is that crisis will be the by-word because the pressure on the old on-going business increases inexorably day by day. There is a kind of Gresham's Law in effect, "Daily work drives out long term work."

We have, in effect, moved the apple a little farther from the tree − but not

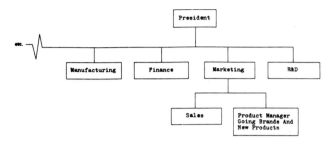

Figure 1. New products developed within regular organization

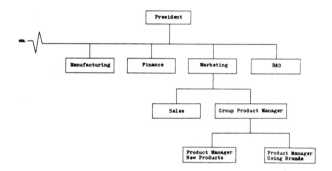

Figure 2. Division of responsibility between new products and going brands

very far. The basic problem is that the group product manager's orientation is still oriented towards known markets and existing brands.

In order to broaden the scope of new product development many companies have established a New Product Committee whose job it is to oversee the corporate effort. This committee meets regularly and reviews all programs to date.

What happens in this case is that the inputs are discussed and evaluated but this committee has very little control over the quality or quantity of inputs, so its deliberations are bounded by what the organization can give it. Therefore, the frailties discussed in Figures 1 and 2 still maintain. However, if the composition of the Committee is broad and it is run democratically we can predict that, because humans are captives of their own environment, a minimum of creativity will abound. After all, the majority of the group will be from areas other than marketing and cannot possible have the proper frame of reference.

In an effort to broaden the scope of new product development some companies have moved responsibility to the Research and Development Department.

It may very well be that in some industries, such as ethical drugs, this system works, but, for packaged goods people, research and development needs strong direction from marketing or there are going to be a lot of products developed

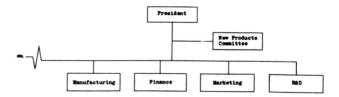

Figure 3. Broadening the scope by establishing a committee

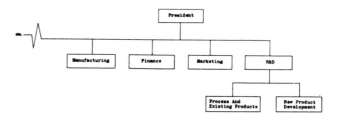

Figure 4. Changing the focus of new product development

that no one wants. A good example of this is an R & D product which was developed in the early 60's that was designed to eliminate "brushing between meals". The assumption was that everyone felt guilty about not brushing after every meal. It was a tablet designed to induce salivation which would cause a "flushing" of the teeth which was in turn supposed to wash the particles of food from between the teeth. An interesting side light of this product, aside from the miserable results in test market, occurred with one of the senior executives of this company. He had just had an eye operation and was forbidden from brushing his teeth because of the shaking involved. What a perfect spot for this tablet! Unfortunately, the product caused him to throw-up.

A fifth system of organization is the "Task Force". In this case a group is assembled from various operating departments and charged with the responsibility of bringing a specific product to market. This method generally assumes that some one else has developed the idea and the Marketing Department or New Product Committee has sanctioned the idea. A serious problem with this method is that each member of the Task Force is, in fact, a representative of the department from which he comes and is bounded by any constraints established by his boss. Also, any expertise developed is not transferable because the group is usually disbanded upon completion of the project.

Finally, there is the New Product Department.

This has the immediate disadvantage of increasing the overhead. "After all, this work used to be done within the regular line groups at no cost." However, when measured against output, the complaint does not hold up. Staffed with experts from several areas of the operation this group can be broad enough to look outside the traditional product line and still be sensitive to the immediate operating needs. Expertise remains as does continuity with the market place.

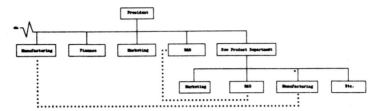

Figure 5. The optimum system

Obviously there are several other possible combinations or permutations but, for the most part, these are the popular organizations.

As was mentioned earlier, the two important measures of new product development are creativity and output. Which of those systems is best for output? Before proceeding it may be best to define output. For the purpose of this paper we will consider any new product to be equal to any other new product in terms of achieving the corporate goals. We are assuming that the corporation has defined parameters which constrain wanton new product introductions. Therefore, with the minimum profitability and probability for success in mind, if a company can increase its output it should thereby increase the number of successful new products.

The hypothesis against which this research was done is "The type of reporting relationships, as delineated by the formal organization structure, is significantly correlated to the number of new products developed by a company." That is, a company with X structure will market more new products than a company with Y structure. This occurs because certain structures vest new product responsibility with line managers who have significant daily responsibility for established products which preclude new product development while other structures have segregated this function and delegated it to specialists who have no other responsibility.

The theoretical framework for segregating specialized duties has been amply established in the management literature. A random selection of this literature clearly sets the ground for our hypothesis.

THE NEED TO ORGANIZE

"The orderly and successful performance of any major human undertaking, of whatever character, requires that a definite sequence of steps be followed in its planning and execution. These steps are: 1) clearly defining the objectives and scope of the undertaking, 2) developing policies necessary to achieve the objective, 3) fixing responsibility, that is, building a logical, workable, organization to do the job, 4) working out a comprehensive approach and plan of action, 5) applying skilled techniques to the work undertaken, 6) maintaining control, from some positive means for measuring results achieved."[1] Within the scope of this paper we are concerned primarily with number 3 and 5 above. Having had the objectives and policies of the corporation clearly delineated the need for the proper organization to translate these into action and results becomes clearly evident.

Obviously, a basic tenent to our theory is that new product development is indeed a specialized function. It is maintained that the work done in developing, nurturing and finally marketing new products is as different from the mainstream of the business' daily operation as the work of a pediatrician differs from that of a general practitioner. It is for this reason that the focus of an analysis of the existing "classical" and "neo-classical" literature is on the basic premises derived for organizing for a specialized task.

Ernest Dale developed the "principle" of specialization in this manner.

Work should be so divided that the incumbent of a position should be able to become a specialist and increase knowledge on the particular job assigned to him. Special ability should be used in full. Groups of people (Divisions, Departments) should comprise a workable, homogeneous and separate field of activity. The nature of their work should be similar or complementary (the former is probably more important in the lower executive ranks, the latter more important in the upper ranks).[2]

The current literature on the ways of organizing for new product development is sparse indeed. Aside from the Johnson & Jones articles in *The Harvard Business Review* (M-J 1957), and articles by Lazo, McFadden and McCarthy, there is nothing of a definite nature on which to base an organizational decision. That is, until now.

HOW THE RESEARCH WAS DONE

New Product Ratios: Through the use of advertising and market auditing companies[3] lists were compiled of the product lines as of year end 1960. All new product additions to the line from 1961 to June 1967 were similarly calculated. In order to check the validity of the reference material several companies were requested to submit price lists (including regional lists) which were then compared to the data gathered from the aforementioned sources. In all cases the secondary data proved to be virtually one hundred percent accurate. A ratio was then developed for each company by dividing the number of new products introduced since 1960 by the number of products in the line as of 1960.

Following the new product ratio calculations the companies were grouped according to type of organization, that is, full-time new product executive, part-time new product executive and no new product executive.

THE FINDINGS

The specific tabulations of the answers to the questions can be found in the full report. The most significant finding, however, is that companies organized with full-time new product executives produce 69.0% more new products that companies with part-time executives and 60.5% more than companies without any new product executives. From this we may conclude that there is not a significant difference between companies organized with a part-time executive and those with no new product executive officially designated. Nonetheless, both methods appear to be decidedly inferior to the full-time new product executive type of organization structure.

ORGANIZATIONAL CHANGES RELATING TO NEW PRODUCT DEVELOPMENT

As the pace of new product development increases and the obsolescence rate of existing product accelerates, the need for new product development becomes more critical. It is, therefore, not surprising that almost all companies in the study indicate that there have been organizational changes relating to new product development activities during the last five years.

While the changes might not necessarily be due to dissatisfaction with the existing system, the fact that 77% of the companies made changes would indicate that there must be a significant desire on the part of management to improve the existing productivity. Of the changes that were made, half the companies indicate that some form of separate new product division was established for the implementation of new product development work. It is interesting to note that the companies which do not have a new product executive have increased the number of committees or task forces at various levels of management. As would be expected, these changes have been accompanied by increased emphasis on the part of management for new product development.

More importantly, however, is the fact that almost two thirds of the companies that have undergone organizational changes believe that this resulted in greater new product idea generation. In only one case was it believed that the number of ideas decreased.

PROBLEMS WHICH PREVENT NEW PRODUCT ACTIVITIES FROM ACHIEVING MAXIMUM RESULTS

There is a remarkable consistency among all three organizational types regarding their views of the major problems. The two overwhelming problems were stated to be attitude and expertise. This would lead one to conclude that a relatively poor management attitude *and* lack of marketing expertise not only pervade most companies but are also the major cause of suboptimal results, and, although a separate division might be established, the same problems tend to remain. In general, the pattern for all problems was pretty similar in all three organizations with the exception of "money" and organizational structure. Lack of funds seems to plague the full-time executive's group considerably more than the company with no new product executive and about twice as much as those companies with part-time executives. Additionally, the companies with part-time and no new product executives felt that their organizational structure was seriously hampering their effort while the companies with full-time executives were not nearly so plagued with this problem. The problem of bad communications with top management seems most pervasive with the no new product executives. This might be the result of lack of time because of the other duties of these executives.

Consistent with the organizational problems, 85% of the companies with part-time executives recommended some kind of organizational change, with nearly three quarters of these recommending a separate new product section. The lack of general marketing expertise on the part of those companies without new product executives becomes apparent when 85% of these companies feel that by increasing their marketing know-how they will be gaining solutions to the problems which prevent new product activities from achieving maximum results. As might be expected the full-time executives felt that many of their solutions lie in adjustments to the budgets.

In reviewing the solutions as given by the respondents one cannot help but be made aware that many of the solutions would be more readily achievable if there were a different organization structure. For example, one of the benefits of specialization is the increase in participation, integration and commitment which, in turn, can lead to better planning, and 40% of the respondents felt the need for better planning. Expertise in any given field comes as a result of continuous operation and marketing is no exception. Thirty-seven percent of the respondents thought that their marketing should be improved. This also holds true for the utilization of personnel.

Two other significant solutions are: 1) the need on the part of the new product executive to have more regularity and routine, and 2) among the part-time executives 85% see some sort of organizational change as necessary to improve their new product work. In that these executives are currently handling "two" jobs their opinion should carry significant weight.

It should be noted that the bulk of the problems fell within the areas of management attitude and marketing. On the other hand, the bulk of the solutions fell within organization changes and planning, with marketing very close behind. This might lead one to believe that many people within corporations see organizational changes and better planning as the solution to a large multitude of problems.

CONCLUSIONS

The research indicates that a great number of the problems associated with new product development seem to be directly related to the way in which a company is organized. The classical management concepts of planning, organizing, staffing, directing and controlling are best served by discrete development sections. The visible advantages of specialization accrue while the not-so-visible communications problem is mitigated. All of these benefits, large and small, react synergistically to increase productivity.

It should be noted that one of the main reasons given for not reorganizing is the lack of trained personnel. This, in fact, may be the effect of bad organization, not the cause. This is cited as an example of a serendipitous benefit which may accrue from the synergism.

Additionally, the findings in this study seem to indicate that the ideal organization would be one in which: 1) all new product work is segregated; 2) the new product department reports as high as possible, in order to have it removed from the press of daily business; 3) the corporation develops specific new product specialists; 4) the new product people have broad backgrounds; 5) reasonably formalized procedures are developed and followed; and 6) top management establishes (and keeps open) good channels of communications.

In reviewing the questionnaire and the notes which were developed during the personal interviews the following additional conclusions seem indicated: 1) that the monies allocated to new product development should be inviolate, that is, these funds should not be diverted for any other purpose. One of the interviews revealed a situation in which the funds for new products came from a general division budget. At the start of each fiscal year a portion was set aside for new product development and marketing, but, as the year progressed, funds from this budget would get transferred to on-going brands to shore-up their merchandising effort. One continuing result was delay of test market introductions to later in the year so the out-of-pocket expenses would be minimized; 2) new product programs should be an integral part of the corporate long range program and there should be "line" responsibility for their output. In other words, the corporate long range plan might state an objective of $10,000,000 increase in sales over the next five years. If existing products can only deliver $5,000,000 then the remaining $5,000,000 can only come from new business, either internally developed or acquired. Assuming it is to be internally developed the new products department is now charged with the responsibility for producing products which will yield this amount of revenue. Once this objective has been set in financial terms it is possible to establish personnel and equipment requirements and, as importantly, it establishes a goal against which objective measurement can be made; 3) the Market Research Departments and personnel should become more "future" oriented rather than "history" oriented. It was never intended that we should dispense with store audits or consumption studies but rather there should be a substantial increase in the amount of research designed to tell us "where we should be in five years" rather than "where we have been in the last five years". There was general agreement that this type of research is very difficult to do with any degree of accuracy but there was almost universal agreement as to its need; 4) finally, managements' actions should be made in line with their stated objectives for new product development. There should be more direct interest on the part of top management in the creation of an atmosphere and corporate attitude which is conducive to an innovative spirit.

NOTES

1. Richard F. Neuschel, *Management by System*. (McGraw-Hill Book Company, Inc., New York, N.Y. 1960) p. 40.

2. Ernest Dale, *Planning and Developing the Company Organization Structure* (American Marketing Association, New York, N.Y. 1952) Report 20, p. 17.

3. Leading National Advertisers, Inc., New York, N.Y. for magazines, Sunday supplements and network television; N. C. Rorabaugh Co., Inc., New York, N.Y. for spot television; Radio Expenditure Reports, Larchmont, N.Y. for spot radio; Broadcast Advertiser's Reports, Inc., New York, N.Y. for network television and network radio; The Advertising Checking Bureau, Inc., New York, N.Y. for newspapers; Media Record, Inc., New York, N.Y. for newspapers.

Marketers today are faced with the dual facts that sales growth is most often accounted for by new products, yet a majority of new products introduced to the market fail. This paper considers strategies to improve the probability of new product success based on diffusion concepts.

15

the new product diffusion process

thomas s. robertson

THE NEW PRODUCT DIFFUSION PROCESS

Product innovation will be critical to survival and essential to growth for American firms in the decade of the 1970s. The pace of technological advances coupled with the American consumer's receptivity to progress and "newness" will shorten the life cycles of established products and place a premium on new products, although product obsolescence rates will continue to vary among industries and among product groups. In general, the less the commodity nature of the product group, or alternatively, the more the opportunity for product differentiation, then the more rapid is innovation and, concurrently, obsolescence.

*Assistant Professor at the Harvard Graduate School of Business Administration. This paper is adopted from a forthcoming book, Innovation and the Consumer (New York: Holt, Rinehart & Winston, Inc., 1971).

Reprinted from Bernard A. Morin (ed.), *Marketing in a Changing World*, Proceedings of the National Conference of the American Marketing Association, published by the American Marketing Association, June 1969, pp. 80-86.

WHAT IS A NEW PRODUCT?

The concern of this paper is with consumer acceptance of product innovations (new products). A major difficulty is in defining what is a new product and at least four definitional criteria have frequently been used: (1) newness from existing products, (2) newness in time, (3) newness in terms of sales penetration level, and (4) consumer newness to the product.

(1) *Newness from existing products.* Many authors argue that a "new product" must be *very different* from established products, although there is little attempt to make such a definition operational. The Federal Trade Commission has rendered an advisory opinion that a product may properly be called "new" "only when [it] is either entirely new or has been changed in a functionally significant and substantial respect. A product may not be called 'new' when only the package has been altered or some other change made which is functionally insignificant or insubstantial."[1]

E. B. Weiss claims that over 80% of new products are not, in fact, "new" but "simply modifications" of existing products.[2] He does not, however, establish guidelines for distinguishing such modifications from new products. It is possible to extend this point of view to the thesis that all new products are modifications or recombinations of existing items. Barnett, an anthropologist who has studied innovation and its effects on cultural change, states that "No innovation springs full-blown out of nothing; it must have antecedents . . . ."[3] This viewpoint, which is quite prevalent in sociological thinking, looks at innovation as the outcome of an evolutionary sequence. Even an innovation such as the computer can be considered to be a recombination of existing elements coupled with a measure of technological insight.

(2) *Newness in time.* Length of time on the market is a second criterion in defining a new product. There has been a pronounced tendency for firms to promote a product as new for as long as two or three years after introduction, under the assumption that the word "new" in advertising or on the package is a positive and desirable sales appeal. The Federal Trade Commission advisory opinion arbitrarily limits the use of the word new to six months after the product enters regular distribution after test marketing.[4]

(3) *Newness in terms of sales penetration level.* Another new product definitional criterion is the sales level which the product has achieved. Bell[5] and Robertson,[6] for example, have arbitrarily defined products as innovations when they have not yet secured 10% of their total potential market.

(4) *Consumer newness to the product.* Yet another criterion for defining a new product is that the consumer must *perceive* it to be new. There is, however,

invariably some consumer who is "new" to the product and it is not particularly useful to talk in terms of any individual consumer; the aggregate consumer is generally what the marketer has in mind. Perhaps a product could be defined as new when a majority of consumers perceive it in such a way, but this is again arbitrary.

These definitions, unfortunately, need not yield the same determinations as to what products are new. For example, using the consumer perception of newness definition, an item can be new without being substantially different in function from existing products, without being particularly new to the market, and while possessing a significant sales penetration level. There is a further difficulty in the discussion to this point, and that is that a simple dichotomy is being used — a product is either new or not new. More logically, a range of "newness" would be the case.

NEWNESS IN TERMS OF CONSUMPTION EFFECTS

The critical factor in defining a new product should be its effects upon established patterns of consumption. It is convenient to think in terms of: (1) continuous innovations, (2) dynamically continuous innovations, and (3) discontinuous innovations.

(1) A *continuous* innovation has the least disrupting influence on established consumption patterns. Alteration of a product is almost always involved rather than the creation of a new product. Examples include: flouride toothpaste, menthol cigarettes, and annual new-model automobile changeovers.

(2) A *dynamically continuous* innovation has more disrupting effects than a continuous innovation, although it still does not generally involve new consumption patterns. It may mean the creation of a new product or the alteration of an existing product. Examples include: electric toothbrushes, electric hair curlers, and the Mustang automobile.

(3) A *discontinuous* innovation involves the establishment of new consumption patterns and the creation of previously unknown products. Examples include: television, the computer, and the automobile.

This definitional framework, while recognizing that innovations are not all of the same order of newness, does not, unfortunately, distinguish new products from non-new products. It is my opinion that this decision is always arbitrary. It may be possible to agree that new sizes, new flavors, and new packages are not new products. Does, however, the addition of sugar to corn flakes, or raisins to bran constitute a new product? Is an instant oatmeal a new product or a variation of the old product? No definition of innovation satisfactorily answers these and similar questions unless we rely on consumer perception, and, as suggested, accept majority consumer opinion of what is and what is not an innovation.

MOST INNOVATION IS CONTINUOUS

Most innovation in the American economy is of a continuous nature. Most innovation, especially in the consumer sector, results as an attempt to differentiate products to increase market share. Few and far between are innovations of a discontinuous nature which significantly alter or create new consumption patterns. The image of innovations resulting from the inspiration of the occasional genius does not fit the typical occurrence and even discontinuous innovations are increasingly the result of planned team research. Most innovation today results from programmed, systematic research efforts.

Some Case Examples

If the first detergent on the market represented a fairly discontinuous innovation, then the succeeding proliferation of brands must represent highly continuous innovations. While one brand may be a low sudser, another possess cold water attributes, another contain bleach, and another contain disinfectant for baby clothes, all are essentially minor variations on the basic product. All of these succeeding brands are *programmed innovations*.

The automobile industry is the leading example of programmed, continuous innovations. New products appear on schedule each year and every three years major design changes occur. This planning and programming of innovation occurs across almost all industries. When a major aircraft manufacturer was considering its next venture into the commercial market, it plotted the various offerings then available in terms of such variables as runaway requirements, flying range, seating capacity, and cost of operation and found the gaps in the market. These gaps were in short-range jets and high-seating-capacity jets. The company then planned to innovate in one of these areas and did so.

THE IMPORTANCE OF INNOVATION TO THE FIRM

Innovation, according to a variety of sources, occurs due to: (1) shrinking profit margins for established products, (2) shorter lives for established products, and (3) excess capacity. Schumpeter has attributed innovation to (4) a search for profit.[7] Barrett has emphasized (5) the pressure of competition and the search for product differentiation as factors leading to innovation.[8]

These reasons for the occurrence of innovation overlap considerably. Analysis of their content also reveals their all-inclusve nature. Innovation, it would appear, is the solution to all business problems. Perhaps Schumpeter's view of innovation as a search for profit summarizes all of the other reasons; although corporate marketers generally cite growth, or forward momentum, as the most important factor encouraging new product development.

Maintaining Momentum

New products are basic to company growth and to profitability. It is seldom possible in today's economy to maintain momentum or even stability with innovations. Mattel Toymakers, for example, grew rapidly with the acceptance of Barbie Doll, but such growth could not be continued without other new products since Barbie Doll soon reached "maturity" on the product life cycle. It is also difficult to maintain profit margins when a product reaches maturity since competition intensifies and product advantages may be neutralized. The typical pattern in the food industry, for example, has been for profit margins to decline while sales are still increasing so that companies must quickly look to other new products for continued profit performance.[9]

Empirical Data

The contribution of new products to the sales growth of various industries has been researched by Booz-Allen & Hamilton, Inc. Expected growth from new products varies from 46% to as much as 100%, with an average of 75%. Innovating industries are also more likely to be high growth industries.[10]

In another study, Mansfield assessed the value of technological innovation to the growth and profitability of individual firms. His concern was with the acceptance of capital goods' innovations by firms of comparable initial size in the steel and petroleum refining industries. He concludes:

> "In every interval and in both industries, the successful innovators grew more rapidly than the others, and in some cases, their average rate of growth was more than twice that of the others."[11]

INNOVATIVE COMPETITION

The importance of successfully marketing product innovations is today being recognized as never before. This is evidenced in the marketing trade magazines and academic journals as well as in the proliferation of consulting agencies devoted to new products and the establishment of new product divisions within existing agencies.

Yet, as more firms become committed to innovation, new product advantages exist for shorter time periods and the "monoply" power of new products is soon overcome. When General Electric quickly followed Squibb in electric toothbrushes, for example, it added innovation to innovation by marketing a cordless version which was then a new usage concept. The new product marketplace is increasingly becoming more competitive as fairly simultaneous innovations often occur and imitation is indeed rapid. Many firms, such as Mattel Toymakers, prefer to jump from product tests to national marketing since test marketing often speeds imitation.

RISKS IN NEW PRODUCTS

Commitment to new products is not without serious problems and associated risks. Research and development expenditures for 1971 should approach $22.4 billion[12] — most of which will be spent on *unsuccessful* new product ideas. Based on responses from 51 prominent companies, Booz-Allen & Hamilton report that is takes almost 60 *ideas* to result in one commercially successful new product and that three-fourths of new product expense funds go to unsuccessful products.[13] These figures, however, must be treated as estimates only, especially since this is a sample of "prominent" companies and we can probably assume greater sophistication in the research and development process.

Buzzell and Nourse, in an extensive study of product innovation in the food industry, report that of every 1,000 new product ideas:

810 are rejected at the idea stage
135 are rejected on the basis of product tests
 12 are discontinued after marketing
 43 are introduced to the market
 36 remain on the market after introduction[14]

According to these figures, food companies would appear to better the across-industry average reported by Booz-Allen & Hamilton. The Buzzell and Nourse figures suggest that over two successful new food products result from every 58 ideas.

New Product Failures

The greatest risk in new products and the greatest potential monetary loss comes at the market introduction stage. Estimates of new product failures run from 10% to 80%. This wide discrepancy in estimates is due largely to three reasons: (1) *definition* of what constitutes a new product — this is seldom stated; (2) *measurement* of what failure means — while one study may include only product withdrawals from the market, another may include all unprofitable or marginally profitable products. While one study may limit itself to measurement within one or two years of introduction, another may choose a considerably longer time span; and (3) the *sample of companies* chosen — large companies are likely to market fewer failures than small companies and companies in sophisticated consumer-oriented industries are likely to market fewer failures than companies in less sophisticated, production-oriented industries.

While it is difficult, therefore, to provide an average new product failure ratio which will uniformly apply, this failure rate can be quite high. It is probably fair to say that a majority of new products fail, although it would be more meaningful to present figures by *industry* if such figures could be obtained.

Why Do New Products Fail?

New product failures are seldom due to bad products. Analysis of the trade literature provides countless examples of basically sound new products failing after market introduction. General Foods failed with a Birds Eye line of frozen baby foods and rejected a forerunner of Instant Breakfast, Brim, in test markets. Ford Motor Company's Edsel is perhaps the classic example of a new product failure. Campbell proved unsuccessful in marketing fruit soup as well as a Red Kettle line of dry soup mixes. Coca-Cola, despite its strong consumer franchise in cola beverages, was initially unsuccessful in marketing a diet cola.

Reasons for new product failures could be discussed at length, but the foremost problem is in *marketing*. More tightly controlled test market and market experimentation procedures are necessary as well as a greater volume of marketing research in advance of new product introductions. Sophisticated models for predicting new product sales levels should be encouraged. The primary focus here, however, will not be on these concerns. It is the thesis of this paper that the probability of new product success can be increased by understanding the factors governing *diffusion* of new products, that is, acceptance by consumers.

NEW PRODUCT DIFFUSION

Diffusion is the process by which something spreads. Anthropologists have studied the diffusion of language, religion, and ideas among tribes and societies. Sociologists, particularly rural sociologists, have study the diffusion of new ideas and new practices within societies. Physicists have studied the diffusion of atomic particles within elements. Marketers have implicitly studied diffusion for many years as they have sought to guide and control the spread of new products, but little research or conceptual thinking has been directed toward an understanding of the diffusion process itself.

The diffusion literature, as developed across a number of disciplines, offers for consideration a fairly well-developed theoretical framework which applies to the flow of information, ideas, and products. It is the integration of this framework with the traditional marketing framework which may advance our understanding of how new products disseminate and gain consumer acceptance and which may suggest means of improving new product marketing strategies.

Components of the Diffusion Process

The diffusion process can be conceptualized as: (1) the adoption, (2) of new products and services, (3) over time, (4) by consumers, (5) within social systems, (6) as encouraged by marketing activities.

Adoption refers to the use of a new item. *New Products* and services will be considered in the broadest sense from highly continuous to highly discontinuous innovations. The *time* dimension distinguishes early adopters from later adopters. The *consumer adoption unit* may be the individual consumer or a family or buying committee, or even a city of consumers. *Social systems* constitute the boundaries within which diffusion occurs. In a broad sense the market segment as a whole can be viewed as a social system, or more narrowly defined, the consumer's friendship group can be considered his social system. Within these systems, communication will occur – both marketer-initiated and non-marketer-initiated. *Marketing activities* are defined as the mix of product, price, promotion, and distribution plans and strategies.

These several aspects of the diffusion process are interdependent. For example: the attributes of the new product will affect the rate of adoption over time, the types of consumers who will adopt, the kinds of social systems within which diffusion will take place, and the marketing efforts needed to achieve diffusion. Alternatively, successful new product diffusion is critically dependent upon the communication of relevant product information and the matching of new product attributes with social system and individual consumer characteristics. Marketing activities can guide and contol, to a considerable extent, the rate and extent of diffusion.

EFFECTS OF MARKETING ACTIVITIES

The opportunities for marketing activities to affect the diffusion process *for a given new product* can be summarized as follows:

Social System

● Marketing decisions can select the social systems (market segments) in which diffusion is most likely to be successful.

● Promotion, pricing, and distribution strategies can be combined to reach specified social systems.

● Marketing activities can, in some cases, chart the diffusion path within a social system to achieve the fastest rate of diffusion. This may be possible by reaching critical individuals first – especially innovators and opinion leaders.

Consumer Adopters

● Marketing decisions can establish the consumer profile most likely to adopt the new product.

● Promotion, pricing, and distribution strategies can be oriented toward this consumer profile.

● Marketing activities can vary by penetration level to specifically reach different kinds of consumers. For example: advertising strategies to reach first adopters should usually be different than strategies to reach later adopters.

Product Meaning

● Marketing activities can help define product meaning and can encourage diffusion by emphasizing the most relevant product attributes. For example: should promotion for a new dessert product emphasize taste, convenience, low cost, or low calorie content?

Time

● Marketing activities can affect *rate* of diffusion. A low price, penetration strategy, a high level of promotional expenditures, free sampling and deal activity, and intensive distribution will generally all encourage a fast diffusion rate.

These opportunities will now be assessed briefly in turn.

Social System

The characteristics of a social system highly influence diffusion patterns for new products. This can be demonstrated by reference to a study by Graham who researched the diffusion of five innovations — television, canasta, supermarkets, Blue Cross, and medical service insurance — across social class levels. His research revealed that no single social class was consistently innovative in adopting all five innovations. Television, for example, diffused more quickly among low social classes while the card game canasta diffused more quickly among upper social classes.[15]

Graham argues that the critical factor in determining diffusion is the extent to which the attributes of the innovation are compatible with the attributes of the culture of the receiving social system. The "cultural equipment" required for the adoption of television, according to Graham, included an average education, a minimum income, and a desire for passive spectator entertainment. This cultural pattern coincided with a lower social class level.

Other researchers have distinguished between communities exhibiting modern versus traditional norms. The modern-oriented community is receptive to innovations while the tradition-oriented community relies on established ways of doing things. The norms in effect in a social system have a sizeable bearing on diffusion rates. This may vary by region of the country and from rural to urban areas.

Innovations may also diffuse at different rates within particular spheres of a social system. A number of studies show that an innovation diffuses more quickly among socially integrated social system members than among socially isolated members. For some products, diffusion may be most rapid among older people.

The marketer has at his discretion the choice of social systems in which to market his product or in which to place heaviest support behind his product. This decision must be based on a matching between the attributes of the new product and social system attributes. Should segmentation be on the basis of social class, ethnic group, age, or ecology? Given the selection of the most relevant social systems, what are the most appropriate promotional, distribution, and pricing strategies to reach these social systems? Finally, is it possible to initiate strategies to reach the most likely buyers within a social system? While this is frequently possible in industrial selling, it is seldom possible in reaching ultimate consumers.

Consumer Adopters

Ultimately, diffusion is dependent upon the individual consumer. He must decide whether adoption of the new product is the appropriate course of action for him. The adoption process refers to the mental sequence of stages through which the consumer passes in arriving at an acceptance (adoption) or rejection decision. It can be conceptualized as awareness, knowledge, liking, preference, conviction, and adoption, although other conceptualizations are also available.

Considerable research evidence indicates that communication sources are not equally effective at different stages of the adoption process. While *advertising* generally has greatest impact at the earlier stages of awareness, knowledge, and liking, the consumer seeks more objective, evaluative information at the later stages of preference and conviction and *personal influence* (word- of- mouth) often becomes the dominant communication source. This, of course, varies by product and holds most when the consumer perceives a good amount of risk in buying. The important point is that a purchase decision results from the cumulative impact of a number of communication sources and the marketer must attempt to move consumers through an entire sequence of information needs.

Not all consumers within a social system have an equal initial propensity toward buying a new product and consumers adopt at different points in time. The earliest buyers, the "innovators," have generally been found to possess different characteristics from later adopters. (A discussion of innovator characteristics is provided by Charles W. King in a paper following this one). An initial goal before marketing a new product should be to establish the profile of the most likely consumer innovators. It may then be possible to design marketing activities in line with this profile. As the innovator level of diffusion is achieved, marketing strategies should then be re-oriented to reach later buyers.

Product Meaning

Extent of a new product's diffusion and its rate of diffusion are, of course, largely a function of the particular attributes of the product. The emphasis given particular attributes and the overall brand image created are critical marketing decision areas.

There are several attribute classification schemes to account for differential diffusion rates. Rogers proposes a set of five characteristics of innovations which he believes are generally relevant. These characteristics are: (1) relative advantage, (2) compatibility, (3) complexity, (4) divisibility, and (5) communicability.[16]

Relative advantage is the degree to which an innovation is superior to the product it supersedes or with which it will compete. While the addition of flouride to toothpaste was considered to add extra product value, many other ingredients had previously been added to toothpaste without the consumer attaching relative advantage to the resulting "new" product. A dominant marketing management function is product differentiation to encourage the consumer to percieve greater product value.

Compatibility refers to how consistent the new product is with existing ways of doing things. The greater the need for consumers to restructure their thinking and to engage in new forms of behavior, the less quickly the item is likely to diffuse.

Complexity refers to the degree of difficulty in understanding and using the new product. In general, the more complex the item, the slower its rate of diffusion and the narrower its potential market.

Divisibility refers to the extent to which a new product may be tried on a limited scale. In-store sampling of a new food product and marketing of small sizes take account of the divisibility factor.

Communicability is the degree to which word of the new product may readily be communicated to others. Conspicuous products, such as clothes, are highest on communicability.

The important point is how these characteristics are *perceived* by consumers since this is what governs response. In summary form, it can be hypothesized that rate of diffusion is positively related to relative advantage, compatibility, divisibility, and communicability, but negatively related to complexity.

Diffusion rates of technological innovations among firms have been studied by Mansfield, who hypothesizes as follows:

(1) Profitability of an innovation relative to others that are available will increase the rate of adoption.

(2) The larger the investment required, assuming equally profitable innovations available, the slower the rate of adoption.

(3) The type of industry will affect the rate of adoption depending on its aversion to risk, market competitiveness, and financial health.[17]

Considerable work remains to be done relating innovation attributes to diffusion rates and further relating innovation attributes to consumer characteristics. For example, to the extent that a product is high on complexity, this may suggest a slower rate of diffusion, but does this also suggest a certain kind of consumer adopter? Also, when is a product attribute important? Relative advantage may be irrelevant for fashion items and for many fad items since their adoption is largely related to the perception of *newness itself* rather than to better functional performance. Diffusion patterns for fashion and fad products show a much more accelerated growth and an equally accelerated decline phenomenon.

Time

The business firm in general wishes to shorten the diffusion time span consistent with profit maximization objectives. At times it may be desirable to gain maximum short-run penetration, while at other times a more deliberate segmentation strategy, often on the basis of price, may be followed. A strategy of maximum diffusion need not be most profitable. It is probably a fair generalization, however, that maximum diffusion (market share) is the goal for most new products. This is especially true for continuous and dynamically continuous innovations and less true for discontinuous innovations.

In a penetration strategy, maximum diffusion is sought as quickly as possible. Price tends to be set relatively low; promotion will lean heavily toward mass advertising; and intensive distribution will be used. This strategy is most necessary if little product differentiation exists for the new product and, therefore, demand is highly elastic. This strategy is also necessary if competitors are likely to introduce similar new product offerings within a fairly short period of time, despite the continuity or discontinuity of the innovation. Rapid diffusion may discourage competition, although it could also have an encouraging effect when high sales are noted — especially if the estimated potential market is large. More importantly, however, rapid diffusion will often lead to a large and brand loyal consumer franchise which is crucial to continuing sales success given the subsequent entry of competition.

A penetration strategy has implications as to the shape of the diffusion curve and encourages high acceleration. In fact, in a number of cases for new convenience *brands*, the diffusion curve is far from S-shaped. In the pre-sweetened cereal market and in the detergent market, for example, a new brand (because of concentrated advertising and deal activity at introduction) may attain its maximum life cycle sales within a matter of a month and then settle down to a lower "maturity" level of sales. It is critical to remember that a varying proportion (sometimes very high) of beginning sales may be for *trial* purposes and need not represent *adoption*, defined in terms of acceptance and commitment to the brand as reflected in repeat purchases. A company must quickly determine its trial-adoption ratio or it can be misled into expanding production for never-to-be-realized repeat sales.

In a sales staging strategy, the typical progression is from generally high "skim the cream" pricing to relatively lower prices, from selective distribution to intensive distribution, and from limited promotion to expanded or mass promotion. Such a strategy is more likely to be successful for specialty and durable items and is generally dependent upon a differentiated product and one which competition cannot readily duplicate. The somewhat discontinuous innovation allows, in effect, a certain degree of monopoly power.

DuPont's "Corfam" shoe material was marketed using the sales staging strategy. It was deliberately introduced to manufacturers of quality shoe products before being made available on a mass basis. Management apparently felt that maximum long-run diffusion for the product would be gained if it was not perceived as a cheap substitute for leather but instead as a quality improvement over leather. DuPont, therefore, by its choice of manufacturers to whom the product was made available, was governing intensity of distribution and pricing and extent of manufacturer advertising.

It is interesting to note that the marketer's diffusion strategy very much influences the shape of the diffusion curve. By the same token, however, the selection of a strategy is a function of the type of product and the competitive situation. A penetration or sales staging strategy must be based on accurate assessment of future market acceptance. Wasson, for example, argues that color television marketers unsuccessfully followed a penetration strategy for their products when sales to support such a strategy were not forthcoming. They misjudged rate of market acceptance and should have been following a sales staging strategy with selective distribution, relatively high price, and limited promotion until the growth segment of the diffusion process was attained.[18] We must also take cognizance of the fact that while a dichotomy of ideal types makes for expository efficiency, a considerable range of strategies between staging and penetration is available to the firm.

CONCLUSION

It is essentially an arbitrary decision as to what is and what is not a new product. Most "new products" on the market today, however, involve only minor changes in consumption patterns; they are of a highly *continuous* nature. Such products are the result of programmed product differentiation.

The critical value of innovation to a firm is demonstrated in many industries where over 50% of sales growth is coming from new products. Yet, the risk of new product failures is high and it is probably fair to say that a *majority* of products which are introduced to the market fail. Furthermore, these failures are seldom due to a technically unsound product but instead are largely the result of poor marketing performance.

It is the conclusion of this paper, however, that the probability of new product success can be increased by understanding the diffusion process. Successful new product diffusion is dependent upon the communication of relevant product information and the matching of new product attributes with social system and individual consumer attributes. Marketing strategies can guide and control, to a considerable extent, the rate and extent of new product diffusion.

NOTES

1. Federal Trade Commission, "Permissible Period of Time During which New Products May Be Described as 'New'," *Advisory Opinion Digest*, No. 120, April 15, 1967.

2. E.B. Weiss "That Malarky about 80% of New Product Failing," *Advertising Age*, Vol. 36, August 2, 1965, p. 101.

3. Homer G. Barnett, *Innovation: The Basis of Cultural Change*, New York, McGraw-Hill, 1953, p. 181.

4. Same reference as 1.

5. William E. Bell, "Consumer Innovators: A Unique Market for Newness." in *Proceedings of the American Marketing Association*, ed., Stephen A. Greyser, Chicago, 1963, pp. 85-95.

6. Thomas S. Robertson, "Determinants of Innovative Behavior," in *Proceedings of the American Marketing Association*, ed. Reed Moyer, Chicago, 1967, pp. 328-332.

7. Joseph A. Schumpeter, *Business Cycles*, New York, McGraw-Hill Book Company, Inc., 1939, Vol. 1, p. 97.

8. Same reference as 3 at p. 73.

9. Robert D. Buzzell and Robert Nourse, *Product Innovation in Food Processing: 1954-1964*, Boston, Division of Research, Harvard Business School, 1967.

10. Booz-Allen & Hamilton, Inc., *Management of New Products*, New York, 1965.

11. Edwin Mansfield, "Entry, Gibrat's Law, Innovation, and the Growth of Firms," *American Economic Review*, Vol. 52, December, 1962, pp. 1023-1051, at p. 1036.

12. "Research: The Cash Pours Out for Research and Development," *Business Week*, 2020, May 18, 1968, pp. 72-74.

13. Same reference as 10.

14. Same reference as 9 at p. 105 and p. 124.

15. Saxon Graham, "Class and Conservatism in the Adoption of Innovations," *Human Relations*, Vol. 9, 1956, pp. 91-100.

16. Everett M. Rogers, *Diffusion of Innovations*, New York, The Free Press. 1962, Chapter 5.

17. Edwin Mansfield, "Technical Change and the Rate of Imitation," *Econometrica*, Vol. 29, October, 1961, pp. 741-766.

18. Chester R. Wasson, "How Predictable Are Fashion and Other Product Life Cycles?" *Journal of Marketing,* Vol. 32, July, 1968, pp. 36-43.

. . . at each stage in a product's life cycle each management decision must consider the competitive requirements of the next stage.

16

exploit the product life cycle

theodore levitt

Most alert and thoughtful senior marketing executives are by now familiar with the concept of the product life cycle. Even a handful of uniquely cosmopolitan and up-to-date corporate presidents have familiarized themselves with this tantalizing concept. Yet a recent survey I took of such executives found none who used the concept in any strategic way whatever, and pitifully few who used it in any kind of tactical way. It has remained — as have so many fascinating theories in economics, physics, and sex — a remarkably durable but almost totally unemployed and seemingly unemployable piece of professional baggage whose presence in the rhetoric of professional discussions adds a much coveted but apparently unattainable legitimacy to the idea that marketing management is somehow a profession. There is, furthermore, a persistent feeling that the life cycle concept adds luster and believability to the insistent claim in certain circles that marketing is close to being some sort of science.[1]

Author's note: This article will appear in a forth-coming book, *Marketing Vision*, edited by Lee Adler.

The concept of the product life cycle is today at about the stage that the Copernican view of the universe was 300 years ago: a lot of people knew about it, but hardly anybody seemed to use it in any effective or productive way.

Now that so many people know and in some fashion understand the product life cycle, it seems time to put it to work. The object of this article is to suggest some ways of using the concept effectively and of turning the knowledge of its existence into a managerial instrument of competitive power.

Since the concept has been presented somewhat differently by different authors and for different audiences, it is useful to review it briefly here so that every reader has the same background for the discussion which follows later in this article.

HISTORICAL PATTERN

The life story of most successful products is a history of their passing through certain recognizable stages. These are shown in Exhibit I and occur in the following order:

Stage 1. Market Development –   This is when a new product is first brought to market, before there is a proved demand for it, and often before it has been fully proved out technically in all respects. Sales are low and creep along slowly.

Stage 2. Market Growth–   Demand begins to accelerate and the size of the total market expands rapidly. It might also be called the "Takeoff Stage."

Stage 3. Market Maturity   – Demand levels off and grows, for the most part, only at the replacement and new family-formation rate.

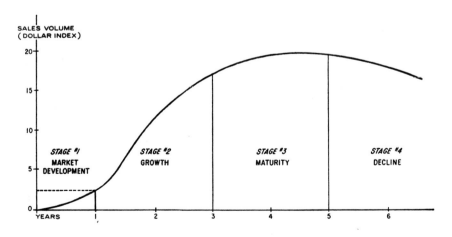

Exhibit I. Product life cycle – entire industry

Stage 4. Market Decline — The product begins to lose consumer appeal and sales drift downward, such as when buggy whips lost out with the advent of automobiles and when silk lost out to nylon.

Three operating questions will quickly occur to the alert executive:

- Given a proposed new product or service, how and to what extent can the shape and duration of each stage be predicted?
- Given an existing product, how can one determine what stage it is in?
- Given all this knowledge, how can it be effectively used?

A brief further elaboration of each stage will be useful before dealing with these questions in detail.

Development Stage

Bringing a new product to market is fraught with unknowns, uncertainties, and frequently unknowable risks. Generally, demand has to be "created" during the product's initial *market development stage*. How long this takes depends on the product's complexity, its degree of newness, its fit into consumer needs, and the presence of competitive substitutes of one form or another. A proved cancer cure would require virtually no market development; it would get immediate massive support. An alleged superior substitute for the lost-wax process of sculpture casting would take lots longer.

While it has been demonstrated time after time that properly customer-oriented new product development is one of the primary conditions of sales and profit growth, what have been demonstrated even more conclusively are the ravaging costs and frequent fatalities associated with launching new products. Nothing seems to take more time, cost more money, involve more pitfalls, cause more anguish, or break more careers than do sincere and well-conceived new product programs. The fact is, most new products don't have any sort of classical life cycle curve at all. They have instead from the very outset an infinitely descending curve. The product not only doesn't get off the ground; it goes quickly under ground — six feet under.

It is little wonder, therefore, that some disillusioned and badly burned companies have recently adopted a more conservative policy — what I call the "used apple policy." Instead of aspiring to be the first company to see and seize an opportunity, they systematically avoid being first. They let others take the first bite of the supposedly juicy apple that tantalizes them. They let others do the pioneering. If the idea works, they quickly follow suit. They say, in effect,

"The trouble with being a pioneer is that the pioneers get killed by the Indians." Hence, they say (thoroughly mixing their metaphors), "We don't have to get the first bite of the apple. The second one is good enough." They are willing to eat off a used apple, but they try to be alert enough to make sure it is only slightly used — that they at least get the second big bite, not the tenth skimpy one.

Growth Stage

The usual characteristic of a successful new product is a gradual rise in its sales curve during the market development stage. At some point in this rise a marked increase in consumer demand occurs and sales take off. The boom is on. This is the beginning of Stage 2 — the *market growth stage*. At this point potential competitors who have been watching developments during Stage I jump into the fray. The first ones to get in are generally those with an exceptionally effective "used apple policy." Some enter the market with carbon-copies of the originator's product. Others make functional and design improvements. And at this point product and brand differentiation begin to develop.

The ensuing fight for the consumer's patronage poses to the originating producer an entirely new set of problems. Instead of seeking ways of getting consumers to *try the product,* the originator now faces the more compelling problem of getting them to *prefer his brand*. This generally requires important changes in marketing strategies and methods. But the policies and tactics now adopted will be neither freely the sole choice of the originating producer, nor as experimental as they might have been during Stage I. The presence of competitors both dictates and limits what can easily be tried — such as, for example, testing what is the best price level or the best channel of distribution.

As the rate of consumer acceptance accelerates, it generally becomes increasingly easy to open new distribution channels and retail outlets. The consequent filling of distribution pipelines generally causes the entire industry's factory sales to rise more rapidly than store sales. This creates an exaggerated impression of profit opportunity which, in turn, attracts more competitors. Some of these will begin to charge lower prices because of later advances in technology, production shortcuts, the need to take lower margins in order to get distribution, and the like. All this in time inescapably moves the industry to the threshold of a new stage of competition.

Maturity Stage

This new stage is the *market maturity stage.* The first sign of its advent is evidence of market saturation. This means that most consumer companies or households that are sales prospects will be owning or using the product. Sales now grow about on a par with population. No more distribution pipelines need be filled. Price competition now becomes intense. Competitive attempts to achieve and hold brand preference now involve making finer and finer differentiations in the product, in customer services, and in the promotional practices and claims made for the product.

Typically, the market maturity stage forces the producer to concentrate on holding his distribution outlets, retaining his shelf space, and, in the end, trying to secure even more intensive distribution. Whereas during the market development stage the originator depended heavily on the positive efforts of his retailers and distributors to help sell his product, retailers and distributors will now frequently have been reduced largely to being merchandise-displayers and order-takers. In the case of branded products in particular, the originator must now, more than ever, communicate directly with the consumer.

The market maturity stage typically calls for a new kind of emphasis on competing more effectively. The originator is increasingly forced to appeal to the consumer on the basis of price, marginal product differences, or both. Depending on the product, services and deals offered in connection with it are often the clearest and most effective forms of differentiation. Beyond these, there will be attempts to create and promote fine product distinctions through packaging and advertising, and to appeal to special market segments. The market maturity stage can be passed through rapidly, as in the case of most women's fashion fads, or it can persist for generations with per capita consumption neither rising nor falling, as in the case of such staples as men's shoes and industrial fasteners. Or maturity can persist, but in a state of gradual but steady per capita decline, as in the case of beer and steel.

Decline Stage

When market maturity tapers off and consequently comes to an end, the product enters Stage 4 — *market decline*. In all cases of maturity and decline the industry is transformed. Few companies are able to weather the competitive storm. As demand declines, the overcapacity that was already apparent during the period of maturity now becomes endemic. Some producers see the handwriting implacably on the wall but feel that with proper management and cunning they will be one of the survivors after the industry-wide deluge they so clearly foresee. To hasten their competitors' eclipse directly, or to frighten them into early voluntary withdrawal from the industry, they initiate a variety of aggressively depressive tactics, propose mergers or buy-outs, and generally engage in activities that make life thanklessly burdensome for all firms, and make death the inevitable consequence for most of them. A few companies do indeed weather the storm, sustaining life through the constant descent that now clearly characterizes the industry. Production gets concentrated into fewer hands. Prices and margins get depressed. Consumers get bored. The only cases where there is any relief from this boredom and gradual euthanasia are where styling and fashion play some constantly revivifying role.

PREPLANNING IMPORTANCE

Knowing that the lives of successful products and services are generally characterized by something like the pattern illustrated in Exhibit I can become the basis for important life-giving policies and practices. One of the greatest values of the life cycle concept is for managers about to launch a new product. The first step for them is to try to foresee the profile of the proposed product's cycle.

As with so many things in business, and perhaps uniquely in marketing, it is almost impossible to make universally useful suggestions regarding how to manage one's affairs. It is certainly particularly difficult to provide widely useful advice on how to foresee or predict the slope and duration of a products's life. Indeed, it is precisely because so little specific day-to-day guidance is possible in anything, and because no checklist has ever by itself been very useful to anybody for very long, that business management will probably never be a science — always an art — and will pay exceptional rewards to managers with rare talent, enormous energy, iron nerve, great capacity for assuming responsibility and bearing accountability.

But this does not mean that useful efforts cannot or should not be made to try to foresee the slope and duration of a new product's life. Time spent in attempting this kind of foresight not only helps assure that a more rational approach is brought to product planning and merchandising; also, as will be shown later, it can help create valuable lead time for important strategic and tactical moves after the product is brought to market. Specifically, it can be a great help in developing an orderly series of competitive moves, in expanding or stretching out the life of a product, in maintaining a clean product line, and in purposely phasing out dying and costly old products.[2]

Failure Possibilities . . .

As pointed out above, the length and slope of the market development stage depend on the product's complexity, its degree of newness, its fit into customer needs, and the presence of competitive substitutes.

The more unique or distinctive the newness of the product, the longer it generally takes to get it successfully off the ground. The world does not automatically beat a path to the man with the better mousetrap.[3] The world has to be told, coddled, enticed, romanced, and even bribed (as with, for example, coupons, samples, free application aids, and the like). When the product's newness is distinctive and the job it is designed to do is unique, the public will generally be less quick to perceive it as something it clearly needs or wants.

This makes life particularly difficult for the innovator. He will have more than the usual difficulties of identifying those characteristics of his product and those supporting communications themes or devices which imply value to the consumer. As a consequence, the more distinctive the newness, the greater the risk of failure resulting either from insufficient working capital to sustain a long and frustrating period of creating enough solvent customers to make the proposition pay, or from the inability to convince investors and bankers that they should put up more money.

In any particular situation the more people who will be involved in making a single purchasing decision for a new product, the more drawn out Stage I will be. Thus in the highly fragmented construction materials industry, for example, success takes an exceptionally long time to catch hold; and having once caught hold, it tends to hold tenaciously for a long time – often too long. On the other hand, fashion items clearly catch on fastest and last shortest. But because fashion is so powerful, recently some companies in what often seem the least fashion-influenced of industries (machine tools, for example) have shortened the market development stage by introducing elements of design and packaging fashion to their products.

What factors tend to prolong the market development stage and therefore raise the risk of failure? The more complex the product, the more distinctive its newness, the less influenced by fashion, the greater the number of persons influencing a single buying decision, the more costly, and the greater the required shift in the customer's usual way of doing things – these are the conditions most likely to slow things up and create problems.

. . . vs. Success Chances

But problems also create opportunities to control the forces arrayed against new product success. For example, the newer the product, the more important it becomes for the customers to have a favorable first experience with it. Newness creates a certain special visibility for the product, with a certain number of people standing on the sidelines to see how the first customers get on with it. If their first experience is unfavorable in some crucial way, this may have repercussions far out of proportion to the actual extent of the underfulfillment of the customers' expectations. But a favorable first experience or application will, for the same reason, get a lot of disproportionately favorable publicity.

The possibility of exaggerated disillusionment with a poor first experience can raise vital questions regarding the appropriate channels of distribution for a new product. On the one hand, getting the product successfully launched may require having – as in the case of, say, the early days of home washing machines – many retailers who can give consumers considerable help in the product's correct utilization and thus help assure a favorable first experience for those buyers. On the other hand, channels that provide this kind of help (such as small neighborhood appliance stores in the case of washing machines) during the market development stage may not be the ones best able to merchandise the product most successfully later when help in creating and personally reassuring customers is less important than wide product distribution. To the extent that channel decisions during this first stage sacrifice some of the requirements of the market development stage to some of the requirements of later stages, the rate of the product's acceptance by consumers at the outset may be delayed.

In entering the market development stage, pricing decisions are often particularly hard for the producer to make. Should he set an initially high price to recoup his investment quickly − i.e., "skim the cream" − or should he set a low price to discourage potential competition − i.e., "exclusion"? The answer depends on the innovator's estimate of the probable length of the product's life cycle, the degree of patent protection the product is likely to enjoy, the amount of capital needed to get the product off the ground, the elasticity of demand during the early life of the product, and many other factors. The decision that is finally made may affect not just the rate at which the product catches on at the beginning, but even the duration of its total life. Thus some products that are priced too low at the outset (particularly fashion goods, such as the chemise, or sack, a few years ago) may catch on so quickly that they become short-lived fads. A slower rate of consumer acceptance might often extend their life cycles and raise the total profits they yield.

The actual slope, or rate of the growth stage, depends on some of the same things as does success or failure in Stage I. But the extent to which patent exclusiveness can play a critical role is sometimes inexplicably forgotten. More frequently than one might offhand expect, holders of strong patent positions fail to recognize either the market-development virtue of making their patents available to competitors or the market-destroying possibilities of failing to control more effectively their competitors' use of such products.

Generally speaking, the more producers there are of a new product, the more effort goes into developing a market for it. The net result is very likely to be more rapid and steeper growth of the total market. The originator's market share may fall, but his total sales and profits may rise more rapidly. Certainly this has been the case in recent years of color television; RCA'S eagerness to make its tubes available to competitors reflects its recognition of the power numbers over the power of monopoly.

On the other hand, the failure to set and enforce appropriate quality standards in the early days of polystyrene and polyethylene drinking glasses and cups produced such sloppy, inferior goods that it took years to recover the consumer's confidence and revive the growth pattern.

But to try to see in advance what a product's growth pattern might be is not very useful if one fails to distinguish between the industry pattern and the pattern of the single firm − for its particular brand. The industry's cycle will almost certainly be different from the cycle of individual firms. Moreover, the life cycle of a given product may be different for different companies in the same industry at the same point in time, and it certainly affects different companies in the same industry differently.

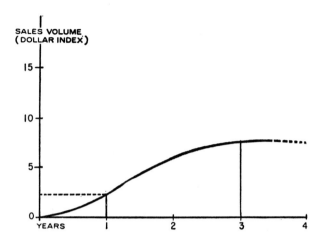

Exhibit II. Product life cycle – originating company

ORIGINATOR'S BURDENS

The company with most at stake is the original producer – the company that launches an entirely new product. This company generally bears most of the costs, the tribulations, and certainly the risks of developing both the product and the market.

Competitive Pressure

Once the innovator demonstrates during the market development stage that a solid demand exists, armies of imitators rush in to capitalize on and help create the boom that becomes the market growth, or takeoff, stage. As a result, while exceedingly rapid growth will now characterize the product's total demand, for the originating company its growth stage paradoxically now becomes truncated. It has to share the boom with new competitors. Hence the potential rate of acceleration of its own takeoff is diminished and, indeed, may actually fail to last as long as the industry's. This occurs not only because there are so many competitors, but, as we noted earlier, also because competitors often come in with product improvements and lower prices. While these developments generally help keep the market expanding, they greatly restrict the originating company's rate of growth and the length of its takeoff stage.

All this can be illustrated by comparing the curve in Exhibit II with that in Exhibit I, which shows the life cycle for a product. During Stage I in Exhibit I there is generally only one company – the originator – even though the whole exhibit represents the entire industry. In Stage I the originator is the entire

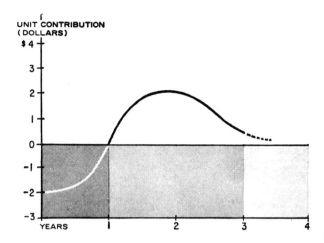

Exhibit III. Unit profit contribution life cycle – originating company

industry. But by Stage 2 he shares the industry with many competitors. Hence, while Exhibit I is an industry curve, its Stage I represents only a single company's sales.

Exhibit II shows the life cycle of the originator's brand – his own sales curve, not that of the industry. It can be seen that between Year I and Year 2 his sales are rising about as rapidly as the industry's. But after Year 2, while industry sales in Exhibit I are still in vigorous expansion, the originator's sales curve in Exhibit II has begun to slow its ascent. He is now sharing the boom with a great many competitors, some of whom are much better positioned now than he is.

Profit Squeeze

In the process the originator may begin to encounter a serious squeeze on his profit margins. Exhibit III, which traces the profits per unit of the originator's sales, illustrates this point. During the market development stage his per-unit profits are negative. Sales volume is too low at existing prices. However, during the market growth stage unit profits boom as output rises and unit production costs fall. Total profits rise enormously. It is the presence of such lush profits that both attracts and ultimately destroys competitors.

Consequently, while (1) industry sales may still be rising nicely (as at the Year 3 point in Exhibit I), and (2) while the originating company's sales may at the same point of time have begun to slow down noticeably (as in Exhibit II), and (3) while at this point the originator's total profits may still be rising because his volume of sales is huge and on a slight upward trend, his profits per unit will often have taken a drastic downward course. Indeed, they will often have done so long before the sales curve flattened. They will have topped out and begun to decline perhaps around the Year 2 point (as in Exhibit III). By the time the originator's sales begin to flatten out (as at the Year 3 point in Exhibit II), unit profits may actually be approaching zero (as in Exhibit III).

At this point more competitors are in the industry, the rate of industry demand growth has slowed somewhat, and competitors are cutting prices. Some of them do this in order to get business, and others do it because their costs are lower owing to the fact that their equipment is more modern and productive.

The industry's Stage 3 — maturity — generally lasts as long as there are no important competitive substitutes (such as, for example, aluminum for steel in "tin" cans), no drastic shifts in influential value systems (such as the end of female modesty in the 1920's and the consequent destruction of the market for veils), no major changes in dominant fashions (such as the hour-glass female form and the end of waist cinchers), no changes in the demand for primary products which use the product in question (such as the effect of the decline of new railroad expansion on the demand for railroad ties), and no changes either in the rate of obsolescence of the product or in the character or introductory rate of product modifications.

Maturity can last for a long time, or it can actually never be attained. Fashion goods and fad items sometimes surge to sudden heights, hesitate momentarily at an uneasy peak, and then quickly drop off into total obscurity.

Stage Recognition

The various characteristics of the stages described above will help one to recognize the stage a particular product occupies at any given time. But hindsight will always be more accurate than current sight. Perhaps the best way of seeing one's current stage is to try to foresee the next stage and work backwards. This approach has several virtues:

> It forces one to look ahead, constantly to try to reforesee his future and competitive environment. This will have its own rewards. As Charles F. Kettering, perhaps the last of Detroit's primitive inventors and probably the greatest of all its inventors, was fond of saying, "We should all be concerned about the future because that's where we'll have to spend the rest of our lives." By looking at the future one can better assess the state of the present.
>
> Looking ahead gives more perspective to the present than looking at the present alone. Most people know more about the present than is good for them. It is neither healthy nor helpful to know the present too well, for our perception of the present is too often too heavily distorted by the urgent pressures of day-to-day events. To know where the present is in the continuum of competitive time and events, it often makes more sense to try to know what the future will bring, and when it will bring it, than to try to know what the present itself actually contains.

Finally, the value of knowing what stage a product occupies at any given time resides only in the way that fact is used. But its use is always in the future. Hence a prediction of the future environment in which the information will be used is often more functional for the effective capitalization on knowledge about the present than knowledge about the present itself.

SEQUENTIAL ACTIONS

The life cycle concept can be effectively employed in the strategy of both existing and new products. For purposes of continuity and clarity, the remainder of this article will describe some of the uses of the concept from the early stages of new product planning through the later stages of keeping the product profitably alive. The chief discussion will focus on what I call a policy of "life extension" or "market stretching."[4]

To the extent that Exhibits II and III outline the classical patterns of successful new products, one of the constant aims of the originating producer should be to avoid the severe discipline imposed by an early profit squeeze in the market growth stage, and to avoid the wear and waste so typical of the market maturity stage. Hence the following proposition would seem reasonable: when a company develops a new product or service, it should try to plan at the very outset a series of actions to be employed at various subsequent stages in the product's existence so that its sales and profit curves are constantly sustained rather than following their usual declining slope.

In other words, advance planning should be directed at extending, or stretching out, the life of the product. It is this idea of *planning in advance* of the actual launching of a new product to take specific actions later in its life cycle — actions designed to sustain its growth and profitability — which appears to have great potential as an instrument of long-term product strategy.

Nylon's Life

How this might work for a product can be illustrated by looking at the history of nylon. The way in which nylon's booming sales life has been repeatedly and systematically extended and stretched can serve as a model for other products. What has happened in nylon may not have been purposely planned that way at the outset, but the results are quite as if they had been planned.

The first nylon end-uses were primarily military — parachutes, thread, rope. This was followed by nylon's entry into the circular knit market and its consequent domination of the women's hosiery business. Here it developed the kind of steadily rising growth and profit curves that every executive dreams about. After some years these curves began to flatten out. But before they flattened very noticeably, Du Pont had already developed measures designed to revitalize sales and profits. It did several things, each of which is demonstrated

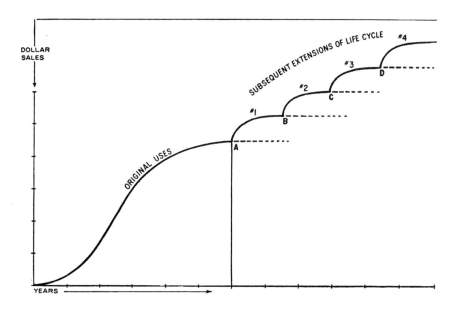

Exhibit IV. Hypothetical life cycle - nylon

graphically in Exhibit IV. This exhibit and the explanation which follows take some liberties with the actual facts of the nylon situation in order to highlight the points I wish to make. But they take no liberties with the essential requisites of product strategy.

Point A of Exhibit IV shows the hypothetical point at which the nylon curve (dominated at this point by hosiery) flattened out. If nothing further had been done, the sales curve would have continued along the flattened pace indicated by the dotted line at Point A. This is also the hypothetical point at which the first systematic effort was made to extend the product's life. Du Pont, in effect, took certain "actions" which pushed hosiery sales upward rather than continuing the path implied by the dotted line extension of the curve at Point A. At Point A action # 1 pushed an otherwise flat curve upward.

At points B, C, and D still other new sales and profit expansion "actions" (# 2, # 3, # 4, and so forth) were taken. What were these actions? Or, more usefully, what was their strategic content? What did they try to do? They involved strategies that tried to expand sales via four different routes:

1. Promoting more frequent usage of the product among current users.
2. Developing more varied usage of the product among current users.
3. Creating new users for the product by expanding the market.
4. Finding new uses for the basic material.

Frequent Usage. Du Pont studies had shown an increasing trend toward "bareleggedness" among women. This was coincident with the trend toward more casual living and a declining perception among teenagers of what might be called the "social necessity" of wearing stockings. In the light of those findings, one approach to propping up the flattening sales curves might have been to reiterate the social necessity of wearing stockings at all times. That would have been a sales-building action, though obviously difficult and exceedingly costly. But it could clearly have fulfilled the strategy of promoting more frequent usage among current users as a means of extending the product's life.

Varied Usage. For Du Pont, this strategy took the form of an attempt to promote the "fashion smartness" of tinted hose and later of patterned and highly textured hosiery. The idea was to raise each woman's inventory of hosiery by obsolescing the perception of hosiery as a fashion staple that came only in a narrow range of browns and pinks. Hoisery was to be converted from a "neutral" accessory to a central ingredient of fashion, with a "suitable" tint and pattern for each outer garment in the lady's wardrobe.

This not only would raise sales by expanding women's hosiery wardrobes and stores' inventories, but would open the door for annual tint and pattern obsolescence much the same as there is an annual color obsolescence in outer garments. Beyond that, the use of color and pattern to focus attention on the leg would help arrest the decline of the leg as an element of sex appeal — a trend which some researchers had discerned and which, they claimed, damaged hosiery sales.

New Users. Creating new users for nylon hosiery might conceivably have taken the form of attempting to legitimize the necessity of wearing hosiery among early teenagers and subteenagers. Advertising, public relations, and merchandising of youthful social and style leaders would have been called for.

New Uses. For nylon, this tactic has had many triumphs — from varied types of hosiery, such as stretch stockings and stretch socks, to new uses, such as rugs, tires, bearings, and so forth. Indeed, if there had been no further product innovations designed to create new uses for nylon after the original military, miscellaneous, and circular knit uses, nylon consumption in 1962 would have reached a saturation level at approximately 50 million pounds annually.

Instead, in 1962 consumption exceeded 500 million pounds. Exhibit V demonstrates how the continuous development of new uses for the basic material constantly produced new waves of sales. The exhibit shows that in spite of the growth of the women's stocking market, the cumulative result of the military, circular knit, and miscellaneous grouping would have been a flattened sales curve by 1958. (Nylon's entry into the broadwoven market in 1944 substantially raised sales above what they would have been. Even so, the sales of

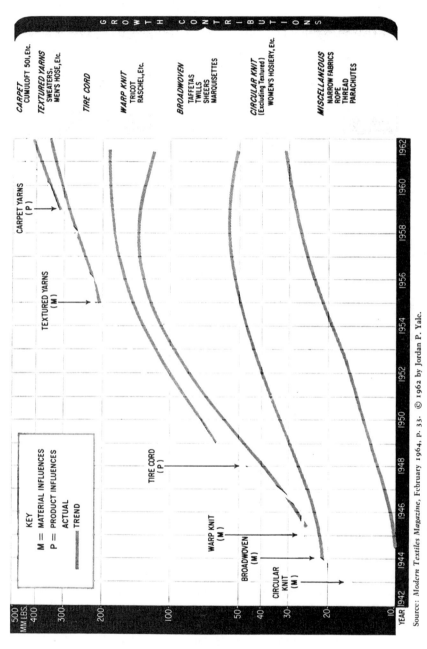

Exhibit V.   Innovation of new products postpones the time or total maturity – nylon   industry

broadwoven, circular knit, and military and miscellaneous groupings peaked in 1957.)

Had it not been for the addition of new uses for the same basic material — such as warp knits in 1945, tire cord in 1948, textured yarns in 1955, carpet yarns in 1959, and so forth — nylon would not have had the spectacularly rising consumption curve it has so clearly had. At various stages it would have exhausted its existing markets or been forced into decline by competing materials. The systematic search for new uses for the basic (and improved) material extended and stretched the product's life.

Other Examples

Few companies seem to employ in any systematic or planned way the four product life-stretching steps described above. Yet the successful application of this kind of stretching strategy has characterized the history of such well-known products as General Foods Corporation's "Jell-O" and Minnesota Mining & Manufacturing Co.'s "Scotch" tape.[5]

Jell-O was a pioneer in the easy-to-prepare gelatin dessert field. The soundness of the product concept and the excellence of its early marketing activities gave it beautifully ascending sales and profit curves almost from the start. But after some years these curves predictably began to flatten out. Scotch tape was also a pioneer product in its field. Once perfected, the product gained rapid market acceptance because of a sound product concept and an aggressive sales organization. But, again, in time the sales and profit curves began to flatten out. Before they flattened out very much, however, 3M, like General Foods, had already developed measures to sustain the early pace of sales and profits.

Both of these companies extended their products' lives by, in effect, doing all four of the things Du Pont did with nylon — creating more frequent usage among current users, more varied usage among current users, new users, and new uses for the basic "materials":

(1) The General Foods approach to increasing the frequency of serving Jell-O among current users was, essentially, to increase the number of flavors. From Don Wilson's famous "six delicious flavors," Jell-O moved up to over a dozen. On the other hand, 3M helped raise sales among its current users by developing a variety of handy Scotch tape dispensers which made the product easier to use.

(2) Creation of more varied usage of Jell-O among current dessert users involved its promotion as a base for salads and the facilitation of this usage by the development of a variety of vegetable flavored Jell-O's. Similarly, 3M developed a line of colored, patterned, waterproof, invisible, and write-on Scotch tapes which have enjoyed considerable success as sealing and decorating items for holiday and gift wrapping.

(3) Jell-O sought to create new users by pinpointing people who could not

accept Jell-O as a popular dessert or salad product. Hence during the Metrecal boom Jell-O employed an advertising theme that successfully affixed to the product a fashion-oriented weight control appeal. Similarly, 3M introduced "Rocket" tape, a product much like Scotch tape but lower in price, and also developed a line of commercial cellophane tapes of various widths, lengths, and strengths. These actions broadened product use in commercial and industrial markets.

(4) Both Jell-O and 3M have sought out new uses for the basic material. It is known, for example, that women consumers use powdered gelatin dissolved in liquids as a means of strengthening their fingernails. Both men and women use it in the same way as a bone-building agent. Hence Jell-O introduced a "completely flavorless" Jell-O for just these purposes. 3M has also developed new uses for the basic material — from "double-coated" tape (adhesive on both sides) which competes with ordinary liquid adhesives, to the reflecting tape which festoons countless automobile bumpers, to marker strips which compete with paint.

EXTENSION STRATEGIES

The existence of the kinds of product life cycles illustrated in Exhibits I and II and the unit profit cycle in Exhibit III suggests that there may be considerable value for people involved in new product work to begin planning for the extension of the lives of their products even before these products are formally launched. To plan for new life-extending infusions of effort (as in Exhibit IV) at this pre-introduction stage can be extremely useful in three profoundly important ways.

1. It generates an active rather than a reactive product policy.

It systematically structures a company's long-term marketing and product development efforts in advance, rather than each effort or activity being merely a stop-gap response to the urgent pressures of repeated competitive thrusts and declining profits. The life-extension view of product policy enforces thinking and planning ahead — thinking in some systematic way about the moves likely to be made by potential competitors, about possible changes in consumer reactions to the product, and the required selling activities which best take advantage of these conditional events.

2. It lays out a long-term plan designed to infuse new life into the product at the right time, with the right degree of care, and with the right amount of effort.

Many activities designed to raise the sales and profits of existing products or materials are often undertaken without regard to their relationship to each other or to timing — the optimum point of consumer readiness for such activities or the point of optimum competitive effectiveness. Careful advance planning, long before the need for such activity arises, can help assure that the timing, the care, and the efforts are appropriate to the situation.

For example, it appears extremely doubtful that the boom in women's hair coloring and hair tinting products would have been as spectacular if vigorous efforts to sell these products had preceded the boom in hair sprays and chemical hair fixers. The latter helped create a powerful consumer consciousness of hair fashions because they made it relatively easy to create and wear fashionable hair styles. Once it became easy for women to have fashionable hair styles, the resulting fashion consciousness helped open the door for hair colors and tints. It could not have happened the other way around, with colors and tints first creating fashion consciousness and thus raising the sales of sprays and fixers. Because understanding the reason for this precise order of events is essential for appreciating the importance of early pre-introduction life-extension planning, it is useful to go into a bit of detail. Consider:

> For women, setting their hair has been a perennial problem for centuries. First, the length and treatment of their hair is one of the most obvious ways in which they distinguish themselves from men. Hence to be attractive in that distinction becomes crucial. Second, hair frames and highlights the face, much like an attractive wooden border frames and highlights a beautiful painting. Thus hair styling is an important element in accentuating the appearance of a woman's facial features. Third, since the hair is long and soft, it is hard to hold in an attractive arrangement. It gets mussed in sleep, wind, damp weather, sporting activities, and so forth.
>
> Therefore, the effective *arrangement* of a woman's hair is understandably her first priority in hair care. An unkempt brunette would gain nothing from making herself into a blond. Indeed, in a country where blonds are in the minority, the switch from being an unkempt brunette to being an unkempt blond would simply draw attention to her sloppiness. But once the problem of arrangement became easily "solved" by sprays and fixers, colors and tints could become big business, especially among women whose hair was beginning to turn gray.

The same order of priorities applies in industrial products. For example, it seems quite inconceivable that many manufacturing plants would easily have accepted the replacement of the old single-spindle, constantly man-tended screw machine by a computerized tape-tended, multiple-spindle machine. The mechanical tending of the multiple-spindle machine was a necessary intermediate step, if for no other reason than that it required a lesser work-flow change, and certainly a lesser conceptual leap for the companies and the machine-tending workers involved.

For Jell-O, it is unlikely that vegetable flavors would have been very successful before the idea of gelatin as a salad base had been pretty well accepted. Similarly, the promotion of colored and patterned Scotch tape as a gift and decorative seal might not have been as successful if department stores had not, as the result of their drive to compete more effectively with mass merchandisers by offering more customer services, previously demonstrated to the consumer what could be done to wrap and decorate gifts.

3. Perhaps the most important benefit of engaging in advance, pre-introduction planning for sales-extending, market-stretching activities later in the product's life is that this practice forces a company to adopt a wider view of the nature of the product it is dealing with.

Indeed, it may even force the adoption of a wider view of the company's business. Take the case of Jell-O. What is its product? Over the years Jell-O has become the brand umbrella for a wide range of dessert products, including cornstarch-base puddings, pie fillings, and the new "Whip'n Chill," a light dessert product similar to a Bavarian Creme or French Mousse. On the basis of these products, it might be said that the Jell-O Division of General Foods is in the "dessert technology" business.

In the case of tape, perhaps 3M has gone even further in this technological approach to its business. It has a particular expertise (technology) on which it has built a constantly expanding business. This expertise can be said to be that of bonding things (adhesives in the case of Scotch tape) to other things, particularly to thin materials. Hence we see 3M developing scores of profitable items, including electronic recording tape (bonding electron-sensitive materials to tape), and "Thermo-Fax" duplicating equipment and supplies (bonding heat reactive materials to paper).

CONCLUSION

For companies interested in continued growth and profits, successful new product strategy should be viewed as a planned totality that looks ahead over some years. For its own good, new product strategy should try to predict in some measure the likelihood, character, and timing of competitive and market events. While prediction is always hazardous and seldom very accurate, it is undoubtedly far better than not trying to predict at all. In fact, every product strategy and every business decision inescapably involves making a prediction about the future, about the market, and about competitors. To be more systematically aware of the predictions one is making so that one acts on them in an offensive rather than a defensive or reactive fashion — this is the real virtue of preplanning for market stretching and product life extension. The result will be a product strategy that includes some sort of *plan for a timed sequence of conditional moves.*

Even before entering the market development stage, the originator should make a judgment regarding the probable length of the product's normal life, taking into account the possibilities of expanding its uses and users. This judgment will also help determine many things — for example, whether to price the product on a skimming or a penetration basis, or what kind of relationship the company should develop with its resellers.

These considerations are important because at each stage in a product's life cycle each management decision must consider the competitive requirements of the next stage. Thus a decision to establish a strong branding policy during the market growth stage might help to insulate the brand against strong price competition later; a decision to establish a policy of "protected" dealers in the market development stage might facilitate point-of-sale promotions during the market growth state, and so on. In short, having a clear idea of future product development possibilities and market development opportunities should reduce the likelihood of becoming locked into forms of merchandising that might possibly prove undesirable.

This kind of advance thinking about new product strategy helps management avoid other pitfalls. For instance, advertising campaigns that look successful from a short-term view may hurt in the next stage of the life cycle. Thus at the outset Metrecal advertising used a strong medical theme. Sales boomed until imitative competitors successfully emphasized fashionable slimness. Metrecal had projected itself as the dietary for the overweight consumer, an image that proved far less appealing than that of being the dietary for people who were fashion-smart. But Metrecal's original appeal had been so strong and so well made that it was a formidable task later on to change people's impressions about the product. Obviously, with more careful long-range planning at the outset, a product's image can be more carefully positioned and advertising can have more clearly defined objectives.

Recognizing the importance of an orderly series of steps in the introduction of sales-building "actions" for new products should be a central ingredient of long-term product planning. A carefully preplanned program for market expansion, even before a new product is introduced, can have powerful virtues. The establishment of a rational plan for the future can also help to guide the direction and pace of the on-going technical research in support of the product. Although departures from such a plan will surely have to be made to accommodate unexpected events and revised judgments, the plan puts the company in a better position to *make* things happen rather than constantly having to react to things that *are* happening.

It is important that the originator does *not* delay this long-term planning until after the product's introduction. How the product should be introduced and the many uses for which it might be promoted at the outset should be a function of a careful consideration of the optimum sequence of suggested product appeals and product uses. Consideration must focus not just on optimum things to do, but as importantly on their optimum *sequence* — for instance, what the order of use of various appeals should be and what the order of suggested product uses should be. If Jell-O's first suggested use had been as a diet food, its chances of later making a big and easy impact in the gelatin dessert market undoubtedly would have been greatly diminished. Similarly, if nylon hosiery had been promoted at the outset as a functional daytime-wear hosiery, its ability to replace silk as the acceptable high-fashion hosiery would have been greatly diminished.

To illustrate the virtue of pre-introduction planning for a product's later life, suppose a company has developed a nonpatentable new product — say, an ordinary kitchen salt shaker. Suppose that nobody now has any kind of shaker. One might say, before launching it, that (1) it has a potential market of "x" million household, institutional, and commercial consumers, (2) in two years market maturity will set in, and (3) in one year profit margins will fall because of the entry of competition. Hence one might lay out the following plan:

I. *End of first year: expand market among current users*
Ideas — new designs, such as sterling shaker for formal use, "masculine" shaker for barbecue use, antique shaker for "Early American" households, miniature shaker for each table place setting, moisture-proof design for beach picnics.

II. *End of second year: expand market to new users*
Ideas — designs for children, quaffer design for beer drinkers in bars, design for sadists to rub salt into open wounds.

III. *End of third year: find new uses*
Ideas — make identical product for use as a pepper shaker, as decorative garlic salt shaker, shaker for household scouring powder, shaker to sprinkle silicon dust on parts being machined in machine shops, and so forth.

This effort to prethink methods of reactivating a flattening sales curve far in advance of its becoming flat enables product planners to assign priorities to each task, and to plan future production expansion and capital and marketing requirements in a systematic fashion. It prevents one's trying to do too many things at once, results in priorities being determined rationally instead of as accidental consequences of the timing of new ideas, and disciplines both the product development effort that is launched in support of a product's growth and the marketing effort that is required for its continued success.

NOTES

1. For discussions of the scientific claims or potentials of marketing, see George Schwartz, *Development of Marketing Theory* (Cincinnati, Ohio, South-Western Publishing Co., 1963); and Reavis Cox, Wroe Alderson, and Stanley J. Shapiro, editors, *Theory in Marketing* (Homewood, Illinois, Richard D. Irwin, Inc., Second Series, 1964).

2. See Philip Kotler, "Phasing Out Weak Products," HBR March-April 1965, p. 107.

3. For perhaps the ultimate example of how the world does *not* beat such a path, see the example of the man who actually, and to his painful regret, made a "better" mousetrap, in John B. Matthews, Jr., R. D. Buzzell, Theodore Levitt, and Ronald E. Frank, *Marketing: An Introductory Analysis* (New York, McGraw-Hill Book Company, Inc., 1964), p. 4.

4. For related ideas on discerning opportunities for product revivification, see Lee Adler, "A New Orientation for Plotting a Marketing Strategy," *Business Horizons*, Winter 1964, p. 37.

5. I am indebted to my colleague, Dr. Derek A. Newton, for these examples and other helpful suggestions.

Businessmen may find the present theory handy as a shorthand method of ascertaining an appropriate marketing mix for a new product.

17

product characteristics and marketing strategy

gordon e. miracle

According to Webster, a science is "any branch or department of systematized knowledge considered as a distinct field of investigation or object of study." By this definition, marketing certainly may be designated as a science, albeit a science in the early stages of development. Scholars and students of marketing are concerned with the collection, analysis, and interpretation of marketing knowledge; and some progress has been made in systematizing and classifying marketing phenomena.

In recent years social scientists have begun to employ a method known in the physical sciences as *systems analysis*. As one social theorist has observed:

> "As judged by history of the physical, biological, and social sciences, study in any field is apt to begin with a none-too-ordered description of phenomena in the field, followed by a cataloguing of them on bases that seem to make sense. As understanding grows, the systems of classification become more closely related to the functioning of interacting elements. Gradually, generalizations about

Reprinted from the *Journal of Marketing*, published by the American Marketing Association, Volume 29, No. 1 (January 1965), pp. 18-23.

functioning are reached which are useful in predicting future events. As the generalizations gain in rigor, they take the form of analytical models of the behavior of the elements being studied. They take the form, that is, of systems."[1]

The development of marketing knowledge seems to be going through similar stages.

A system is a set of interdependent or interacting elements. The investigation of the factors that determine the state of the system is called systems analysis. This type of analysis may be applied to a business firm as well as to a society or other organization. Exogenous and endogenous factors may be examined to determine their influences on the firm in its movement toward an equilibrium.

Exogenous factors influencing the business firm include a profusion of economic, sociological, political, and cultural circumstances and trends. Endogenous factors influencing the movement of a firm toward equilibrium include the several elements in a firm's marketing program, usually described as the firm's marketing mix. The marketing mix, in its general form, includes decisions and activities of business firms in the areas of product policy, channel policy, promotional policy, and pricing policy.[2]

The term "marketing mix" suggests a relationship between interacting elements. The development of the term constituted a step forward in the classification of interrelated marketing efforts. Although more is becoming known about the relationships among elements of the marketing mix, it is still common practice to think of it as a blend of marketing efforts, essentially nonquantifiable, the development of which often depends on experience, judgment, and perhaps a measure of good fortune.

The concept of a system provides a means of improving further the framework within which we think about the interrelationships between and among marketing activities. After all, a business firm engages in marketing activities (endogenous factors in the system) in order to adapt to its environment (exogenous factors). This adaptation is intended to move the firm toward an equilibrium in which the level of operation is such that the goals of the firm are being achieved.

THE CHARACTERISTICS OF GOODS THEORY

An observable relationship exists between the characteristics of a product and the approximate marketing mix for that product. This is by no means a startling assertion. However, up to the present, there appears to be no systematic statement of the relationships between product characteristics and *each* of the elements in the marketing mix.

Historically, one of the most widely accepted classification of goods has been that of convenience, shopping, and specialty goods. The definitions of these goods are based on consumer buying habits.[3] They focus on consumer behavior and assist in answering questions as to why the consumer "shops" for some goods but not for others. Although the classification is helpful in guiding marketing policies, it is not altogether satisfactory.[4] If a businessman classifies his product in the traditional manner, the relationships between product classification and marketing policies still may be quite uncertain.

The theory presented here is a revision and an extension of "The Characteristcs of Goods Theory" proposed by Leo V. Aspinwall.[5] But whereas Aspinwall discusses the characteristcs of goods theory only in respect to channels of distribution and promotional policy, the theory presented here is broadened to include the areas of product and pricing policy.

Definition of Product Characteristics

If product characteristics are to be utilized to explain marketing policies and methods, each distinguishing characteristic must be reasonably stable during the period of time the explanation is to be valid. Also, each characteristic must be universal in the sense that it is to some degree a feature of all products.

A product is defined by most modern marketers as the sum of the physical and psychological satisfactions the buyer receives when he makes a purchase.[6] For example, when he makes a purchase the consumer receives an article with certain physical characteristics, or a service with certain features; he receives the item at a convenient location; he is able to purchase at a convenient time; he receives an item about which he has some knowledge (from the salesperson or from consumer advertising).

While the product may not be absolutely perfect from the point of view of each consumer, producers and sellers usually attempt to offer a "total product" that suits a large number of consumers reasonably well. The "bundle of utilities" purchased by the consumer is "collected" by incurring product development costs, channel costs, promotional costs, and other marketing costs. The "total product," in a broad sense, includes all of the features and conveniences for which the consumer pays in the retail selling price of the item.

Considerable ambiguity often exists in the definitions of product characteristics, consumer characteristics, and market characteristics. The amount of time and effort spent in purchasing a product may *seem* to be a consumer characteristic. But if convenience of location is part of the "bundle of utilities" and hence part of the "total product" for which the consumer pays, it seems reasonable that the "short" length of time the consumer spends searching for a place to buy a pack of cigarettes is a characteristic of the product. The "convenience" is provided as one feature in the "bundle of utilities." Another way of stating this point is that the nature of the product determines how much time (or what kinds of effort) consumers will wish to spend in buying the product. Thus, "consumer" and "market" characteristics may be described in terms of product characteristics.

Redefining consumer and market characteristics in terms of product characteristics permits development of a single list of characteristics instead of several.

Classification of Products

Observation of a large number of "products" indicates certain "product characteristics":

1. Unit value
2. Significance of *each* individual purchase to the consumer
3. Time and effort spent purchasing by consumers
4. Rate of technological change (including fashion changes)
5. Technical complexity
6. Consumer need for service (before, during, or after the sale)
7. Frequency of purchase
8. Rapidity of consumption
9. Extent of usage (number and variety of consumers and variety of ways in which the product provides utility)

By reviewing a list of products (for example, candy bars, hardware, radios, automobiles, and electronic computers) the variations in product characteristics can be observed in detail. Unit value ranges from low to high; the significance of each individual purchase to the consumer ranges from low to high; and so on down the list.

Products such as candy bars would be rated low for the first six characteristics, and high for the last three. For electronic data processing equipment, the opposite would tend to be true for each product characteristic. Hardware items or radios would be rated somewhere between. Thus, if products are arrayed on a continuum, they might range from such items as cigarettes and razor blades at one extreme, to steam turbines or large specialized machine tools at the other.

For convenience in exposition, it was decided to "break up" the array of products into five arbitrarily chosen groups, ranging from one extreme to the other, and including in each group some examples of items with similar product characteristics. The following groups were chosen:

Group I: Examples are cigarettes, candy bars, razor blades, soft drinks.

Group II: Examples are dry groceries, proprietary pharmaceuticals, small hardware items, industrial operating supplies.

Group III: Examples are radio and television sets, major household appliances, women's suits, tires and inner tubes, major sporting and athletic equipment.

Table 1
Product Characteristics of Five Groups

Product characteristic (see list)	Group I	II	III	IV	V
1	Very low	Low	Medium to high	High	Very high
2	Very low	Low	Medium	High	Very high
3	Very low	Low	Medium	High	Very high
4	Very low	Low	Medium	High	Very high
5	Very low	Low	Medium to high	High	Very high
6	Very low	Low	Medium	High	Very high
7	Very high	Medium to high	Low	Low	Very low
8	Very high	Medium to high	Low	Low	Very low
9	Very high	High	Medium to high	Low to medium	Very low

Group IV: Examples are high quality cameras, heavy farm machinery, passenger automobiles, high quality household furniture.

Group V: Examples are electronic office equipment, electric generators, steam turbines, specialized machine tools.

Table 1 shows the variation in product characteristics for each group.

It is, of course, an artificiality to classify products by groups; and it would be more accurate to place products on a continuum, or within a spectrum ranging from one extreme to another. Leo Aspinwall utilizes the "color classification" to express the idea of gradation of products on the basis of their characteristics. He utilizes red and yellow as the extremes of the spectrum, indicating that the blend of these colors produces orange — in fact, various shades of orange. Products in Group I would be classified as "red" goods. Products in Groups II, III, IV, and V range from orange to yellow.

A product might not always remain in the same classification. It might fall initially into Group III or IV; then, as larger numbers of consumers gradually accept it, as time and effort spent in purchasing is reduced, as consumer needs for service decline, and as other characteristics change, the product may move into Group II, or even Group I. At a later time marketers may succeed in improving or differentiating a product so that it is again in Group III or IV.

Table 2
Product Policy

Product group	Degree to which a manufacturer offers product varieties (for example: style, color, model, flavor, price) to consumers				
	Only one, or very few varieties	Few varieties	Several varieties	Many varieties	Different variety for every sale
I	X				
II		X			
III			X		
IV				X	
V					X

Table 3
Marketing Channel Policy

Product group	Intensity of distribution				
	Intensive	Moderately intensive	Some selectivity	Considerable selectivity	Highly selective, or direct sale to customers
I	X				
II		X			
III			X		
IV				X	
V					X

PRODUCT POLICY

An important aspect of marketing is the determination of the number of variations in products that are to be offered: the degree of product homogeneity or heterogeneity.

The problem for the businessman is to determine the effective demand for various product features — for example, style, color, model, quality level, and durability. The marketer must communicate this knowledge effectively to designers and production personnel, so that a product line can be developed that is consistent with the desires of consumers, the state of technology, the firm's capabilities, and other uncontrollable factors.

If the *unit value* or size of purchase is low, frequently the product will be highly standardized; perhaps only on variety within a brand category will be offered for sale — for example, Baby Ruth candy bars or Lucky Strike cigarettes.

Likewise, if the *significance of each individual purchase* is low, and if the *time and effort spent in the purchasing process* is low, product variety offered by each manufacturer tends to be low. Also, when the *rate of technical change* is low, few varieties tend to be offered; manufacturers are able to develop a product that remains suitable to consumers for an extended period of time.

Also, *technically simple* products often tend to be standardized to few varieties or a single variety. Likewise, a lack of *consumer need for service* often is associated with a standardized product. These characteristics with a rating of low or very low are typical of products in Group I.

On the other hand, *very high frequency of purchase, rapidity of consumption*, and *broad usage of the product* by a large number of consumers of diverse types, typically are associated with products in this group. Therefore, as indicated in Table 2, *a suitable product policy for products in Group I is to keep very low the varieties of products offered for sale.*

For products in Groups II, III, and IV, with successively higher values of characteristics 1 through 6 and successively lower values of characteristics 7, 8, and 9, the number of varieties offered tends to increase. At the other extreme, for products with a very high value for characteristics 1 through 6, and a very low value for characteristics 7, 8, and 9, the other extreme is reached in respect to the number of varieties offered.

Usually each product is "custom built" or "custom installed" according to the needs of each customer; every product sold is different from that sold to another customer.

MARKETING CHANNEL POLICY

Channel policies include selection of the types of distributors and number of each type. Intensity of distribution usually refers to the number of distributors utilized, from among those which might be suitable. A policy of intensive distribution means utilization of all available outlets regardless of their characteristics.

The selection of distributors according to their capability and suitability is called selective distribution. A policy of highly selective distribution is understood to mean the utilization of only a few (selected) outlets. The extreme case would be for a manufacturer to utilize no middlemen at all, that is, to sell directly to consumers or users, and either assume the wholesale and retail functions or pass them on to the consumer or user.

Intermediate policies, between the extremes of intensive and selective distribution, are indicated in Table 3. Moderately intensive distribution refers to the situation in which products are sold in a wide variety of outlets, but somewhat limited to certain classes. Some selectivity in distribution refers to the policy of selling products through a large number of outlets but limited somewhat to those with desired characteristics. Considerable selectivity means that the number and types of outlets are limited to those with specifically desirable characteristics.

When the unit value is very low; when the significance of each individual purchase is low; when little time and effort are spent in the purchasing process; when the rate of technological change is low; when the product is not complex technically; when consumers need little service; and when the frequency of purchase, rapidity of consumption, and extent of usage are high, highly intensive distribution usually is preferred over selective distribution. At the other extreme, when the values of characteristics are just the opposite, highly selective distribution is the rule. Various intermediate values of characteristics for products in Groups II, III, and IV suggest a range of policies between the extremes.

Note also that products in Group I typically are sold through a relatively long channel of distribution, while products in Group V often are sold through the shortest of channels – direct to user or consumer.[7] In fact, in Table 3 the phrase "length of channel" could be used with some validity instead of "intensity of distribution."

PROMOTIONAL POLICY

A major aspect of promotional strategy is to decide how much effort is to be placed on mass media consumer advertising vis-a-vis the amount of effort on personal selling.

For products in Group I, observation suggests that the emphasis usually is on consumer advertising. In the extreme case a firm may have no salesforce at all. On the other hand, products in Group V depend almost entirely upon personal selling effort, although advertising in trade magazines may play a supplementary role. Products in Groups II, III, and IV require a combination of consumer advertising and personal selling, as illustrated in Table 4.

PRICING POLICY

The pricing policy of a firm depends upon the degree to which a firm has control over price. If the firm has no control, if prices are set "in the market place" by custom or by any other means beyond the control of the firm, there is no need for the firm to have any pricing policy at all (except to sell or not to sell at the going price).

Thus, a starting point in establishing a firm's pricing policy is to specify the degree of control which the firm has over price. It is only after this has been ascertained that the businessman can turn to the specific tasks of price determination and price administration.

Table 4
Promotional Policy

Relative emphasis on mass media consumer advertising and
personal selling

Product group	Sold almost entirely by consumer advertising	Sold primarily by consumer advertising	Consumer advertising and personal selling both needed; neither of predominant importance	Sold primarily by personal selling	Sold almost entirely by personal selling
I	X				
II		X			
III			X		
IV				X	
V					X

Table 5
Pricing Policy

Degree to which seller controls price

Product group	Very little	Sightly	Moderately	Significantly	Substantially
I	X				
II		X			
III			X		
IV				X	
V					X

The degree of control that a firm has over price of its products seems to vary according to the enumerated product characteristics. As shown in Table 5, firms have little control over prices of items in Group I, relatively more control in the middle groups, and the highest degree of control in Group V.

Pricing policies are established with regard to (1) the degree of variation from customer to customer, and (2) the degree of adherence to list prices versus dependence on negotiating the price for each sale. As can be observed in Table 6, products in Group I usually show little variation in price, whereas prices of products in Group V change relatively more frequently and often are substantially different for different customers purchasing similar products. Concomitantly, the prices of products in Group V are likely to be established

Table 6
Pricing Policy

Product group	Stable	Variations in prices over time, short term, seasonally, cyclically, or by customer categories.			
		Slight variation	Moderate variation	Significant variation	Substantial variation
I	X				
II		X			
III			X		
IV				X	
V					X

independently for each sale. The prices of products in Group I are not often negotiated in this manner.

THE MARKETING MIX

By way of summary, the marketing mix for products in Group I should be substantially as follows:

1. Relatively little effort and money spent on product development. Since a standard variety of the product is suitable for a broad group of customers, there is relatively less need for frequent change than for products in other groups.
2. Considerable effort spent in achieving intensive distribution. Products must be available quickly and conveniently.
3. Heavy consumer advertising — little or no personal selling. Consumers typically are pre-sold by advertising.
4. Relatively little effort and time spent on pricing. Firms have little control over price; variations in price are relatively infrequent; prices are not negotiated between seller and consumer.

At the other extreme, we would expect to find that products in Group V usually are:

1. Custom built.
2. Sold directly from manufacturer to user.
3. Sold primarily by salesmen, rather than advertising.
4. Sold on the basis of an individually negotiated price.

The marketing mix of products in Group V would involve relatively heavy efforts in the area of product policy; the marketing channel would be short, perhaps direct; personal selling is relatively more important than mass media; and considerable time and effort are spent on the determination and negotiation of price.

The marketing mix of products in Groups II, III, and IV can be characterized as modifications of the two extremes.

CONCLUSIONS

Knowledge of the product characteristics can be utilized to predict the nature of the marketing mix which is suitable for a given product. The prediction is, of course, an approximate *ideal* for a product with given characteristics. As a practical matter, the ability of a firm to engage in the indicated marketing methods may be limited in a number of ways, such as financial capabilities, or availability of personnel with the requisite skills, or management talent.

The primary contribution of the present theory is a modest increase in the analytical character of the marketing mix. Hopefully the next steps will be to develop more precise measures of the functional relationships among the elements in the marketing mix.

Businessmen may find the present theory handy as a shorthand method of ascertaining an appropriate marketing mix for a new product. Or if policies not in accordance with the theory are being followed. a businessman may be well advised to review carefully the reasons for his policies. It may even happen that the characteristics-of-goods theory will point the way to profitable policy changes.

As another example, a firm faced with the need to justify in a court of law its past marketing methods might use the theory as a broad framework to illustrate the reasons for its past decisions. Or the model might serve to direct the attention of researchers into relevant channels, or provide assistance to executives in the tasks of organizing marketing facts as a basis for making marketing decisions.

NOTES

1. Everett E. Hagen, *On the Theory of Social Change* (Homewood, Illinois: The Dorsey Press, Inc., 1962), p. 4.

2. Neil H. Borden, "A Note on the Concept of the Marketing Mix," in Eugene J. Kelley and William Lazer, Editors, *Managerial Marketing: Perspectives and Viewpoints* (Homewood, Illinois: Richard D. Irwin, Inc., 1958), pp. 272-275.

3. Melvin T. Copeland, "Relation of Consumers' Buying Habits to Marketing Methods," *Harvard Business Review*, Vol. 1 (April, 1923), pp. 282-289.

4. Richard M. Holton, "The Distinction Between Convenience Goods, Shopping Goods, and Specialty Goods," *Journal of Marketing*, Vol. 23 (July, 1958), pp. 53-56.

5. Leo V. Aspinwall, "The Characteristics of Goods Theory," in William Lazer and Eugene J. Kelley, Editors, *Managerial Marketing; Perspectives and Viewpoints* (Homewood, Illinois: Richard D. Irwin, Inc., 1962), pp. 633-643.

6. Harry L. Hansen, *Marketing: Text, Cases, and Readings* (Homewood, Illinois: Richard D. Irwin, 1961), p. 312.

7. Aspinwall, same reference as footnote 5.

III UTILITIES - SUGGESTED ADDITIONAL READINGS

Leo Aspinwall, "The Characteristics of Goods and Parallel Systems," 2nd ed., William Lazar and Eugene J. Kelley, eds., Homewood, Illinois: Richard D. Irwin, Inc., 1962, 633-643.

William E. Cox, Jr., "Product Life Cycles as Marketing Models," *Journal of Business*, 40, October 1967, 375-384.

Ernest J. Enright, "Market Testing," *Harvard Business Review*, 36, September-October 1958, 72-80.

Ronald E. Frank, Susan P. Douglas and Rolando E. Polli, "Household Correlates of Package Size, Proneness for Grocery Products," *Journal of Marketing Research*, 4, November 1967, 381-384.

Alan H. Gepfert, "Business Logistics for Better Profit Performance," *Harvard Business Review*, 46, November-December 1968, 75-84.

Herbert S. Kleiman, "A Case Study of Innovation," *Business Horizons*, 9, Winter 1966, 63-70.

Philip Kotler, "Phasing Out Weak Products," *Harvard Business Review*, 43, March-April 1965, 107-118.

R. William Kotrba, "The Strategy — Selection Chart," *Journal of Marketing*, 30, July 1966, 22-25.

Herbert E. Krugman, "White and Negro Responses to Package Designs," *Journal of Marketing Research*, 3, May 1966, 199-200.

Alfred A. Kuehn, "Measuring the Effectiveness of Advertising," Robert M. Kaplan, ed., *Marketing Concept in Action*, Chicago: American Marketing Association, 1964, 275-281.

John H. Kunkel and Leonard L. Berry, "A Behavioral Conception of Retail Image," *Journal of Marketing*, 32, October 1968, 21-27.

J. Douglas McConnell, "The Price Quality Relationship in an Experimental Setting," *Journal of Marketing Research*, 5, August 1968, 300-303.

William R. Mason, "A Theory of Packaging in the Marketing Mix," *Business Horizons*, 10, Summer 1958, 91-95.

Stuart U. Rich and Bernard Portis, "Clues for Action From Shopper Preferences," *Harvard Business Review*, 41, March-April 1963, 132-149.

Thomas S. Robertson, "Consumer Innovators: The Key to New Product Success," *California Management Review*, 10, Winter 1967, 23-30.

Daniel Starch, "Do Ad Readers Buy the Product?" *Harvard Business Review*, 36, May-June 1958, 49-58.

John B. Stewart, "Functional Features in Product Strategy," *Harvard Business Review*, 37, March-April 1959, 65-78.

John F. Stolle, "How to Manage Physical Distribution," *Harvard Business Review*, 45, July-August 1967, 93-100.

Chester R. Wasson, "How Predictable Are Fashion and Other Product Life Cycles?" *Journal of Marketing*, 32, July 1968, 36-43.

IV

Operations

Coordinating
and Evaluating
Marketing Effort

Many of the preceding readings include some operational aspects. Methods of searching for want-satisfying utilities and designing products which will provide these utilities to a maximum degree, have been suggested throughout. Psychological, sociological, and other behavioral techniques for analyzing people individually and in groups have been introduced.

Similarly, the writings in this section, can be related in some way or other to people, or to utilities, or to both. They differ from the others in that they are more applicable in the area of marketing administration. More emphasis is placed on the effective performance of some marketing task than on the people who do it or the utilities produced.

The article by Doremus is concerned with the policy which precedes implementation; this provides a basis to understanding the rationale developed in the other articles of this section. Quantitative methods have rivaled the behavioral sciences in recent years. Both areas are contending for consideration by marketers seeking new dimensions. Operations research has vied with motivation research for the attention of marketing specialists. In selecting readings in such areas as marketing science, the editors did not have as their objective, the presentation of those readings which describe any specific techniques in detail; rather readings were selected which emphasize understanding.

Since marketing to segments of the population is receiving increased attention, the selections also suggest various ways to segmentize, of which the surveying of characteristics is only one. For instance, approximately 20 per cent of the population changes residences each year. Geographic viability as a profitable dimension for segmenting consumer markets is evaluated. Weiner segments by a regional market concept; Wells segments according to willingness to buy induced by promotional strategies. Emerging marketing ideas rarely receive unanimous acceptance. To give representation to a divergent viewpoint on the usefulness of segmenting approaches, we have included a critical overview of market segmentation by Bieda and Kassarjian.

Obviously, marketing has drawn freely from other disciplines and sciences. But this has not been a parasitic or sterile process. Drawing from other sciences has created additional knowledge which should provide the basis for generally accepted strategies in marketing, and which may, in addition, shed some new light on aspects of other disciplines.

Business policy is essentially a system of values that govern types of decisions to be made by management. Based partly on interviews with top executives, Professor Doremus suggests that the market can be the prime mover as well as the goal of a business as an organizational system. Even technically-oriented firms, like Litton Industries, can be marketing-centered. "The market furnishes the businessman with a raison d'etre: *a goal-directed purpose more real than dollars and more fundamental than profits, although not necessarily out of harmony with either."*

18

policy, the core of business commitment

william l. doremus

Policy is a focal point for planning and decision making. This article stresses the rationale of policy rather than its implementation. A marketing orientation prevails throughout.

I. THE POLICY RATIONALE

Policy is afflicted with imprecision. Frequently when no justification can be found for an act or decision, line executives guardedly rationalize with the comment, "It's company policy." The term is used loosely, even by otherwise sophisticated scholars of business administration. Relatively little has been written about it. Perhaps business policy as a depth study is not subject to a problem/solution reference. Perhaps, too, the subject fits economist J. R. Sargent's observation to the effect that occasionally one must carry out the ritual of showing that a question is unanswerable before it is actually answered.[1]

Reprinted with permission from the *University of Washington Business Review*, a publication of the University of Washington, Volume 4 (Summer 1967), pp. 5-18.

Seeking an approach to policy formation is the critical task. One wonders what the term policy means to the businessman. Often it is explained by the use of illustration rather than by a statement of its essence. During an interview with the author several executives responded by providing illustrations of how policy is carried out. Such a response is of limited help to the investigator trying to get at the nub of the thing, even though some sympathy can be extended to these entirely competent and skilled executives by arguing, along with Bergson, that the brain serves to bring about a choice that shows us less the thing itself than the use we can make of it.[2]

Policy, Common Understanding in Decision Making

Often the firm's policy resides in a senior management sanctuary – the mind of the executive. Indeed, one management authority has gone so far as to define policy as an understanding by members of a group that makes the actions of each member of the group in a given set of circumstances more predictable to other members.[3] It is necessary to basic operating conduct that there be general agreement among top management about a kind of overall corporate purpose. This is recognizable in a creed, a faith, a kind of basic belief which, although lacking in precision, serves as foundation for further development and ultimate general understanding among senior executives and on down the chain of authority. It implies common understanding of goals. Policy becomes a guide for making decisions and the attainment of goals. Focus, understanding, and agreement on goals as viewed among the members of the management are the catalysts for decision making.

Economist J. N. W. Oanh has provided us with something of a definition when, in his "Keynes Today," he observes that Keynes, like other great figures in economics, was concerned with policy, and that economists look upon policy as a reflection of their individual systems of values.[4] He also feels that when taking a policy position economists are motivated by a desire to promote changes that will better the environment in which they live. Clearly, there is a strong ethical value judgment in this approach.

The Precept of Ethical Value in Business Policy

The root of business policy seems to tie in with *values*. In this context policy becomes a realization of what the business firm holds as its value position. There is an implied ethical extension here.

Policy now becomes a philosophy of basic business determination, evidenced in a collection of precepts or rules of action which give uniformity and direction to business conduct.[5] Perhaps the term *precept* is central in this approach, since it implies guiding behavior considered beforehand as a kind of moral injunction upon management to observe a maxim. This does not preclude the fact that any given executive group may engage in policy determination that results in corrupt conduct. The term policy is therefore not exempt from being based in odious purpose.

Policy and the Moral Base

There have been celebrated instances in which proper policy promulgation would have prevented patent mismanagement at the lower echelons. In these cases submanagement was alleged to be in violation of what senior management held as agreed policy decision practice. The so-called electric cases of the early 1960's are instances in which some of the nation's leading electric equipment companies engaged in price-fixing agreements. Failure of senior management to communicate policy down the chain of command resulted in failure by middle management to employ the standards and norms which could have prevented illegal sales engagements. These companies lost more in reputation than in treasure, but more important, caused serious damage to the image of American business.

Even senior management has not always been free of participation in price-fixing monopolistic conduct. The Temporary National Economic Committee, 1938-1941, investigated a common form of monopoly practice called price leadership, in which it was freely admitted by the president of United States Steel that his firm set prices for steel, and by the president of Bethlehem Steel, that his firm followed the lead while blandly calling the act "meeting a competitive situation."[6] In the face of some of these facts, one is tempted to become aphoristic and observe that business policy, along with politics, may well qualify as the moral man's compromise, the swindler's method, and the fool's hope.

Corporate Objectives at the Root of Policy

What appears to be a constructive, realistic approach to a study of business policy is grounded in an attempt to give articulation to the basic *objectives* of the company. Profit optimization, major share of market, decentralization of product and profit responsibilities, may be looked upon as examples of basic long-run objectives. If we view corporate policy as progressing from corporate objectives, we argue that policy is the articulate *spokesman* for the firm's reason for being. Now policy is a form of business communication carrying the authoritative fillips of top management.

How specific should a corporate objective be? Some students of business policy have argued that company objectives are allowed to degenerate into vague statements ". . . which describe the goals in broad general terms such as increased sales, increased profits, a broader base of operations, a better environment for the growth of personnel, and so forth. Such expressions of objectives are, indeed, neither meaningful nor useful."[7] On the other hand, "broad purpose" and "wide range" are terms specifically used by marketing vice presidents and corporate planning vice presidents in billion dollar corporations when they refer to corporate objectives.[8] The position of these men can be summarized by observing that the rationale at the objective/purpose level of thought must be general, since it is at the core of the structure. The rationale at the policy level, on the other hand, becomes more specific because policy is the base upon which plans are laid.

In practice it may be difficult to differentiate objective from policy. If a corporation vice president holds that one of the marketing objectives of the firm is progressively to increase relative share of market, how is this translated into policy without substantially repeating the words and the essence of the objective upon which the policy is based? If this question is answered affirmatively, are not objective and policy the same thing? Some senior executives claim that, in day to day practice, operating management uses them interchangeably, and that it is not material to look upon company objectives and company policies as mutually exclusive concepts.

II. RATIONAL INSPECTION OF TERMS: POLICY, OBJECTIVE

In a mid-twentieth century world of rapid scientific evaluation, it would seem that some management terms and their meanings are out of focus when they are subjected to rational inspection. Such a condition leads an investigator to the celebrated polemic between science and art. The scientist argues, along with Socrates, that if one would discuss a subject he must define his terms. The scientist looks upon business management as more a science than an art, and therefore the scientifically centered individual seeks to align elements according to the requirements of an organized body of knowledge having specific classifications and consequently mutually exclusive definitions of terms. Such a view would force a clear differentiation between business objective and business policy and each would be defined in mutually exclusive terms. On the other hand, an artist such as Paul Gauguin, seeing things in a more detached manner, may well contend that business management is predominantly the art of handling people and would undoubtedly invite a spillover of definitions by advising that we not finish our work too much and that an impression is not sufficiently durable for its first freshness to survive a belated search for infinite detail. On such a scale of values, business terms, like art, have no final boundaries.

At this point, along with John Ciari, one might feel a need to be wary of compounding innocence with a pedantic solemnity. Perhaps stress on science, semantics, and the attending requirement for strict definition may develop into solemn narrowness far short of the wide parameter we may hope for.[9]

III. POLICY DECISION: NARROW-GAUGED AND BROAD-GAUGED

A narrowness, solemn or not, has pervaded much of the policy decisions in American business because of what might be characterized as a unilateral dealing from strength. D. Ronald Daniel tells of a venerable chairman of a five-man board of directors who invited a personal friend to attend a board meeting. At the meeting a proposal to build a new plant was made and the vote went four to one against the chairman not to go ahead. "The ayes have it. We'll proceed with construction," said the chairman crisply, and adjourned the meeting. Later the startled friend asked the chairman about his arithmetic and the old man replied, "Francis, some days we count the votes around here, other days we weigh them. Today we weighed them." The chairman was the firm's largest single stockholder.[10]

Professor Suojanen in his *Dynamics of Management*[11] is hardly narrow when he makes the broad observation that policy is essentially a *system of values* that governs types of decisions to be made by management. Such a system of values in a given case may well manifest itself in an understanding among members of the management group, as Professor Massie points out.[12] When decisions are made, based upon such a joint understanding, they are policy decisions that set precedents, thus providing guidelines for future action – policy decisions.

These policy decisions, based upon (1) previous multiparticipant problem solving of proven effectiveness and upon (2) joint understanding of approaches and methods by fellow members of the management team, are apt to be far more scientific than the vaunted intuitive, single-handed solutions rendered by a veteran administrator. As Perrin Stryker has observed, "The ability of managers to solve problems and make decisions rationally has long been assumed to be one of the valuable products of experience on the job. But close observation of their actual practices has shown that even veteran managers are likely to be very unsystematic when dealing with problems and decisions. And their hit-or-miss methods often produce decisions based on erroneous conclusions, which means that the decision must also be wrong.[13]

From the Center Outward

Inspection of the accompanying target-like design (Figure I) shows that the firm's objectives are the goals at the core of its being. From this center the firm structures its values, and guidelines are drawn. The formulation of guidelines and their decimation are policy.[14] Planning projects into the future is an extension of company values – thus, it is hoped, providing an efficient and effective mode of operation.[15] The plan is made operative through the melding (management) of human and material resources. The terminal act of appraising the performance of management is accomplished by an audit of operational feedback. Here is a philosophy of business management that is brought together by weighing the fact, the theory, the alternatives, and the ideal.

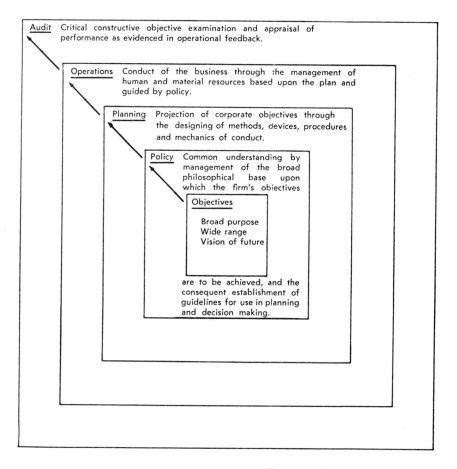

Figure 1. Corporate Policy Posture

From the Pragmatic to the Scientific

". . . the age of horseflesh is gone — that of engineers, economists and calculators has succeeded." These words were written by Thackeray in 1840[16] when, as now, it was alleged that great changes were taking place. More than 125 years later we say with conviction that much of the decision making accomplished by the executives in giant corporations has moved from the subjective pragmatic to the objective automatic. Policy making is predicated upon the realization that rapid scientific development is moving business at a pace well ahead of the capacity of those who came to management by way of the exercise of outstanding practical "horseflesh." An engineering-oriented manager, as an example, in past years, could be expected to be a man of practical action. Such a man may well solve problems in distribution logistics with high functional skill, but this may not be enough today. The current revolution in management dictates that the engineer draw heavily upon the physical sciences — upon the knowledge developed in the laboratory by scientist-engineers. Data processing with the consequent economic implications of the fore-shortening of time scale is a case in point, and this is especially applicable in policy determination in relation to logistics in channels of distribution. As with the engineer, so too with the marketing man. The pure sciences and more especially the social sciences recently have been spilling over into the technology of business management. As Dr. H. A. Stratton, president of the Massachusetts Institute of Technology observed, the progress of these changes has been so swift that we have in fact a management revolution on our hands.[17]

Firm Policy and the Innovation Revolution

The changes in business management are much deeper than those that have occurred in the past when action was directed primarily toward improving and expanding what already existed — an effort to achieve more of the same. Nearly the full spectrum of the sciences have come forward to give aid and direction to the formulation of innovation-centered business policy. "Of the basic disciplines it appears that history, philosophy, religion, the social sciences, the physical sciences and political science have some meaningful applications to business policy. In addition to developing a more sensitive awareness of environmental factors, the methods of research, analysis and evaluation in these fundamental areas are invaluable in the decision making processes of business policy."[18]

The innovation revolution has taken hold at policy levels among many of the giant corporations, even though these big companies might logically be looked upon as less likely to embrace it. Their large capital investment in present structure and strong consumer franchise in present products and methods make them qualify as tending pathologically toward playing it safe while employing conventional people, using conventional ideas, and retaining conventional operating practices. Nevertheless, these corporate policy makers show an active, demonstrated interest in the broadest spectrum of business participations that reshape life, tastes, values and needs. Innovation influencing considerations include the physical, social, and life sciences; aesthetics, mass culture and technology; a panoramic cluster of ideas, theories, facts, and events.

In some case, methods of achievement and the policy guidelines have become extravagantly permissive, with innovation seeking a better way while believing that it is still better to be better, even if it increases the risk of becoming worse! A policy line that dares not to take the risk of making the new happen results in management taking, by default, the greater risk of being surprised by what happens.

The Highest Human Effort

Ideas, the product of creativity, are latent in most policy makers as they seek to implement corporate objectives. Creativity has been called the highest human effort and its consequences man's great legacy. At a meeting in 1962, J. B. McKitterick, manager of marketing research, General Electric Company, made two significant policy recommendations when he said: "The real challenge to marketing people is to get hold firmly of the idea that changing a business – finding it new roles, new customers, new markets – is even more important than operating it efficiently. If the corporation's aim is to outlive the markets upon which it is founded, then marketing must replace the lost function of the entrepreneur in the business planning process. Far too many of our companies today are filling their top management ranks with executives skilled in problem solving, when they should be seeking problem formulators – people to specify tasks worthy of the organization's best efforts, to see what the country really needs and be more dedicated to that vision than to forever attempt to repeat some past success."[19]

Reason for Being: the Market

It has been argued that marketing is an all-encompassing thing and that in point of fact the market represents the prime mover as well as the goal of business, broadly viewed. Since this thesis is relatively new, there is a paucity of tradition backing it. The band-wagon sounds in current support of it, however, are loud. When business is directed toward society, customers and other people, the firm is given significant moral as well as practical justification for giving marketing the prime position in executive thinking and policy making. It provides a break from such concepts as the parochial view that profit resides essentially in low-cost full production. The market furnishes the businessman with a *raison d'etre*: a goal-directed purpose more real than dollars and more fundamental than profits, although not necessarily out of harmony with either. A market-centered or people-centered basic policy as against a profit-centered policy for the individual business holds promise of a continuing breakthrough in business thinking. While there is ground for saying that a market-centered policy and a profit-centered policy may obtain simultaneously, the audacity and daring attached to specifying market-centered policy orientation as primary throws critical light upon the traditional selection of profit optimization as an element of basic policy. More than forty years ago, in 1923, Henry Ford showed the way to such a policy breakthrough when he announced that, "Our policy is to reduce the price, extend the operations and improve the product." There is strong market orientation here. In any case, the best leadership opinion in mid-20th century seems to have moved to the view that market is *central* to overall business making.

Market Overview in the Policy of Technically Oriented Firms

Roy Ash, President of Litton Industries, can speak with authority. His company's revenues have grown at an average annual rate of 60 percent, 1955-65, from $9 million to $916 million, with earnings growing at a rate of over 30 percent a year! When he states that *commercial potential* is the basic policy criterion for the introduction of a new product, such a policy statement is worthy of examination. He makes the point that determination of commercial potential is based upon three thresholds. First, make sure the product works in the field, not just in the laboratory. Second, check out totally the economics of the new product. In the marketplace, costs are crucial. The third threshold is founded in public acceptance: will it sell? Policywise, before Litton places the "go" label on a new product it asks, what do we do with the product? Is there a market? What is it? Can we reach it? How? Can the venture be profitable? These are marketing questions. Even though Mr. Ash observes that ". . . technology is the common denominator of just about all the things we do – or plan to do," when it comes down to establishing basic policy, he is clearly a marketing-centered executive.[20]

Company Totality and Interdepartmental Policy Rationale

The market as central to overall corporate policy determination poses organizational and operational problems. As the marketing organization in a given firm assumes more responsibility for corporate success, the marketing executives tend to make greater demands upon other departments of the company. Often, marketing people justify their actions on the premise that marketing is the elite factor and must not be subordinated. Hostility between members of the management team and costly power struggles frequently follow. Meeting the demands of the marketing department may well impose a loss of operating efficiency upon other departments, thereby doing violence to their cost guidelines. Top management, in functioning as arbiter, is faced with resolving what the marketing department regards as required conditions for the attainment of sales goals on the one hand, and the cost-centered efficiency goals of the several nonmarketing departments on the other. Top management must view the policy of the firm in terms of what the company as a whole is trying to achieve.[21]

It is inevitable that each department within a firm will look upon its contribution to the enterprise in terms of the means it requires to meet the challenge. "Consider the desires of certain departments with respect to length of product line. The marketing group wants a long product line because it means a better position in the market-place. But the production people want long production runs in order to minimize manufacturing costs. The financial executives want to minimize capital investments in inventory and the extra production equipment needed to produce the longer line."[22] In four of the country's giant billion-dollar corporations whose executives were interviewed by the author, this situation was resolved in an entirely logical manner, the rationale of which became the base for related future policy decisions. It became a matter of reducing emphasis on narrow, unilateral, departmental operations and increasing emphasis on the development of interdepartmental policies that pointed toward overall company objectives.[23] This is a systems approach.

Systems Thinking: Focus on the Total Picture

A business that is centered in people, the market as an end purpose or totality, suggests an examination of another concept presently being pursued at business policy levels: the idea of an organizational system, an encompassing totality. For example, in the marketing sector, the best thinking does not permit advertising, merchandising, pricing, sales promotion, selling, and other market-oriented activities to be appraised as segmented components. They are to be viewed collectively as a systematic whole — as the marketing contribution. In like manner, only a short while ago businessmen focused attention upon finance, production, accounting and marketing as components of the enterprise, to be treated separately and in relative isolation. Today, stress is laid upon the contribution of these several parts, interacting and made manifest as a net delivery. This is systems thinking.

An example of the effectiveness of systems thinking in corporate policy is found in the success of the product manager or brand manager concept in the packaged goods field.[24] The $2 ¼ billion Proctor and Gamble Company, whose volume and net earnings have more than doubled over the most recent ten years, has continued to operate under the policy that each brand is a separate business and is expected to stand on its own feet competitively and financially. As Howard J. Morgens, President of Proctor and Gamble, commented, ". . . it gives us assurance that no one brand will be neglected and that the work on each will have behind it the kind of single-minded drive [i.e., systems thinking] [25] that it needs if it is going to have a chance to succeed in the highly competitive fields in which we operate." [26]

The discipline imposed by a policy of systems thinking does not limit freedom. It steadies the direction of the individual participant, as well as providing him with a key to the relationship he bears to the total picture. J. A. Stratton has likened it to a graduation from the anatomy of components to the physiology of an organic whole.[27]

IV. MANAGERIAL ATROPHY, THE MONOPOLY SPECTER, AND CORPORATE EXPANSION POLICY

Reasonable mastery of the firm's on-going operations, especially at the marketing, production, and financial levels, forces policy-forming management into a position in which it must seek expanding employment for the company's human resources. Without the challenge of more and greater problems there is real danger of managerial atrophy and loss of some of the more highly talented personnel. In addition to the need to further exploit its management and technological talents, the firm may be enjoying substantial return on capital, an excessive cash position, strong product demand, and a burgeoning market potential. Expansion, ergo growth, vertically, horizontally, or both, becomes the issue. The parochial approach is to develop more products for the line or seek to acquire companies turning out products that are immediately or closely related. To travel this route may result in long and costly government monopoly litigation. Many corporate acquisition policy guidelines direct management toward diversifying by seeking ownership in firms sufficiently removed from its kind of operation to make inquiry by governmental antimonopoly administration quite unnecessary.

High Stakes and Acquisition Policy

When the stakes are high enough, management invariably will go ahead with an acquisition in the face of a strong likelihood of attack by federal authorities on monopoly grounds.

International Telephone and Telegraph Corporation attempted to acquire American Broadcasting Company, knowing full well that the Federal Communications Commission would seriously question the antitrust characteristics of the marriage. This acquisition would tie in two important electronic/communication companies, adding some $375 million in sales to IT&T's already substantial $2,125 million total. Harold S. Geneen, president of the corporation, in a statement before the New York Society of Security Analysts,[28] stated that the policy on acquisitions is to maintain a higher-than-average rate of growth and concentrate on businesses in which earnings have stability as well as growth. He might have observed, too, that apparently another IT&T policy rationale is to widen the corporate base by diversifying across a wide range of enterprise: Avis car rentals, life insurance, small loans, mutual funds, educational publishing, telecommunications, farm publications, and military, space, and avionics products.

Policy Dilemmas: The Surgeon General, Dissipation, and the Curse of Cash

In the face of the Surgeon General's report and a flood of health warnings on the dangers of the smoking habit, one can hardly blame senior officers of the major tobacco companies for being less than sanguine about the future of their business. E. F. Hoover, Manager of Corporate Development for the American Tobacco Company,[29] recently observed during an interview that an important consideration in the active search for likely corporate acquisitions is the unpromising outlook for his firm's products. It is interesting to observe that some four hours following that interview, the radio carried the news that more cigarettes had been consumed during the immediate past twelve months than in any time in history!

Among other policy guidelines being observed by American Tobacco Company in relation to corporate acquisitions are:

1. Because the American Tobacco Company has well-developed skill in the manufacture and marketing of packaged consumer goods, only companies of that type are given acquisition consideration.

2. Because the American Tobacco Company has a background in both the manufacture and marketing of packaged consumer products, and is of the opinion that being in full control of both these activities offers optimum profit and promise of potential expansion, only companies that offer for acquisition both manufacturing and marketing assets are given consideration. A comparative illustration of this approach is the fact that Liggett & Myers Tobacco Company bought control of Paddington Corporation (J & B Rare Scotch Whisky), which places L & M in the import/distributor business, a marketing operation only. American Tobacco Company, on the other hand, has acquired a majority interest in James B. Beam Distilling Company, both a manufacturing and marketing firm.

(Parenthetically, it would seem, tobacco and whisky are natural associates. As the wag observed, It's a dissipation marriage!)

3. Since the American Tobacco Company continues to remain in an excess cash position, special consideration is given to searching out companies which favor a high cash transfer in the process of acquisition.

4. Because a fixed objective of the company is to avoid litigation with government, commitments are avoided that may develop into lengthy government regulatory or statutory investigation.

V. POLICY INITIATION: SOME BOTTOM-UP INFLUENCES

In 1911 Henry Sturgis Dennison gave 200 employees of the Dennison Manufacturing Company controlling participation in the management of the business.[30]   Although not entirely parallel, this famous first in business policy making was a forerunner of the current trend toward an acceptance by senior management of increasing participation by operating line management in the establishment of corporate policy. An example of this reasoning in top management circles today is evident in statements by both a senior vice president and a vice president of marketing in one of the nation's largest business service organizations, Dun and Bradstreet, Inc. They expect operating executives at the middle and junior range to think imaginatively, solve problems with some daring, and thus introduce piecemeal changes in policy that are based upon lessons learned through feedback evaluation of conditions in the field. As Carl E. Treiber, a 35-year veteran, put it, "We hold that policy must be adjusted to the needs of the marketplace. In this sense much of our policy changes are initiated by operating personnel."[31]

This sort of bottom-up management is in harmony with the sophistication presently found down the line in the executive hierarchy. "Today, managers must manage educated people, who are less docile, who demand reasons for what they are asked to do and who insist on participating in the determination of objectives as well as choosing means for reaching these goals."[32] This is the way Douglas McGregor sees the inevitability of continuing acceptance, if not the encouragement, of a policy rationale that allows for participation from the bottom up to the top of the management scale. In some cases, top management has responded by decentralized decision making, multiple management, participative management and consultative management approaches.

NOTES

1. *Oxford Economic Papers*, Vol. 15. No. 1, p. 1.

2. Henri Bergson, *The Creative Mind* (Wiston Library, 1946), p. 137.

3. J. L. Massie, *Essentials of Management* (Prentice-Hall, Englewood Cliffs: 1964), p. 40.

4. J. N. W. Oanh, "Keynes Today," *Harvard Business Review*, May-June, 1960, p. 98.

5. J. Jones and W. L. Doremus, *Sales Management*, Alexander Hamilton Institute, 1958, p. 17.

6. *Hearing Before the Temporary National Economic Committee* (Washington, D.C.: Government Printing Office), Part 19, pp. 10586-10588.

7. M. L. Mace, "The President and Corporate Planning," *Harvard Business Review*, January-February, 1965, p. 51.

8. International Paper, Alcoa, Westinghouse, Continental Can; author interviewed senior officers in these and eleven other billion dollar corporations.

9. L. F. Urwick, "The Problems of Management Semantics," *California Management Review*, Spring, 1960.

10. D. Ronald Daniel, "Team at the Top," *Harvard Business Review*, March-April, 1965, p. 77.

11. W. W. Suojanen, *The Dynamics of Management* (New York: Holt, Rinehart, and Winston, 1965), p. 15.

12. Massie, *op. cit.*

13. Perrin Stryker, "Can You Analyze This Problem," *Harvard Business Review*, May-June, 1965, p. 73.

14. C. L. Jamison, *Determination of Objectives* (Englewood Cliffs, N.J.: Prentice-Hall, 1953), p. 103.

188   ESSENTIALS OF AN EFFECTIVE MARKETING PROGRAM: READINGS

15. T. J. McNichols, *Policy Making and Executive Action* (New York: McGraw-Hill, 1959), p. 12.

16. *The Paris Sketch Book* (London: Smith, Elder & Company, 1869), p. 14.

17. Address before the International Management Congress, New York City, September 18, 1963.

18. Thomas Moranian, Donald Grunewald and Richard C. Reindenbach, *Business Policy and Its Environment* (New York: Holt, Rinehart, and Winston, Inc., 1965), p. 4.

19. 45th national conference of the American Marketing Association, as quoted in *Advertising Age*, June 25, 1962.

20. "How Litton Keeps It Up – The View From Inside," *Fortune*, September, 1966, pp. 152-153.

21. Seymour Tilles, "How To Evaluate Corporate Strategy," *Harvard Business Review*, July-August, 1963, p. 112.

22. Charles West Churchman, Russell L. Ackoff, and E. Leonard Arnoff, *Introduction to Operations Research* (New York: John Wiley & Sons, Inc., 1957), p. 5.

23. Philip Kotler, *Marketing Management Analysis, Planning and Control* (Englewood Cliffs, N.J.: Prentice-Hall, 1967), pp. 138-139.

24. R. M. Fulmer, "Product Manager: Panacea or Pandora's Box?" *California Management Review*, Spring, 1965.

25. Author's insertion.

26. H. J. Morgens, "The Proctor & Gamble Company," Speech before the New York Society of Security Analysts, November 2, 1966.

27. J. A. Stratton, "Science and the Process of Management," International Management Congress, New York City, September 18, 1963.

28. As reported in *The Wall Street Journal*, November 8, 1966, p. 8.

29. Interviewed by the author on December 30, 1966.

30. "Famous Firsts: Bringing Brainwork to the Fore," *Business Week*, February 15, 1964, p. 54.

31. Author interview with Carl E. Treiber, Senior Vice President, and R. W. Bechtel, Vice President Market Services, Dun & Bradstreet, Inc., January 12, 1967.

32. Douglas McGregor, *The Human Side of Enterprise* (New York: McGraw-Hill, 1960).

*. . . increased insight and expanded under-
standing of management processes, rather than
the analytic techniques themselves, constitute
the really important contribution of the quantitative approach to management science.*

19

qualitative insights
from quantitative
methods

robert h. hayes

FOREWORD

To an ever-increasing extent, modern management is adopting and applying
quantitative techniques originally developed in fields such as science,
engineering, and economics. These techniques are certainly proving their
usefulness; but in addition to that, the clear, analytic thinking that underlies
them is beginning to leaven administrative attitudes at large and to cast new light
on the general processes and problems of management itself, as a kind of
"intangible" bonus value. In this overview of the uses that management is
making of quantitative methods, the author stresses the point that this increased
insight and expanded understanding of management processes, rather than the
analytic techniques themselves, constitute the really important contribution of
the quantitative approach to management science.

Reprinted from the *Harvard Business Review*, Volume 47, (July-August 1969) pp.
108-117, © 1969 by the President and Fellows of Harvard College; all rights reserved.

Mr. Hayes is Associate Professor of Management at the Harvard Business School. Formerly, he served as Acting Assistant Professor at Stanford University and as consultant in management to McKinsey & Company, Inc. His fields of interest are managerial economics and operations management, and he is conducting research on acquisitions and divestitures and on procedures for reviewing control policies.

What does top management need to know about quantitative methods? The traditional response to this question is not particularly encouraging. At best, one gathers that quantitative analysis (under the name of *operations research, management science,* or whatever) has been able to develop a handful of tools that are sometimes useful in attacking certain types of management problems. This traditional view fails to see that there is a special *qualitative* difference between these methods and the other kinds of tools that managers use in problem solving. Because it fails to see this difference, the traditional view seriously understates the ultimate impact these methods are going to have.

I believe that the greatest impact of the quantitative approach will not be in the area of problem solving, although it will have growing usefulness there. Its greatest impact will be on problem formulation: *the way managers think about their problems* – how they size them up, bring new insights to bear on them, relate them to other problems, communicate with other people about them, and gather information for analyzing them. In this sense, the results that "quantitative people" have produced are beginning to contribute in a really significant way to the *art* of management.

Consider what the real impact of the computer has been. A few years ago, the computer was thought of as just a "very fast bookkeeper," really not much different from any other piece of expensive equipment. But management is beginning to recognize that the computer has the potential to exert a fundamental influence on business organization, communications, and control, and that its original view of these machines was almost painfully naive. It is unwise to underestimate the final, total effect that computerization or any other analytical, quantitative technology will have.

I want to examine in some detail three areas of vital interest to top managers in which quantitative techniques are contributing dramatic new insights – namely, management control, information evaluation, and executive motivation. Before doing so, however, I want to spell out by examples what I mean by the "transfer of insight" from one discipline to another via quantitative analysis – because this, in my opinion, is the key to understanding the broad significance, for the business world, of what the quantitative people are doing today.

TRANSFER OF INSIGHT

Many people are aware that quantitative methods can be immediately useful in improving our communication, even about traditional problems. For example, one executive has described a meeting of his company's planning board as follows:

"We argued for 45 minutes about what we should do right now and what it would cost to postpone a decision, but it wasn't until we put a decision tree on the board that people began to realize that we had all been talking about different problems!"

It is also well known that quantitative methods are useful in dealing with problems of unusual scale. To help management come to grips with problems that are so large and complicated that many people must work on them simultaneously, quantitative people have developed entirely new structures for describing and talking about them. PERT networks[1] and decision trees,[2] for example, are two ingenious frameworks for thinking and talking about certain types of large, complex problems and for gathering information needed to resolve them. Such structures represent valuable progress, but they are by no means the end of the story.

On a higher and more conceptual level, quantitative analysis is facilitating communication where it never existed before. When a problem has been stated quantitatively, one can often see that it is structurally similar to other problems (perhaps problems in completely different areas) which on the surface appear to be quite different. And once a common structure has been identified, insights and predictions can be transferred from one situation to another, and the quantitative approach can actually increase communication. Let us look at a couple of examples.

Inventory and Electrical Circuits

Suppose a company produces an item for which the demand is constant over time. It costs money to set up a production run, and it also costs money to carry items in inventory. Relatively, long production runs (large "lot sizes") decrease the first cost but increase the second. Now what is the appropriate compromise between the two types of expenses? In other words, what is the most economical lot size?

It has been found, analytically, that minimizing total costs leads to a square-root formula,

$$Q = \sqrt{CD},$$

where Q is the optimal lot size, C is a cost ratio that describes the internal system, and D is the demand rate. One insight this formula gives us is that a change in the demand rate for a given item does not ordinarily have a *proportionate* impact on either the lot size or the company's inventory of the item. For example, if the demand rate doubles, then the average inventory should increase by only about 40%.

What is more interesting for my purposes, however, is the fact that variants of this same formula crop up in a variety of seemingly unrelated contexts. The names of the variables are different, but the structure of the problem is similar. For example, the formula for finding the optimal time *between* production runs (that is, between economic lot sizes) is given by

$$T = Q/D = \sqrt{C/D},$$

which is similar to the formula for finding the time between swings of a pendulum:

$$T = 2\pi \sqrt{C/D},$$

where C represents the length of the pendulum (a *system parameter*, so-called), and D the acceleration due to gravity. Electrical engineers have arrived at the same basic formula in analyzing certain simple types of electrical networks, using C to represent an appropriate system parameter and D to represent the force of an external voltage.

After quantitative formulation revealed the basic similarity between the lot-size problems and those associated with certain types of electrical networks, new lines of communication opened up. People began to ask if they could apply engineering knowledge about the behavior of electrical networks in which, say, the *voltage* is changing, to the problem of maintaining stability in an inventory control system in which the *demand level* is changing. They have found that to some extent this is possible. I shall discuss this particular transfer of information more thoroughly later.

Allocation and Distribution

A production manager who is trying to allocate scarce resources (for example, manpower and machine capacity to product lines, or products to various markets) in an efficient fashion faces much the same problem as the advertising executive who must allocate limited funds to presentations in different media. The investor who must allocate limited funds to different capital projects faces this same problem in a different guise. Although this similarity tends to be concealed by different jargons, different units of measure, and so on, it shows up clearly when the problems are formulated quantitatively. Moreover, quantitative analysis has provided radically new and powerful solution techniques for this basic, common problem, under the imposing name "mathematical programming."[3]

As an added bonus, an analysis of the logic behind these solution techniques shows that the problem of establishing appropriate prices for intracompany transfers is also similar in structure to the problem of efficiently allocating scarce resources — really just another way of looking at this same basic problem. Economists since Adam Smith, of course, have been claiming that a price system established by the supply-demand interaction in a free market provides the most efficient way for allocating goods to consumers. Hence this analytical thinking has established a common interest — and a *line* of communication — between the economists, on the one hand, and the production manager, the advertising executive, the investor, and the interdivisional manager of a corporation on the other. Any of these men can now begin to weigh the usefulness that the others' insights may have for him.

Insight is Contagious

Once such techniques as mathematical programming have taken hold in one area, the useful effects and results in other areas can outrun all original expectations — even within a single company. Consider the following case:

■ Five years ago a large wood-products company faced a logistics problem which its personnel couldn't seem to handle adequately by traditional methods. The problem was this: given the locations and volumes of its logging operations, the locations and capacities of its lumber processing plants, and the costs of transporting logs between different locations, how could its plants be supplied most efficiently? The problem was complicated by the fact that each type of log had a different degree of suitability for each of the company's final products. Moreover, each of its mills produced more than one of these products.

The company decided to innovate, and began using a mathematical programming model to guide its log-allocation decisions.

Once the model had proved its effectiveness, the next step was to hook it into the demand side of the company's business. Given the current demands for its various final products, their prices, and the supply (and mix) of logs currently being provided by the logging operations, which products should each mill produce? The mathematical programming model was therefore extended to provide guidance in this more comprehensive type of allocation decision. As a by-product, it began providing information which improved the scheduling of the processing plants' day-to-day operations. Again, the model "proved out."

As executives gained a clearer view of the interrelationships between the processing and demand sides of their business, it occurred to them that perhaps more care should be taken in the supply side — that is, in deciding what kinds of trees at which locations should be harvested. They found that the kind of analytical thinking that linear programming had fostered in other areas was helpful here as well, and the model was accordingly expanded to integrate logging practices with the new downstream requirements. The company's whole activity, from forest to finished product, was improved as a result.

The model is now having its effects throughout the company. For example, it provides inputs into the company's cost accounting system, and hence is having an impact not only on product pricing and marketing decisions, but on internal-transfer pricing as well. It is also beginning to affect longer-term decisions about such things as land purchase, leasing, and plant construction.

In addition to increased efficiency, the use of mathematical programming in all these different areas meant that the personnel working in these areas had a new means of communication – almost a new language for communication. This communication was the key to the expansion of the original model; and this, in my opinion, is the vital point in the long run.

THREE AREAS

This transferability of insight between scientists, engineers, and managers is a very important phenomenon — not because these groups necessarily have a *lot* of problems in common, but because they now have a way of recognizing the ones that *are* common and they now share a language for talking and thinking about them. Furthermore, transfer of information between these groups has been accompanied by a slowly dawning recognition that the same transferability of insight is possible between different functional areas of management.

Why is it that this recognition is coming so slowly? Well, many in management feel that quantitative people are themselves poor communicators, and that they tend to get bogged down in their own techniques – they can't see the managerial forest because of all the decision trees. Quantitative people are likely to reply to such criticism by accusing nonquantitative people of carelessness and imprecision. This mutual hostility is just a fragment of the age-old antagonism between artists and engineers.

I must acknowledge that quantitative people have been partly responsible for this limited view of their contribution. Even though they have at times concerned themselves with major issues, by and large they have contented themselves with making small improvements in efficiency rather than investigating the larger conceptual issues that influence the way a top manager looks at his job.

For example, in "Practical Slants on Operations Research,"[4] Harvey M. Wagner suggests that 3%-10% is a typical range for the cost savings to be expected from a successful operations research study. Often the savings that quantitative people produce are of this nickel-and-dime kind, and such savings contrast strongly with the economic consequences of a merger or an acquisition, or a new-product decision. This state of affairs tends to diminish the real significance and validity of the quantitative approach in management's eyes.

Whatever the "rights" of this controversy are, it is time to drop these childish hostilities and look ahead to future developments.

Organization Structure and Control

The area of management control is one of the best examples of a managerial preserve that is beginning to feel the impact of new insights from a seemingly unrelated discipline. Until fairly recently, much of the attention focused on the problems of management control was directed at its purely mechanical aspects — that is, at constructing information-flow systems and report systems that would provide the right man at the right level with the right information. As these problems were brought under some control, highly significant *second-level* problems began to emerge:

- Organizational and motivational problems associated with using these systems.
- Disruptive effects caused by the time lag between the moment that an event occurs and the time that it is sensed, transmitted, and finally acted on.
- Difficulties in predicting and protecting against a whole gallery of "unforeseen repercussions" — combinations of circumstances, in other words, which would cause the control system to malfunction.

Electrical engineering analogies: For over 30 years, however, electrical engineers have been working on the problem of accurately predicting and directing the responses of complicated operating and communications systems in uncertain environments. (In fact, the term "control system" is derived from engineering terminology.) A number of management theorists noted the similarity between this problem and some of their own. Following this clue, they have explored the possibility of transferring insights and solutions from the engineering context to the managerial context. The man most closely associated with this investigation is Jay W. Forrester of the Massachusetts Institute of Technology, an electrical engineer who assimilated the administrative point of view during his experience as head of the Whirlwind Computer development at M.I.T., just after World War II, and of the SAGE Air Defense Computer System a decade later.

Forrester used the fundamental concept of "feedback" to link the fields of electronics and management. The concept of feedback is, of course, fundamental to the analysis and design of electrical networks, where it denotes that a portion of the output of the network returns to the network as one of its inputs. In management, a decision made at one point in time affects the environment in which later decisions will be made, and in this sense feedback is a natural management concept.

In terms of an organizational network, feedback occurs in two readily definable ways: (a) formally, through the preparation of reports and projections based on past experience, and (b) informally, through the human tendency to remember past successes and mistakes and to adjust present behavior accordingly.

Expanding the analogy, one can see that industrial systems — organizational, operational, and logistic — have counterparts of many of the other ingredients of electrical networks:

- Flows of raw materials, finished goods, and information correspond to the flow of electricity.
- Both types of systems have delay components. I have already mentioned the obvious production, transportation, data processing, and transmission delays that exist in an industrial system. The use of economical order quantities introduces another kind of delay, by introducing a time lag between the occurrence of a demand at one level of an organization and the recognition of that demand, through a replenishment order, at a higher level.
- Both systems have elements that act to amplify or dampen the flows through them. In a management system this effect might be as informal as the human tendencies to "play it down" and "blow it all out of proportion," or as formal (and measurable) as scrap losses and inventory deteriorations. Like many convenient analogies, this one can be pushed too far. Forrester and his disciples tend to accept it literally, and over the past decade they have reported a number of attempts to construct models of actual organizations from this point of view — apparently with mixed success. Here, however, I shall discuss it simply as a valuable source of insight into the often puzzling behavior of of complex industrial-economic systems.

The electrical engineering analogy, first of all is helpful in distinguishing between the total system and its parts. Engineers have long been aware that an electrical network formed by connecting several subnetworks is likely to have entirely different characteristics from any of its parts. To understand the entire network's performance and alter it in a desired direction, the engineer must look at it in *toto* — this, in fact, is the basic rationale of all systems analysis. The same is ordinarily true of industrial systems, even those that seem relatively uncomplicated. For example:

- A three-part system that is composed of (a) a simple demand-forecasting procedure, combined with (b) a simple inventory-production scheduling rule that responds to demand orders filtering up through several levels of a distribution hierarchy, and (c) a simple cost-control system that governs and supervises the other two subsystems — even this relatively simple system may have highly unstable properties.

Quantitative formulation and analysis of such systems can often help to identify the sources of instability and offer clues for correcting it. In the absence of such an analytical framework "tampering with the system" on a piecemeal basis can be disastrous.

This type of systems analysis can also assist control by showing where a company is working at cross-purposes with itself. The familiar economic lot size, despite its mathematical virtues and its history of successful uses, is a frequent villain here. Although using such lot sizes may smooth the operation within one department, it may cause disproportionate and undesirable fluctuations and inefficiencies in other departments. In fact, in the parlance of electrical engineers, economic lot sizes can act as amplifiers, and thus substitute an erratic series of large shocks for a smooth series of small ones. In many cases this is an effect that is compounded with each additional level of a company's distribution system.

General systems analogies: Systems analysis can contribute a good deal to control by dispelling misleading illusion. For example, in his article, "Industrial Dynamics: A Major Breakthrough for Decision Makers,"[5] Forrester described a very reasonable-looking production-distribution complex in which a level demand pattern (with small random fluctuations about the average) resulted in a *highly cyclical* production pattern! The illusion of such a "seasonal" production cycle might very well affect every level of the organization, including the highest policy levels. A merger or acquisition might be consummated, for example, that is unjustifiable on economic grounds but seems necessary as a "counter-cyclical measure."

The behavior of the national economy provides examples of similar phenomena. Of necessity, economists have been forced to adopt the systems approach. Some of their experiments show that if a simple, realistic model of the economy is subjected to random shocks (a strike here, a drought there, a police action over there), then the model responds by simulating a "business cycle." *Fortune's* description of the recent "profit squeeze," for example, has a familiar ring to control engineers:

"In 1967 economic analysts stopped hailing the demise of the business cycle . . . After five year-to-year increases in a row, the earnings of the 500 largest industrial corporations dipped 2.6 percent. What happened was that the year's moderate increase in sales — total revenues of the 500 advanced 8.9 percent — fell short of manufacturers' great expectations. In 1966, looking forward to boomy demand in 1967, manufacturers invested heavily in new capacity and in inventory accumulation. But a slowdown in sales began in the last quarter of 1966 and lasted through the third quarter of 1967. Burdened with excess inventories, manufacturers cut back on orders to their suppliers. . . .

"Unit labor costs went up too. So did interest costs, largely because companies had borrowed heavily at high rates to finance investment in plant and equipment. With these three kinds of costs going up, the total costs for the 500 rose by 9.7 percent. . . . A 9.7 percent rise in costs combined with an 8.9 percent rise in revenues led, by inescapable arithmetic, to a decline in profits."[6]

Good businessmen, of course, are not unaware of the conflicting currents at work in their businesses and the economy. They often use words such as "momentum," "overshoot," and "countervailing forces" to convey their qualitative awareness of the dynamic interplay of action and reaction. But a deeper understanding of this interplay, and possible means for controlling it, requires a more organized, quantitative approach.

Analysis can also be immediately helpful to companies that want to direct their progress and growth. Some corporations, for example, appear to thwart the best efforts of management to change their direction. A company may introduce new information and control systems, develop new sales procedures, define and implement new corporate policies, and so forth, but the same old problems may continue to plague it. A company of this kind resembles a bell, which will ring at the same frequency no matter how hard or how often it is struck. What is required here is a *systematic analysis and revision of the basic internal structure of the organization itself.* To get the frequency it wants, management may have to change the structure of the bell.

New Insights into Information

Everybody talks about information these days. Since the dawn of commerce, in fact, managers have been asking for more accurate, up-to-date, and relevant information. Today, however, the requests are somewhat more sophisticated. The need now is for "better information *systems*" or "better information *processors*" (usually some form of computer). This attitude is certainly understandable; information is the glue that holds organizations together. Moreover, since the quality of communication in the modern corporation depends on the quality of information, to a very large degree this demand for better information is really a demand for a more accurate basis for communication.

As technology has responded to these needs, some thoughtful managers have realized that there is just as much danger in too much information as there is in too little. The real need is not just for information but for the *right type* of information. Since different types of information cost different amounts of money, the main problem is to balance the value of potential information against its cost. Otherwise, the natural tendency is to seek as much information as one can get for a given cost — a sure prescription for generating mountains of information of the cheapest and least useful kind.

But while businessmen have their own unique informational requirements, the need for pertinent information is common to all types of decision making, and other disciplines have long been grappling with such basic questions as: "What is information?" "How does one go about measuring and evaluating it?" "How can one predict the value of a system set up to provide information?" Within electrical engineering, in fact, a whole new area called information theory has grown up in the past 20 years. What is taught at many graduate business schools as "statistical decision theory" could perhaps more properly be called "evaluation of information for management decision making." A consensus is now emerging from the various studies on information being carried on in engineering, statistics, and economics — a consensus that has surprising relevance to management thinking.

What is information? Information is now defined as anything that serves to affect the uncertainty associated with some quantity. This is not an operational definition, of course, until we define "uncertainty," but note the generality of this statement. Information, under this definition, could be obtained in a business context through preparing financial reports, sampling, doing research, seeking the advice of a consultant, or simply delaying a decision "until the situation clears a little." Note also that the definition says "affect," and not "reduce," uncertainty. Information can confuse as well as enlighten.

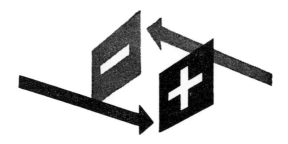

A precise and often convenient way to describe uncertainty is in terms of probabilities — that is, by assigning a weight to each possible value of a quantity to reflect its relative likelihood of occurring. Let us consider a simplified example:

■ A potential buyer of a certain company's common stock is interested in its earnings per share during the current year. In light of his present information, he feels that only three possible values are worth considering: $2.00 per share, $2.50 per share, and $3.00 per share. He also feels that the third value is twice as likely to occur as the first, and just as likely as the second. "Normalizing" these relative assessments so that the total of the probabilities is 1.0, he obtains this result:

Value	Probability
$2.00	.2
$2.50	.4
$3.00	.4
	1.0

Increasing the number of possible outcomes would complicate the assessment problem a little, but the basic idea remains the same.

Tomorrow he may read that his company has just landed a government subcontract and revise his probabilities as follows:

Value	Probability
$2.00	.1
$2.50	.5
$3.00	.4
	1.0

The next day a labor spokesman voices a strike threat, and the probabilities change again:

Value	Probability
$2.00	.3
$2.50	.4
$3.00	.3
	1.0

The first peice of news made this potential buyer both more optimistic and more certain, and the second made him less certain and a trifle more pessimistic. Both pieces of news represent information in that they effect the set of probabilities he assigns to the various outcomes.

Conversely, if neither bit of news affects the probabilities (possibly because he knows someone in the company who has informed him about both events *before* he assesses our original set of probabilities), neither is "information" under the present definition. Like many other reports, they are merely words and numbers or, to use a particularly descriptive term coined by electrical engineers, "noise."

What is its value? Theorists use a lot of formulas in measuring the economic value of information, but the basic idea is still straightforward. By changing the probabilities associated with a certain event, new information causes decisions to change. Hopefully these decisions will be better — that is, more profitable. And it is the increased profitability of the decision made on the basis of the new information, as distinguished from the decision that would have been made without it, that gives the information its value.

For example, suppose a company is thinking of bringing out a new product. The initial investment required is $1,000,000. For simplicity, assume that there are only two possible outcomes:

1. If the product is "successful," then the discounted present value of the cash flows resulting from the new product will be $1,200,000.
2. If it is not "successful," then this value will be only $800,000.

Assume that the probability of the favorable outcome is .7 (in other words, 70%). Then the probability of an unfavorable outcome is .3. Thus the company has a .7 chance of making $1,200,000 and a .3 chance of making $800,000 on its $1,000,000 investment. It therefore can *expect* to make, as a *weighted average*,

$$.7(\$1,200,000) + .3(\$800,000) - \$1,000,000 = \$80,000.$$

On the other hand, if it does not introduce the new product, it can expect to make nothing.

Now suppose a new market survey (call it Study I) indicates that the probability of the new product being successful is only .4 (or 40%). The chance of its being unsuccessful would therefore be .6, and the company could expect to *lose money* since.

$$.4(\$1,200,000) + .6(\$800,000) - \$1,000,000 = -\$40,000.$$

The company would probably reverse its decision to introduce the product, on the basis of the new information. Hence the value of this new market study is the expected "saving" to the company of $40,000.

This approach may sound simplistic, until one understands its corollary: *information that doesn't affect a decision is valueless.* To illustrate:

■ Several years ago I developed a new salesforecasting procedure for a manufacturer of women's sportswear. I did a rather good job, I thought. The average error in my estimate of total season sales only three months into the season was about half that of the old forecasting procedure. I was certainly providing information, in the sense that I could guarantee considerably more certainty than the old procedure could; yet the information I was providing turned out to be almost valueless. It was having virtually no impact on the *really important* decisions — fabric commitments, marketing decisions, and initial production decisions that had actually been made much earlier in the season. My new information was all after the fact.

■ Another good illustration of this approach involves one of the most "valuable" pieces of information of all time. This information was received by Nathan Rothschild in England via special family courier (some say by messenger pigeon) from the Continent on the morning of June 20, 1815. Realizing that it would be several hours before the same news would reach his countrymen, Rothschild hurried to the London stock exchange and proceeded to sell consols (British State Bonds). He was only 38 years old, but already the prosessor of an awesome reputation for financial wizardry, and his action therefore attracted immediate suspicion. The rumor began to spread: "Napoleon has beaten Wellington. Rothschild has learned of it." A selling panic commenced and soon reached epic proportions. Then, just before the official news from Waterloo arrived, Rothschild's agents began buying back enormous quantities of consols at bargain prices.

Some say that Rothschild doubled his fortune on that day. The point is that only somebody in his position would have been able to capitalize on it. To a poor man, the same information would have been valueless.

How can one predict its value? So far, I have shown how one can establish the value of a given piece of information, such as that provided by market research or a consultant's report. The next problem is to predict the value of information *before* it is received. This, of course, generalizes to the problem of trying to determine the value of an *information system*. The logic loses a bit of its directness here, but in rough terms it simply says that the decision maker should take into account, in advance, the likelihood that the information to be obtained *will change* a proposed decision by its impact on the probabilities involved, and that he should calculate its value if it does change the decision. This often represents an enormous computational task, but one entirely within the capabilities of a computer.

Let's return to an earlier example. Suppose the company, after obtaining the result of Study I, is debating whether or not the expenditure of an additional $15,000 for further market research (call it Study II) is warranted. Also, suppose this new study will:

▼ Either confirm that the previous study was correct, and that the new product has only a .4 chance of success.

▲ Or reject the results of the previous study and affirm the accuracy of the original assessment that the product has a .7 chance of success.

Finally, suppose the company management now feels that the first outcome is twice as likely to be obtained as the second.

From the previous discussion it should be clear that if Study II indicates that the previous decision (*not* to introduce the new product) is still the correct one, the new information will have been valueless (i.e., worth $0.00) to the company. On the other hand, if Study II refutes Study I (that is, if it indicates that the product's chance of success *is* .7, after all), the company should once again decide to introduce the product. If the company *does* introduce the product, then, as we have seen, it can expect to make $80,000 on it. This figure therefore represents the expected discounted value that this outcome of Study II would have. Now the question is: Should the company put up the additional $15,000 for Study II?

Since the respective probabilities of the two alternative outcomes are .333 and .667, the expected value that Study II has *before* it is undertaken is

$$.667(\$0.00 + .333(\$80,000) = \$26,667.$$

Study II is therefore worth more to the company than it would cost (only

$15,000). Hence $15,000 would appear to be a reasonable amount to pay for the additional information it would provide.

I could have made this example more realistic by including a variety of other possible outcomes from Study II, but the basic procedure would stay the same. That is, for each possible outcome, determine:

- What the decision should be if that outcome were to occur.
- The expected value of the new information under that new decision.
- The expected value of the new information under the previous decision.

Multiplying each of these values by the probabilities we originally assigned to the various outcomes and summing provides a measure of the potential value of the new information.

Summarizing, then, from this qualitative framework:

1. Information is something that reduces uncertainty, usually at a cost.

2. Information only has value in the context of a specific situation.

3. The amount a decision maker should be willing to pay for information depends on the likelihood that it will change his decision.

These insights are perhaps little different from those that good, hardheaded "common sense" might have dictated. Yet, in the absence of this quantitative framework for evaluating the potential of new information, the decision whether to buy it is often governed more by fear of the unknown than by a rational assessment of the costs and benefits.

Management has much to gain from this area of quantitative analysis, especially in clearer thinking and more accurate communication about *risk,* for this is what is ultimately in question here. Broadly speaking, it is safer and wiser to weigh risk in the scales of probability than in the scales of personal intuition.

Risk and Motive

Many management theorists believe that if a group of rational people are each given the same information about a decision problem, they will arrive independently at about the same decision. Anybody who has sat on a committee knows that this is not necessarily so.

A variety of reasons are usually advanced to explain divergence of opinion, and these generally fall into either of two categories:

1. Different people usually have different amounts of information about, or experience with, any given situation.

2. Different people have different, and often directly conflicting, goals.

The first reason is both acceptable and correctable. If two people have basically different levels of understanding about a problem, they can generally discuss away their differences. A subtler aspect is that sometimes they have different perceptions of the *uncertainty* in a problem — a circumstance which is often fostered by reporting schemes which, in an effort to be concise, rely on single point estimates or predictions of uncertain quantities. This often lulls managers into a false sense of precision — particularly those high up the communication ladder.[7]

The second reason, on the other hand, has a faintly sinister ring, carrying as it does dark hints of power struggles. Decision theorists suggest, however, that it may just as likely be due to the fact that different people have different psychological attitudes toward risk taking. Most of us know people who are highly conservative in the face of a risky decision; bankers and accountants are familiar stereotypes for this type of attitude. At the opposite end of the scale are the "plungers"; marketing people tend to fit this stereotype.

Corporate decisions are frequently made by a group of individuals whose risk attitudes fall everywhere in the spectrum between these two extremes, and it should not be surprising that they disagree. I have recently been doing some research on decision processes associated with acquisitions and divestitures, where this phenomenon shows up quite clearly. This phenomenon also frequently lies at the root of friction between the headquarters of a diversified corporation and a recently acquired subsidiary. For example, one often hears such comments as these: "He doesn't understand. He's not a little company any more; he's a little part of a big company!"

Ralph O. Swalm has described actual situations where not only do different individuals within a company have different risk attitudes, but also each one tends to use the same risk attitude in making corporate decisions as in making personal decisions — and this virtually guarantees a variety of opinions.[8]

Pinpointing the *source* of disagreement sometimes helps resolve it, but not always. What should be done if it doesn't? How should one go about reconciling disagreement? One way, of course, is to centralize all decision making in one person. But then, which person? Rather than choose one individual to reflect the "corporate" attitude toward risk, shouldn't a company's top management attempt instead to *define* in advance what that attitude will be? There is some evidence that this is already being done informally — for example, in such statements of corporate goals as "maximum growth consistent with prudent risk."

Finally, how does one go about evaluating individual decision-making capabilities? And how do we motivate individuals to have risk attitudes that are more consistent with the corporate one? Empirical evidence indicates that most individuals are more risk-averse than the companies they work for. Although stock options are one common device for encouraging individuals to accept more risky projects, most other reward structures within a corporation — primarily the promotion system — tend to do just the opposite.

Here management seems to have blundered its way into a conceptual framework that asks more questions than it answers. I don't think this is really true, of course; what the concept of risk aversion has accomplished really, is to bring into sharper focus a number of fundamental issues that already existed, to facilitate communication about them, and possibly to suggest avenues for further research by more traditional management theorists.

FINAL WORD

The crucial point is that these questions have been raised, and their answers are currently being pursued, by *quantitative* people. The focus of these questions is communication, taken in its broadest sense: between different parts of an organization (the "systems approach" to organizational design), between an organization and its environment (the valuation of information) and between individuals participating in a decision process (the analysis of risk aversion). Because of their backgrounds in exact disciplines, and because the quantitative approach tends to focus on the basic *structure* of a problem rather than its situational uniqueness, they tend to think about these problems in precise terms and use precise techniques in analyzing them. The result, in many cases, is not just a new management tool but a new conceptual framework for management, a new way of thinking.

NOTES

1. Arch R. Dooley, "Interpretations of PERT," HBR March-April 1964, p. 160.
2. John F. Magee, "Decision Trees for Decision Making," HBR July-August 1964, p. 126.
3. Alexander Henderson and Robert Schlaifer, "Mathematical Programming: Better Information for Decision Making," HBR May-June 1954, p. 73.
4. HBR May-June 1963, p. 61.
5. HBR July-August 1958, p. 37.
6. June 15, 1968, p. 2.
7. See Pearson Hunt, "Fallacy of the One Big Brain," HBR July-August 1966, p. 84.
8. "Utility Theory – Insights Into Risk Taking," HBR November-December 1966, p. 123. (For a detailed discussion of the impact of risk attitudes on decisions and of methods for measuring an individual's risk aversion, see John S. Hammond, III, "Better Decisions With Preference Theory," HBR November-December 1967, p.123.)

The authors emphasize that model builders must overcome prejudice against the use of models in the marketing organization. This can be done by proper communication and by providing models that make marketing sense.

20

practical applications of marketing models

emanuel demby and louis cohen

One of our clients, a prominent maker of packaged goods, informed us, "I know you're going to build a model to solve this next problem. But don't tell us about it. There is a fair amount of prejudice against models in this organization."

Another of our clients, a well known marketing consultant, invariably goes in the other direction. No matter how we might approach the solution of the problem, he invariably asks that we build a model — and no amount of persuasion will convince him that anything less than a model can solve his problem.

I think, as we approach the practical application of marketing models, we ought to start, first, with the practical problem of semantics and people.

The term, model, can be glamorous or deadly depending upon the biases and backgrounds of the people with whom you are talking. And when you try to define the term — as a mathematical representation of a real-life situation — you only reinforce either the receptivity or the negative feelings about the model.

From our experience, I would say the problem is that the model presents a

Reprinted from Bernard A. Morin (ed.), *Marketing in a Changing World*, Proceedings of the National Conference of the American Marketing Association, published by the American Marketing Association, June 1969, pp. 118-120.

challenge in conceptualization that is difficult to get not only for marketing men, but for researchers as well.

Really, everything we do in marketing research is a model – even the cross-tab to some extent, if we care to work out the mathematics of relationships between the variables we are studying or if we do a double cross tab. Or, in doing a discriminant function analysis, a Q-Analysis, or a cluster analysis, we are model building. The model is a re-ordering of data so that we can visualize the dynamics in a given situation; we can see the impact of A upon B and B upon C and so on. Or, the model is a constant re-ordering of data so that we can play what-if games, simulate, and begin to understand better the potentials of cause and effect – not that we ever really say that we have found the cause, but that we have used a causal combination of data and theoretically produced an effect.

The problem is in the word "Model". It attracts and detracts depending on the listener's orientation.

Recently, we pioneered in the development of psychographics. Some have said that our national probability sample of the U.S., in which the marketplace for the spending of discretionary income was segmented into Creative and Passive Consumers, was really the first large-scale psychographic study ever conducted. Now we could have said that we built a model, a model of discretionary income use in the U.S. But we did not; the trend (the fad if you will) in marketing and marketing research has been towards segmentation studies. And so, we said what we had accomplished was the psychological segmentation of the U.S. consumer. Indeed, that is what it was. If we had called our work a model, there would have been very sharp segmentation among those who responded favorably and those who responded unfavorably. Fortunately, aware of the temper of the times, we said we had done segmentation research, and the acceptance of the psychographic approach is growing.

What I am getting at is that the model builders (ourselves included) have been the beneficiaries and victims of semantics, depending upon who was the communications target.

What I should like to do, then, in this paper is two things:

1. Discuss practical applications of models to marketing;
2. Discuss a practical way of getting marketing management to work with models.

There are a number of complaints about the model:

"The findings are unrealistic."
"How do you know this is so?"
"Models have formulas all right, but just try to apply them in real life."
"The Model builders," runs another form of complaint, "are not practical people."

Well, lets admit it, a lot of complaints are true.

When the model is in the hands of a mathematician who is not marketing oriented (by our standards, not his), you are liable to get some unusual output.

For example, consider the mathematician who recommended that a cosmetics manufacturer optimize his advertising by concentrating on 28 year old women. (We patiently explained to him that while 28 year old women might, indeed, represent the optimal age group in the marketplace, there were not enough 28 year olds to support a national advertiser.)

Another problem of the mathematician in Operations Research for marketing is that he speaks a language of his own, making it difficult for the plain-talking marketing executive to learn whether the model-makers are for real or whether they engage in complex computer exercises.

Finally, we have the pure-research model problem experienced by a major record company. Their mathematician built a model which found that the name of the artist on the label had nothing to do with how well the record sold. The computations may have been technically correct, but as any marketing man or researcher who knows his salt will tell you most records depend on the glamour and name of the star on the label.

So much for the flip side.

Building a model is not, of course, an automatic process. It is not, really, very much different from doing good research, except that your tools are so powerful you need to know what you are doing before you do it.

Some of our most successful marketing models do not come up with revolutionary findings, but I hope all make marketing and common sense. If the findings do not make marketing sense, we go back to the drawing board to find out why they do not. A recent project will show what I mean.

We built a model of usage of a particular toiletries product not long ago. Several mathematicians wise in the ways of operations research theory worked on it, and the construction was sound. When we looked at the printout, however, we saw at once that something was likely wrong.

Early in our work on the product, we had carried out classic motivation and marketing research, and we already knew quite a bit about the product. The model findings did not coincide with what we knew.

When we went back to the early steps in the model, we realized the problem: Men and women were lumped together as a single group — and a single model was built — but in reality they are two very different markets, with different buying motivations.

Once we separated the sample into these two natural market segments — a separation apparent to a marketing man, but not so obvious to a mathematician — we were able to build a model for each. The models, with this assistance, unearthed a previously untapped market. The client is preparing a new campaign to reach this market right now.

Some of our most productive models do not produce totally new findings.

This was the case in the model we have just discussed. The project was conducted in a European country. As we were developing the recommendations based on the model output, we realized the marketing approach recommended was exactly the same as that used five years ago by a brand in the United States to move from a low-share-of-market to the number one position. Of course, the approach would be new in the country in which the study was made. The fact that our recommendation was not completely new, that there was a substantial success story in the U.S. using a similar marketing concept, was a key point in management's decision to go ahead with the new approach suggested by a marketing model.

One point we are making here is that in many cases, a single marketing model is not enough to explain all consumer behavior.

An implication of this point is that the mathematician or statistician who builds the model needs the marketing-oriented researcher as much as the researcher needs the model builder. A great deal of marketing judgment and knowledge of the marketing problem is necessary before a successful marketing model can be built. The mathematician and the researcher need each other.

Another important implication is that preliminary research is necessary — marketing and motivation research — before a successful model can be built. We have found that only through immersing ourselves in knowledge of the subject area are we likely to build a marketing model which offers practical solutions to pressing marketing problems.

Basically, the preliminary depth and marketing research is needed for the following three reasons.

The first is to determine the important marketing segments for a product about which to develop models. Earlier, we spoke about a toiletries product, for which sex was an important factor for segmentation. In one project for a mail order gift company, we found that what they thought was a single business was really two businesses, one where they sold gifts through catalogs and one where they sold gifts through advertising in publications, even though both involved mail order gifts. By combining the "catalog" business and the "publications" business in a single model we obtained results which related to neither. Only by constructing separate models for each business were we able to move toward solving the marketing problems of each.

The second reason why preliminary research is necessary is to discover *all* the factors with possible relevancy to sales, so that they are included within the model framework. In a model we built of operating room supervisors (nurses), one of the critical variables explaining sales of surgical supplies was "attractive salesmen." Without preliminary research, I have to admit we would not have included this factor in the model, and if you do not include a factor in the model, you cannot test its importance.

The third reason for preliminary research is to be sure you can understand the model output. We built a model of canned processed meat. One factor which the model showed critical to sales was that the product be seen as "not salty." If we had not done preliminary depth research, we would have taken this finding too literally. In reality, the factor explained why women used the canned product mainly for guests, despite its having a poorer image than the fresh smoked meat. Our preliminary research showed that the regular smoked meat is sometimes too salty and the result is a cooking debacle, which not even the best cook can save. To paraphrase a famous slogan, women feel they can be sure if they use the canned product. There are many marketing implications to this "not salty" factor which are not apparent unless you have researched the product area.

Another check we have developed to ensure that a marketing model project will result in practical findings is to make the project a *team* effort, with management very much on the team.

We find that making management a part of the project team has three very positive results:

First, management's expertise about their company and their product keeps us on the track.

Second, management's involvement with the project practically ensures that the results of the project will be used rather than filed.

Third, some of the most creative members of the project team are the very involved people of management. An approach we often use is to present the final report to management — *without recommendations or practical applications*, scheduling another meeting in two or three weeks. The management members of the team are given the task of developing practical applications of the findings. We at MPI do the same. In the final meeting, we thrash out a final set of practical applications.

Here is an example of how this team approach works in helping to ensure success for the model. We were conducting a study for a company selling industrial products.

Our preliminary research indicated that the company's business potential centered around six important market segments. However, the management members of the team informed us that their sales force was limited and could not be increased at the present time. Without this advice from management, our project might have produced some interesting, but perhaps not too useful, findings. The management members also developed some excellent practical applications of our findings, and the entire marketing efforts for the ensuing year are a direct offshoot of the marketing model developed for the company.

The marketing model is a powerful technique which can be used to understand some of the forces acting in the marketplace. However, it is too easy to make the mistake of viewing the model not as a technique, but as the marketplace itself. I recall the words of one model theoretician who said he saw life as a series of multiple correlations, and another who saw it as "dimensional space." It is too easy to make the mistake of moving from the simile to the metaphor.

Seeing the marketing model as being the marketplace, rather than as just a technique, leads to error, because it may place the researcher in an unquestioning or unskeptical mood.

In summary, we have discussed the fact that the mathematical model can be an extremely powerful tool whose use in the marketing department has been stalled because of *a gap in communicating our story to marketers* — we do not state our story clearly enough and we do not state it in the language of marketers; and because of *a credibility gap* — too many of the findings and recommendations which result from marketing models do not make marketing sense and some do not even make common sense.

*Currently we are witnessing the first, frequently
painful efforts to extend the application of the
management sciences to sensitive and critically
important issues of marketing strategy*

21

marketing and management science - a marriage on the rocks?

john j. cardwell

> We have a good-sized OR group, and we've been in computers ever since 1960, so
> we're certainly not fighting progress. But if you know of anybody who's solved a
> major marketing problem with operations research or computers, I'd like to hear
> about it. We never have.

This remark, made recently by the chief executive of a half-billion-dollar
packaged goods company, underlines a serious question of many senior
executives: Can management sciences be practically and profitably employed in
marketing? Many top marketing men are frankly skeptical about the possibilities. They have heard plenty of promises, but except for the area of

marketing logistics — inventory control and the like — they have yet to see much in the way of performance.

Their attitude is an understandable one, for marketing success hinges on logistics less often than on the critically important strategic decisions. And here, to date, management sciences have provided little real help.

To explore the reasons for this poor record and possibly to develop some insights of practical value to top management, McKinsey & Company recently undertook a research study into the experiences of fourteen companies, with annual sales ranging from $300 million to more than $2 billion, who were reputedly among the leaders in their efforts to apply the management sciences to marketing.

From extensive interviewing in these highly diverse companies, balanced with analysis of the existing literature, some findings have emerged that have implications for every marketing manager. Most importantly, the evidence makes it clear that no key marketing executive in any sizable company can afford to ignore or belittle the computer's potential — any more than he can afford to take the more overblown claims of management science enthusiasts without a healthy pinch of salt. Our study indicates that management sciences, **realistically applied**, can offer unique, yet economic, solutions to certain kinds of marketing strategy problems.

EVOLUTIONARY PROCESS

Marketing applications of management sciences are an evolutionary development rather than a radical new departure. For at least the past decade, the main thrust of progress in marketing management has been toward fact-founded, research-oriented decision making and the replacement of intuition or "hunch" by a serious effort to quantify marketing variables. First, marketers learned to make heavy use of consumer and market research. Next came computer applications in inventory forecasting and control and other aspects of marketing logistics. In these projects, typically, not marketers, but manufacturing engineers or other staff groups provided the leadership; nonetheless, marketers adapted to the new systems and learned to use them effectively.

Currently, we are witnessing the first, frequently painful, efforts to extend the application of the management sciences to sensitive and critically important issues of marketing strategy. These applications are really at an embryonic stage. No one can predict with assurance what will happen over the next few years. But there is already evidence to suggest that, at least under certain conditions, management sciences can play an important role in planning marketing strategy. In fact, our study shows that a few companies have already achieved substantial payoffs by applying management sciences to certain problems in these areas.

Before discussing strategic applications further, however, a brief review of some of the more commonplace computer contributions to marketing systems may be useful.

EXAMPLES OF CURRENT ROLE

Management sciences and marketing systems.

From a managerial point of view, it is useful to view marketing as comprising a spectrum of activities ranging from broad over-all strategic decision making to more or less mechanical administration. By looking at marketing in this way instead of viewing it as a collection of separate functional categories (distribution, advertising, pricing, etc.), one may see the entire function, in all its complexity, as a single orderly decision-making process. (See Fig. 1.)

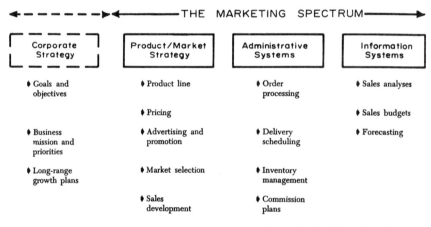

Figure 1. The Marketing Spectrum

This concept of a marketing spectrum is helpful in enabling us to position the current role of the management sciences. For it becomes immediately obvious that the principal contribution of management science to date has been made on the mechanical, systems side of marketing, that is, to the activities grouped in Figure 1 under "Administrative Systems" and "Information Systems."

Most of the large and well-regarded companies participating in our study had successfully computerized at least some of these systems (Fig. 2), in some cases with striking success. Consider these two examples:

One company with an immense product line and a total finished goods inventory of over $100 million, characterized by a complex pattern of withdrawals found

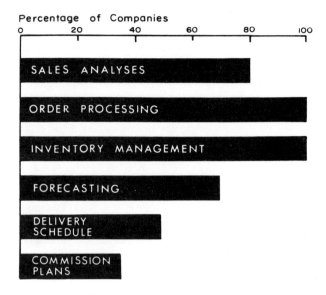

Figure 2. The Type and Extent of Applications
in Survey Companies

that by carefully analyzing fluctuations in inventory levels and reorder times with
the aid of management science techniques it could rather easily construct a set of
"decision rules" that actually decreased stockouts while significantly lowering the
safety stock requirements. It thereby achieved over-all inventory reductions of
more than 20 per cent, along with improved balance among products and sizes.
Assuming it cost only 10 cents to carry each dollar's worth of inventory –
including the cost of capital, warehouse overhead, obsolescence, and pilferage –
this meant annual savings of more than $2 million.

By improving its sales forecasting methods by the application of management
science techniques, another manufacturer sharply reduced outages and achieved
tangible improvement in customer service levels and sales effectiveness. This
company's delivery performance had deteriorated as its sales had grown – a not
uncommon problem. Reliability of delivery was far more important to its
customers, however, than elapsed time from order to receipt. By applying
relatively straightforward statistical analyses, management succeeded in sharpen-
ing the reliability of its forecasts. The results: far more accurate production and
delivery scheduling.

A CONTINUING TREND

Despite some disappointments and difficulties, therefore, it seems inevitable that
more and more companies will seek to apply management science concepts and

techniques to a growing range of problems at the systems end of the marketing spectrum. The cost-reduction potential, improved accuracy, and increased machine capabilities all argue strongly for a continuation of the trend. And the techniques, fortunately, are known and tested.

From the viewpoint of the marketing executive, then, it will become increasingly necessary to computerize systems activities in marketing. His competitors have done so or soon will, and his customers will expect it. More immediately, the opportunity to save money is too evident to be ignored.

MARKETING SUCCESS

The payoff in marketing strategy.

Despite the impressive contributions of the management sciences in marketing systems, however, success or failure in the market place is more often determined by activities at the opposite end of the marketing spectrum. Miles Laboratories, for example, reportedly gives a new advertising campaign — not superior information or administration — most of the credit for the recent increase in Alka-Seltzer's sales volume and market share. Similarly, Pet Milk management is said to believe that Sego's success stems from a strategic decision to distribute mainly through food chains rather than through the traditional drug outlets preferred by its chief competitor. In most businesses, decisions such as these are the key to marketing success and often even to survival, while the downstream systems activities merely determine how efficiently these strategy decisions are carried out.

Why have management science applications in the administrative and informational support systems been so much more successful than applications at the strategy end of the spectrum? The evidence of our study suggests that the answer lies in the nature of the applications themselves — specifically, in the contrasting nature of the inputs, the relationships, and the outputs involved. Let us consider the systems and strategy applications in turn.

SYSTEMS APPLICATIONS

Marketing systems.

Systems applications such as inventory control and scheduling of delivery fleets are a direct and logical extension of the traditional engineering-oriented systems from which the management sciences grew. A linear program developed to aid in managing a petroleum refinery, for example, is not really very different from a linear program designed to allocate a delivery truck fleet to best meet customer demands.

More generally, traditional techniques of the management sciences exhibit three key characteristics, all of which are typically present in marketing systems applications:

- **Accurate inputs.** The necessary input data — such as current inventory status, cost of storing inventory, cost of a new order, lead time, and patterns of inventory withdrawals — either are known precisely or can be estimated with a high degree of accuracy.
- **Well-defined relationships.** For example, this relationship between a beginning inventory, the rate of inventory withdrawal, and the ending inventory can be precisely stated in mathematical terms.
- **A measurable (optimum) end product.** The desired result can also be stated quite specifically. For example, the objective might be least total cost at some given level of customer service, defined in terms of the number of outages or back orders management regards as tolerable. (The higher the specified customer service level, the higher the required inventory minimum, and consequently the cost.)

THE STRATEGIC END

Strategic applications.

Problems at the strategic end of the marketing spectrum, however, rarely display these characteristics. Input data — e.g., on competitor promotional plans or consumer buying intentions — are usually imprecise, if they are not missing altogether. Relationships are too numerous or too complex for useful definition; e.g. print media and television are likely to have quite different impacts on sales results in any given market, and the difference cannot be explicitly and exhaustively defined. The end product rarely lends itself to definition in conventional management science terms; for example, how would a grocery executive go about specifying an "optimum" pricing policy? In fact, the whole concept of mathematical optimality seems dubious in the strategy area, precisely because of the nature of the data and the almost overpowering variety and complexity of relationships.

In sum, because strategic marketing problems differ fundamentally from the more traditional problems of marketing operations, management science techniques developed to deal with systems problems are largely inappropriate for marketing strategy.

NEW ORIENTATION NECESSARY

This means that a different approach is necessary. The evidence of our study suggests that the key lies in **substituting a problem orientation for the technique orientation** that has proved so successful in the systems area. Instead of seeking solutions from the application of the techniques at hand, which may not be appropriate to the problem, marketers should start from the nature of the given problem and try to shape the techniques to fit.

One company learned the hard way. Determined to capitalize on the occult computer arts, this company charged its OR staff with developing a workable system for selecting advertising media. The result was a mathematically elegant linear program which, to the best of my knowledge, has never been used. Finding too many holes in the input assumptions, the product management group refused to even try the new system. Instead of turning immediately to the computer, this company should have allowed its marketing people to analyze the problem and call in computer expertise at their discretion.

Failure to understand and practice this problem orientation largely explains marketing executives' prevailing disenchantment with the management sciences. It lies, I believe, at the root of what are frequently referred to as communications problems, fear of new technology, or the other administrative reasons cited to account for the fact that the management sciences have not yet made substantial inroads into marketing strategy. Some of these administrative problems, of course, are real and pressing. But there are many instances where the "fear of new technology," to take one frequently mentioned difficulty, ought to be interpreted not as an indictment of marketing managers but as an indication of the inadequacy of the technology.

TWO EXAMPLES

A handful of companies have already applied a problem orientation to strategic management science applications with considerable success. I cite two examples from among the fourteen companies surveyed.

> The first, a major oil company, is now making far more profitable service station location decisions as a result of a management science application.
> The second, a food retailing chain, has built a better image and improved its profits through a new approach to pricing.

Each of these applications had some limitations, but each represented a substantial success. And in each case the key point to that success was the problem orientation.

Example: expansion of retail locations. Three years ago a major petroleum refiner and marketer faced a serious problem: A $20 million expenditure on new service station locations wasn't paying off. The new stations were failing at a rate of 15 per cent a year; even in the successful units, the gallonage sold was barely at the industry average. Further analysis showed that actual gallonage in the 588 newest units that had been in operation at least a year was averaging only 70 per cent of preconstruction estimates, but the discrepancies between estimate and performance varied so widely from one station to the next that the possible causes could only be guessed at.

THE MOST CRITICAL FACTOR

As almost any gasoline marketer or other retailer will agree, the selection of new sites (i.e., locations for service stations) is the single most critical factor for success in the business. Not only do new stations account for a considerable current cash outlay, but their number and location are the principal determinants of future profits and, often, of future survival. Little wonder, then, that the management of this company was deeply concerned.

Against this background, management launched an intensive study with the single purpose of devising a feasible and practical approach to upgrading the entire expansion effort. Although this project ultimately resulted in a reasonably sophisticated computerized model, the study team's original charter did not even mention the management sciences – the sole objective was to solve a real and immediate business problem. And **the problem was solved**. Today, failures have been reduced to under 3 per cent, and the average gallonage sold has doubled.

The study team began by attempting to work out possible correlations between actual gallonage sold and any factor or combination of factors that could be ascertained before purchase of the site. If such correlations could be found, the team reasoned, then future site selection decisions could obviously be built around them.

Two hundred and thirty-nine widely dispersed service stations were used in the analysis. Traffic counts, number of nearby competitors, visibility measures, required land investment, and other conventional measures taken from the company's own "reconnaissance reports" were among the factors considered for possible correlation with gallonage sold.

Surprisingly, no significant relationships were discovered between actual gallonage and any of the factors considered. Except on interstate highways and other major thoroughfares, for example, traffic volume past a site showed little direct relation to gallonage. In fact, all the factors in combination accounted for less than half the variations in volume.

The total impact of all factors on ultimate gallonage varied widely from market to market and from area to area within markets. Moreover, the potential of a given site seemed to depend on whose gas was being sold.

INTENSIVE ANALYSIS

Accordingly, several metropolitan markets were selected for intensive analysis by marketing teams to test the impact of demographic characteristics (e.g., income level and population density) and competitive characteristics (e.g., market share and share of outlets). The most significant of the new factors uncovered by these analyses was the relationship between market share and a unit's gallonage performance.

It would normally be expected that as a company's share of outlets increased, its share of market would increase proportionately (the dotted line in Figure 3). Analysis showed, however, that below a certain share of market, incremental new outlets were substantially below average in gallonage, while above this point their performance rapidly climbed. Above the critical share of market, in effect, each new station located in an area not only added its own volume to the company's total but apparently increased the average of all units in the area as well.

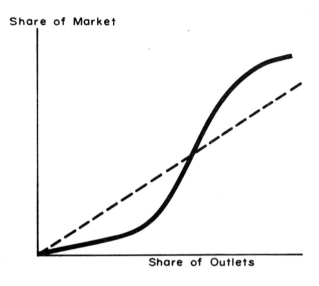

Share of Market

Share of Outlets

Figure 3.   Relationship of Outlets to Market Share

Other factors than market share, of course, must be considered in allocating market expansion money profitably. Such factors include profit contribution per gallon, average investment requirements (involving a series of management assumptions on site availability, costs, available capital, price stability, etc.), assumed growth potential, and competitors' assumed expansion intentions. These factors were first developed and tabulated in the study to serve as a basis for ranking the attractiveness of each market area. The resulting priority listing, however, failed to take into account many complex interrelationships — for example, what growth rate is adequate to offset a low netback (gross margin for the product, area by area) in a market where the company controls only an 8 per cent share? Nor did it suggest the level of investment likely to yield the optimum over-all return on investment in each of the selected expansion areas.

EXPANSION MODEL

Here it was necessary to turn to management sciences to develop a computerized "expansion model" by means of which management could quickly compute and compare all the various alternatives in order to determine the most appropriate investment allocations. (See Fig. 4.)

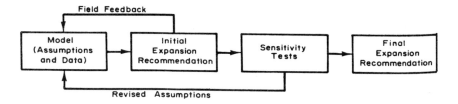

Figure 4. Expansion Model

The model incorporates statements about the effect of current market share, netback, and population growth, together with corporate policies on available expansion money and desired return and assumptions about expected volume and costs. These factors are run through the computer to generate an "initial expansion recommendation," which may then be tempered by field feedback on such factors as site availability, as well as by the results of sensitivity testing (determining the responsiveness of the results to changes in any one or a combination of the input factors). From all of this, the computer then generates a "final expansion recommendation." The real value of this model lies in three related capabilities:

1/ It allows management to test a wide variety of alternative assumptions and strategies and to approximate the effect of each, **before committing funds**.

2/ Through sensitivity testing it helps management to assess the risks attendant on various expansion alternatives.

3/ Recognizing that no mechanical system can cope by itself with the bewildering array of variables in a typical marketing strategy problem, it provides for managerial input at several points along the way.

RESTRUCTURING THE APPROACH

Notable in this success story was the "problem orientation" displayed by management. The marketing vice-president had no preconceptions about the value of the management sciences in his site selection decisions; he was interested only in a workable solution. But when that solution turned out to require mathematical sophistication and computing capacity beyond what a clerical staff could offer, he did not hesitate to add the appropriate skills to his study team.

Even then, however, he and his immediate subordinates stayed with the problem. Together with the technicians, they restructured the traditional approach in three ways:

- They used assumptions and probability estimates to allow for imprecise input data and uncertain relationships.
- They verified their estimates, where needed, by simulation and experimentation (sensitivity tests).
- Instead of "answers" in the form of mathematical optimums, they sought to develop feedback systems that could provide for: manipulation of more data than could have been handled manually; continuous automatic surveillance of results against plan — a kind of mechanical "management by exception" to spotlight potential problems and opportunities more quickly; and storing of "experience" so that each new decision could be as good as the last, or better.

PATTERN REPEATED

Every successful application of the management sciences to marketing strategy analyzed in our study has exhibited this same pattern. Perhaps more important, we have found no practical successes built on the more conventional approach. The problem-oriented approach — simple enough in principle but nonetheless a dramatic departure from traditional practices — can be seen again in the second example.

Example: setting pricing policy. To maintain its price image and control its margins, a large food chain had to review literally thousands of items almost weekly. Like most of its competitors, this chain was struggling through a difficult profit squeeze, aggravated by customer and government pressures to reduce its "unreasonably high" prices — which routine price surveys of its seven major competitors showed were no higher than average.

In the markets it served, however, pricing conditions were chaotic. Arbitrarily assigning an index value of 100 to its own prices, the company found that its competitors' indexes ranged from 98 to 102. However, trying to meet the lowest competitive price on every product would have brought the company's index down to 90 — a sure way to go out of business in an already low-margin industry. (The corresponding highest-price index would have been 108.)

PRICING CHAOS

How could the company price to ensure an equitable return and at the same time stay competitive? It was clear that prices on 6,500 to 7,000 items would need to be reviewed, and so many supplier cost changes and competitor price changes occurred each week that no manual system could do the job. Obviously, a computer would have to be part of the solution.

The company listed all the factors bearing on price, including manufacturer's cost, direct handling and selling costs, competitor prices, and movement of the product. They then developed a set of rules to govern pricing decisions for each major merchandise category. (For instance: "Nationally branded canned peas must generate a gross profit of 25 per cent, provided the resulting retail price does not exceed the local average price of the three lowest competitors.") At the same time, "exception criteria" were specified to guard against undesirable consequences. (For instance: "Single out for judgmental review items on which the machine-computed price reduced movement by 5 per cent or more during the previous reporting period.")

EARLY RESULTS PROMISING

The model thus developed proved to be a powerful pricing and management information tool. Each week the computer generates a series of suggested prices and an exception list that is passed to buyers and merchandisers for review. Product movement, new competitor prices, and supplier cost changes are entered into the system weekly, together with any indicated changes in pricing rules or exception criteria, and the cycle is repeated.

Although this system is too new for conclusive evaluation, the early results have been highly promising. In addition to a mechanism for setting and implementing pricing policy, the system provides a simulation capability for pretesting new pricing strategies, as well as data collection files for evaluating advertisements, promotions, and other price decisions. It constitutes, in short, a highly useful management-oriented (and largely management-defined) information system with considerable potential future expansion in such areas as monitoring performance on features and displays.

CONCLUSIONS AND FORECAST

Implications for the future.

What does all this add up to for marketing executives? Obviously, the management sciences can make a highly profitable and sometimes unique contribution to the solution of certain kinds of marketing strategy problems. Beyond this, as the examples suggest, one condition of success is the active involvement of the marketing executives themselves. In neither of the two cases cited did the management sciences enter into consideration until well along in the process.

In short, the place to start is not with the operations research or computer capability but with business itself: the competitive and economic environment in which it operates, its own strengths and weaknesses, and the opportunities and problems they engender. More specifically, **five management guidelines** can be drawn from our study:

Focus on specific key marketing problems, not global issues or pure research. Efforts by management scientists in universities (and to a lesser extent in corporations) to construct computer-based "total marketing models" that simulate the entire complex marketing decision process have not yet, to my knowledge, produced very useful results. Unsupported claims for such systems have probably contributed, in fact, to business skepticism about the management sciences in general, particularly in the light of corporate experience with some of these sweeping systems revisions.

Almost five years ago, for example, a large and successful manufacturer embarked on an effort to computerize most of his marketing process, from order entry to stock replenishment. As management envisioned the system, an order filed by a salesman anywhere in the world would be sourced automatically at the most profitable manufacturing location or warehouse and scheduled for delivery. With each transaction, inventory levels, sales statistics, and accounting records would be automatically updated. Any executive would routinely be able to interrogate the central processing unit and be informed of current sales and profitability by customer and by product, plant operating rates, and so on. Today, more than \$2 million down the road, the project has yet to produce a workable set of computer programs to implement this concept. Understandably, the entire management sciences effort is less than well regarded by top management.

For the next several years, it seems clear, the real opportunity for management sciences lies in selective strategic uses, where the nature of the problem dictates the tools to be used.

Seek out recurring problem situations, not isolated decisions. To date, successful strategic applications of the management sciences have been almost wholly confined to recurrent problems, not one-time decisions such as whether or not to enter a particular business or make a major change in distribution channels. Assumptions, simulation and experimentation, and feedback systems are most appropriate and can offer the most significant improvement over raw judgment where the decision is one that recurs periodically in a reasonably stable environment, so that experience can be accumulated and used to improve future decisions. Food store pricing, for example, exhibits all these characteristics: pricing decisions must be made weekly; they are affected by manufacturer's cost, competitive prices, movement, and the company's own desired "image." All these elements can be stated, measured, programmed, and periodically fed back through the system to update decisions. Advertising spending levels similarly meet most of these tests in a number of businesses. The problem of predicting next year's fashions, on the other hand, meets none of them.

Select only areas where the company is willing to make aggressive changes in strategy. In both of the successful applications discussed, the company was deliberately acting on its environment, not reacting to it. Successful strategic applications of the management sciences inevitably result in change, extending more often than not beyond the area of immediate application. The service station site selection project, for example, changed not only the headquarters budgeting and planning operation but also the jobs of field real estate people, territory managers, and even division managers who had previously been responsible for allocating expansion money.

Such changes are often felt in functional areas outside the marketing organization. They can require modifications in manufacturing practices or financial policy. The problem singled out for study, therefore, ought to be one about which management is actively unhappy and willing to endure the pangs of change in return for a solution.

Precisely because the desired end products cannot be rigidly defined, a considerable measure of risk inevitably attends most new applications. This risk has at least three dimensions: the chance that no adequate technology can be devised for economic solution of the problem; the possibility that sufficiently accurate data cannot be made available at reasonable cost; and the possibility that the solutions, even when they can be economically developed, will not be implemented — perhaps because the price of change is too high.

Even unqualified success, it should be noted, can be uncomfortably long in coming. The site selection model described above, for example, was nearly two years in development. And since some failures — perhaps a good many at first — are bound to be mixed in with the successes, the profit return requirement should probably be set quite high: three or four to one, or even higher, depending on management's own assessment of the likelihood of success.

A corollary point that warrants mention, although its significance is far from clear, is that none of the companies that have had real success in marketing strategy applications of the management sciences is among the generally recognized leaders in American industry. The companies most frequently noted as "most advanced," "best managed," and the like are notably absent from the management sciences honor roll. This is a curious finding, for which we have no ready explanation. The answer may be simply that the leader companies feel they are performing so well that they need not rush into largely uncharted fields. In any event, this finding does tend to underscore the vital importance of an active desire for change.

Be alert to opportunities to expand an initial application to broader marketing uses. The food pricing system described earlier appears to have considerable potential for expansion into a comprehensive marketing data system. Its capacity to remember costs, competitor prices, and movement is now being used in various ways — as a framework for collection of these data on an ongoing basis, a simulator to evaluate new pricing decision rules and explore alternative promotional and feature policies, a mechanism to ensure that pricing policies are implemented, and a device for the conduct of experiments. In short, the basic system seems capable of performing far more than was realized at first. The same is generally true of other successful applications we have seen.

Although it is too early to generalize very usefully about this feature of successful strategic applications, one clear rule does emerge: **Seek opportunities to install uniform coding and programming standards and to capture available marketing information on a disaggregated basis.**

One fairly large company, generally regarded (with some justice) as a leader in computer technology, recently had to embark on a massive project to accomplish precisely this. The company is multidivisional, but the product codes vary from division to division, as do customer codes, destination codes, and programming languages. There is even variation of this kind within some of the larger divisions. Thus, for example, computer programs written for inventory management are not compatible with those written for marketing forecasts. The company has spent a considerable amount of money in recent years to collect data. Yet the data collected are, in a very real sense, neither available nor useful except for the special purposes for which they were collected — purposes too often dictated by accountants, not managers.

Evidence indicates, moreover, that many other companies are in much the same predicament. And the problems they confront are far from trivial. In addition to the excessive cost of incompatible data systems, valuable information is frequently lost. Had the project teams in the site selection application or the pricing application been hampered by this problem, it might have taken them another year to accumulate the data and perform the analyses necessary to design and implement the model.

This is not to suggest that every company should immediately start building a massive data bank before reasonably precise uses for the data are known or payoffs have been estimated. But it does suggest the wisdom of making sure that the routine data normally collected are processed and stored in an orderly way, so that they will be available for other uses in the future.

Recognize that much of the leadership burden will inevitably fall on marketing

men, not management scientists. A few companies have already achieved substantial payoffs by applying the management sciences to certain problems of marketing strategy. But the methods by which they have achieved success are neither easy nor obvious. They involve a dramatic shift from much of what has gone on in the past. Most importantly, they show that the key to future success lies less with the management scientists than with the marketers. Only marketing executives have the judgment and managerial "feel" necessary to ensure the successful application of computers to marketing. Only they are in a position to focus efforts on the real "make-or-break" payoff opportunities, provide the necessary judgments and market knowledge needed to define the relationships, and make the application work by using and improving it over time.

However, since marketers will need to rely on computer specialists and operations researchers for technical assistance, it makes good sense to begin building management science capabilities into the marketing operation early, even in the absence of specific problems. In the considerable period of mutual education that lies ahead, the management scientist himself can provide useful advice on how his skills can be best employed. But it is marketing men who must supply the real leadership.

One knowledgable executive summarized the situation, perhaps a little too neatly, by saying: "The computer isn't going to take over marketing; in fact, nothing much is going to happen until marketing men take over the computer." Probably a better answer lies in a cooperative effort between management scientists and marketing personnel. Such a joint effort could lead to an earlier fulfillment of the promise that some of us see in the application of computers to marketing programs.

Most economic theory relating to business behavior emphasizes pricing. Also, the economist traditionally attempts to explain marketing strategy in terms of monopolistic and competitive market structures. This approach is challenged by the author of this article.

According to his research, the product and the customer are the determining factors in a company's marketing strategy.

22

how important is pricing in competitive strategy?

jon g. udell

In an effort to ascertain the key elements of business success in the market place, the author conducted a study among 200 producers of industrial and consumer goods. A sample of fairly well-known and successful manufacturing companies was selected from *Martindell's Manual of Excellent Management*. Listed are companies which are supposedly well managed, evaluated according to the criteria developed by the American Institute of Management. The use of the manual seemed appropriate in that the two most heavily weighted criteria are sales vigor and management efficiency.

The present study attempted to answer the question: "What are the key policies and procedures common to successful marketing managements in various manufacturing industries?"

Management's interest in the study was reflected by a 75% response to a 4-page mail questionnaire. The first section of the questionnaire listed 12 general policy areas of marketing management — among them, sales research, and sales

Reprinted from the *Journal of Marketing*, published by the American Marketing Association, Volume 28, No. 1 (January 1964), pp. 44-48.

planning, pricing, management of sales personnel, and product service. The respondent, usually the vice president in charge of marketing, was asked to select the five areas which he regarded as most vital in his company's marketing success.

Importance of Product Development

The results indicate that product research and development, selected by almost 80% of the respondents, is most important in modern-day competitive strategy. Four other policy areas, relating to either product or sales effort, were selected by more than half of the respondents. Table 1 presents a percentage analysis of the responses.

Table 1
How Management Ranks the Factors
of Marketing Success

Rank	Policy areas	% of firms selecting the policy area[a]
1	Product research and development	79
2	Sales research and sales planning	73
3	Management of sales personnel	59
4	Advertising and sales promotion	56
5	Product service	52
6	Pricing	50
7	Organizational structure	44
8	Distribution channels and their control	41
9	Marketing cost budgeting and control	17
10	Financing and credit	14
11	Transportation and storage	7
12	Public relations	7

[a]Based on a tabulation of 135 usable questionnaires. Percentages here are rounded.

It appears that business management did not agree with the economic views of the importance of pricing — one-half of the respondents did *not* select pricing as *one of the five* most important policy areas in their firm's marketing success.

Also, the two major facets of nonprice competition (product and sales effort) were subdivided into a number of policy areas; for example, sales effort was subdivided into sales research and sales planning, management of sales personnel, and advertising and sales promotion. In short, *the competitive activities relating to the product and to sales effort were selected as most important in the success of these firms.*

Pricing

The emphasis on product and sales effort does not imply that price is unimportant. Three factors probably account for the relatively low ranking of pricing:

1. In today's competitive economy, *supply* – or production capacity – *generally exceeds demand*; and, therefore, nearly all sellers are forced to be either completely competitive or almost collusive in their pricing. Because there may be little or no freedom for a company to deviate from the market price, heavy reliance must be placed on product differentiation and sales effort.

2. *The relatively well-to-do consumers of today are interested in more than just price.* They are interested in product quality, distinctiveness, style, and many other factors which lead to both physical and psychological satisfaction. Consumers not only can afford but want product differentiation and sales promotion. From them the consumer receives a great deal of psychological satisfaction and utility. It is only logical that consumer-oriented managements would choose to emphasize products and sales efforts in an attempt to satisfy consumer desires.

3. *It is through successful product differentiation that a manufacturer may obtain some pricing freedom.* Products known to be identical must be priced identically in the market place. A departure from identical prices would result in all patronage going to the seller or sellers with the lowest price.

MARKETING STRATEGIES ACCORDING TO PRODUCTS AND CUSTOMERS

Economists have proposed several theories that give recognition to the nonprice factors of competitive strategy.[1] However, they have not credited the nature of the product and the characteristics of the buyers as the dominant factors in explaining how companies organize to market their products. Instead, the dominant factor is usually assumed to be the market structure of the industry (competitive, oligopolistic, or monopolistic).

A producer of machine tools would not be expected to compete in the same manner as a producer of perfume; and a comparison of the structures of the machine-tool and perfume industries would not explain the differences in their marketing strategies. *Common business sense would lead one to believe that a company's use of nonprice competitive strategy should vary according to the nature of a firm's product and the characteristics of the buyers for that product.*

Accordingly, the data were classified according to the respondents' type of industry: industrial goods, consumer durable goods, and consumer non-durable goods.

Producers of Industrial Goods

The producers of industrial goods stressed the product facet of competitive strategy.

Two of the policy areas listed in the marketing management study pertain directly to the product — product research and development, and product service. (Product service refers to those activities performed by a manufacturer in the attempt to guarantee that a product gives satisfactory performance to its users.)

As shown in Table 2, both of these policy areas were selected by about 80% of the industrial users.

Table 2
Policy Areas Selected by Industrial
Goods Producers

Policy areas	% of firms selecting the policy area[a]
Product:	
Product research and development	79
Product service	79
Average product selection ratio	79
Sales efforts:	
Sales research and sales planning	63
Management of sales personnel	49
Advertising and sales promotion	37
Average sales efforts selection ratio	50
Pricing	47
Other areas:	
Organizational structure	50
Distribution channels and their control	34
Financing and credit	18
Marketing cost budgeting and control	12
Transportation and storage	9
Public relations	7

[a]Based on the questionnaires of 68 industrial goods producers.
Percentages here are rounded.

The policy areas relating to sales effort were relegated to a lesser role by the successful manufacturers of industrial goods. The average selection for the policy areas pertaining to sales effort was 50%, as compared with the average product selection of 80%.

The industrial-goods producers' primary emphasis on the product facet of marketing strategy was also emphasized in letters received from various respondents. A Pratt & Whitney Aircraft executive said: "Our two most valuable assets sales-wise are the technical excellence of our products, and our policy of rendering the best possible product service to our customers both before and after the sale."

Producers of Consumer Goods

The manufacturers of consumer goods placed a much greater emphasis on the sales effort facet of competitive strategy. This emphasis was especially great in the case of the firms producing nondurable goods.

As shown in Table 3, the nondurable goods producers had an average sales effort selection of 85%, as compared with an average product selection of 45%. Durable goods producers had an average sales efforts selection of 79%, as compared with the product selection of 60%.

Table 3
Policy Areas Selected by Consumer Goods Manufacturers

Policy areas	Manufacturers of nondurable goods	Manufacturers of durable goods[a]
Sales efforts:		
Advertising and sales promotion	89	73
Management of sales personnel	64	91
Sales research and sales planning	82	73
Average sales efforts selection ratio	85	79
Product:		
Product research and development	83	75
Product service	14	36
Average product selection ratio	45	60
Pricing	50	46
Other areas:		
Distribution channels and their control	54	46
Organizational structure	39	27
Marketing cost budgeting and control	29	9
Financing and credit	11	9
Transportation and storage	4	9
Public relations	7	— —

[a]Based on the questionnaires of 28 nondurable goods producers and 11 durable goods producers. Figures here are rounded.

The differences were accounted for by the low selection ratios for product service, in that most consumer goods manufacturers selected product research and development.

It is understandable that consumer-goods producers selected product research and development with such a high degree of frequency in light of their emphasis on sales efforts. It is less difficult to promote a differentiated product than it is to promote an undifferentiated product.

Product research and development are important, but sales efforts are *most* important to manufacturers of consumer goods.

Product research and development was not broken down into research related to physical (real) product improvement and research related to psychological (fancied) product improvement. It would be immaterial to the consumer-goods manufacturer if a product change were *real* or *fancied*, so long as the change was regarded as an improvement by his customers.

The second section of the questionnaire subdivided the general areas of policies and procedures into more specific categories of business activities. When product research and development was subdivided into three categories of activities, the following selections were obtained:

	Industrial goods	Manufacturers of Consumer nondurables	Consumer durables
Technical research and development	75	54	56
Marketing research related to new products	30	62	56
Product evaluation	16	19	22

As might be expected, the technical development of products was most emphasized by the industrial-goods producers, whereas marketing research related to new products was most emphasized by the consumer-goods producers.

This analysis indicates that all three groups of manufacturers — industrial, consumer durable, and consumer nondurable — stressed the nonprice facets of competitive strategy, and that *the relative emphasis on product and sales efforts varied according to the nature of the products and the characteristics of the buyers.*

To further test this proposition, the questionnaires were grouped according to specific industries. If the proposition were valid, there should have been a high degree of similarity in the marketing strategies of respondents of a specific industry. That is, the respondents of a given industry, producing similar products for like customers, should select similar policy areas as most important in their marketing success.

Here are three examples that demonstrate the validity of this proposition.

Case No. 1 — Capital Goods Industry

The most homogeneous grouping of companies with similar products and similar customers consisted of 12 producers of major installations — capital goods. As Table 4 illustrates, *all 12 producers selected product research and development and product service.*

Table 4
Selection of Major Policy Areas
Twelve Producers of Major Installations

Rank	Policy areas	Selection ratio—%
1	Product research and development	100
2	Product service	100
3	Distribution channels and their control	67
4	Organizational structure	42
5	Management of sales personnel	42
6	Sales research and sales planning	42
7	Advertising and sales promotion	33
8	Pricing	25
9	Financing and credit	17
10	Public relations	17
11	Marketing cost budgeting and control	8
12	Transportation and storage	8

Distribution channels and their control was selected by 8 of the 12 producers. This may be because sales servicing before and after is often performed by the distributors of capital goods.

The 100% selection for product research and development and for product service were high. Statistically one would expect such an occurrence only twice in 100,000 trials due to random sampling error.

Assuming that each policy area is actually of equal importance, there is a .00002 probability of getting a policy area with a 100% selection ratio due to random sampling error (binomial theorum used). The fact that *both* of the policy areas pertaining to product were selected by all 12 respondents provides further statistical proof that the selection ratios are *not* due to chance.

Case No. 2 – Metals Industry

Another grouping of companies was comprised of producers of steel, zinc, aluminum, and other processed metals, The companies have similar markets and similar products, in that their products are the raw materials for the manufacture of other goods.

It would be anticipated that the product facet of competition would have prevailed in the competitive strategies of these companies; and Table 5 shows that this was true.

Table 5
Selection of Major Policy Areas by
Eight Producers of Metals

Rank	Policy areas	Selection ratio—%
1	Product service	100
2	Product research and development	75
3	Sales research and sales planning	63
4	Pricing	63
5	Distribution channels and their control	50
6	Management of sales personnel	38
7	Organizational structure	25
8	Transportation and storage	25
9	Financing and credit	25
10	Public relations	13
11	Advertising and sales promotion	13
12	Marketing cost budgeting and control	——

Case No. 3 – Chemical Industry

A third grouping of companies highlights the importance of customers in determining marketing strategy. Of the six chemical manufacturers participating in the study, three produced for the consumer market and three for the industrial market.

All six firms responded by selecting product research and development, but at this point the similarities ceased.

As shown in Table 6, the average product selection ratio of the industrial chemical manufacturers was much higher than that of the consumer chemical manufacturers. The average sales effort selection ratio of the consumer products manufacturers was higher than that of the industrial producers.

Table 6
Selection of Major Policy Areas by Chemical and Drug Producers

Policy areas	Selection ratio of industrial chemical producers (3)		Selection ratio of consumer chemical producers (3)	
Product research and development	100		100	
Product service	67		——	
Average product selection ratio		83		50
Advertising and sales promotions	——		100	
Sales research and sales planning	100		67	
Management of sales personnel	33		67	
Average sales efforts selection ratio		44		78

HOW IMPORTANT IS SIZE?

To ascertain the influence of company size on management's selection of the facets of marketing strategy, the responses were classified according to the sales volume of each company: less than $50 million, $50 to $100 million, $100 to $500 million, and over $500 million.

The differences among the selection ratios of the various size classifications were so small that none was found to be statistically significant. Apparently size had little influence on the relative importance that a company attached to the various facets of its marketing mix.

IN CONCLUSION

The ranking method provided only a rough measure of the importance of price, product, and sales efforts; *but it was a measurement*.

As for another possible limitation — lack of differentiation between responses related to "what is" and what the respondents felt "should be" — one might ask, "Who is better qualified to select the most important areas of a successful firm's marketing program than the firm's marketing management?"

The study reported illustrates two major points:

1. In today's market, the nonprice facets of competition occupy a prominent role.

2. The explanation of the roles of nonprice competitive facets does *not* lie solely in the structure of the industry (or the size of the firm), but instead primarily in the nature of the product and its market.

The importance of the nonprice aspects of the marketing mix and the variations among industries can be explained by the nature of today's economy. To compete successfully in a setting characterized by oligopolistic firms offering rival products to a customer-dominated market, the firm must be customer-oriented. In appealing to the customer, management finds success in utilizing the nonprice facets of competitive activity, adjusting its strategy to the needs and desires of the buyer.

NOTES

1. Lawrence Abbott, *Quality and Competition* (New York: Columbia University Press, 1951); Hans Brems, "The Interdependence of Quality Variations, Selling Effort and Price," *Quarterly Journal of Economics*, Vol. 62 (May, 1948), pp. 418-440; C. A. Stocking, "Advertising and Economic Theory," *American Economic Review*, Vol. 21 (March, 1931), pp. 43-55.

. . . has offered empirical evidence for the hypothesis that geographic mobility experience is a useful dimension for segmenting consumers for formulating courses of marketing action.

23

geographic mobility
and market
segmentation

alan r. andreasen*

The concept of market segmentation has been advanced in recent years as a promising way to improve marketing efficiency and effectiveness in expanding markets. [6, pp. 3-8]. Essentially, the concept is that by separating buyers into groups having different knowledge, attitudes, and behaviors toward a given product or service, then differentiating marketing strategies in both quality and quantity among them, marketers can increase profits beyond what they would by using strategies treating buyers as a mass.

Variables used in segment buyer markets may be grouped according to : (1) content into geographic, economic, social, and personal variables, (2) composi-

*Alan R. Andreasen is an assistant professor of marketing and business organization, State University of New York at Buffalo. He wishes to express appreciation to the Marketing Science Institute and to its technical director, Michael H. Halbert, for advice and assistance on this project. The present study is only part of an ongoing, long-term study of geographic mobility at the Institute.

Reprinted from the *Journal of Marketing Research*, published by American Marketing Association, Volume 3, No. 4, November 1966, pp. 341-8.

tion into simple or complex variables, and (3) time perspective into measures of present status and measures of changed status over time. Geographically, the possibilities are shown in the figure.

A number of studies, both published and unpublished, treat both simple and complex variables in all four content areas. These variables, however, have been treated mainly in their present status. As measures of change, only occupational and social class mobility and family life-cycle change variables have received much attention, at least in the literature.

Although marketers will readily agree that present geographic location or residence is sometimes a most important determinant of consumer attitudes and behavior, it is surprising that change in residence (geographic mobility) has not yet received the theoretical or empirical attention that, say, social mobility has. It is our intention to explore this variable. The principal objective of the article will be to discover whether geographic mobility might be a profitable dimension for segmenting consumer markets.

GENERAL DIMENSIONS OF GEOGRAPHIC MOBILITY

First one may ask, how important is geographic mobility in the national economy? Introductory data about the incidence of geographic mobility for the civilian population from the 1960 census is shown below. Several general characteristics of geographic mobility are:

1. The geographically mobile segment of the population is *large*. Approximately 20 percent of the population changes residence each year.

2. About two-thirds of all movers move within the same county (locally) and about one-third between counties (long distance). Of the between county movers, about one-half move within a state.

3. The highest incidence of mobility both local and long distance is in the young, 18 to 34, segment of the population.

4. Mobility is about identical for males and females.

5. While the incidence of mobility is higher among non-whites, they are less likely to move long distance than the white segment of the population.

One might infer from the above findings that, compared with nonmovers, the mobile segment of the population, because of its size and its relative youth, could be an important market segment for products in general or for specific kinds of goods and services. The remainder of the article will explore this hypothesis through a detailed analysis of some exploratory-descriptive data gathered on a sample of *long-distance* geographic mobiles. These data were generated in the course of an exploratory study I conducted under the

Market Segmentation Variables

Content	Type	Measures of present status	Measures of change
Geographic	Simple	Region neighborhood } 	Geographic } mobility
	Complex	Urbanity	
Economic	Simple	Income, occupation	Occupational mobility
	Complex	Social class	Social class mobility
Social	Simple	Marital status, children	{ Family life Cycle growth
	Complex	Family life cycle	
Personal	Simple	Age, sex	Growth
	Complex	Personality	Maturation

sponsorship of the Marketing Science Institute on a sample of 148 households moving into the Philadelphia Metropolitan area during the summer of 1964. It will be assumed that this hypothesis will be supported if it can be demonstrated that the long-distance mover group, when compared with the combined local and nonmover group (i.e., the remainder of the consumer population), is found to be significantly superior or inferior according to four criteria: level of present spending power, potential for future increased spending power, present purchase behavior, and potential for change in future purchase behavior.[1] It will further be assumed that the most useful analysis of the geographic mobility variable for practitioners, theorists, and researchers will be based on theory.[2]

The first part of the article presents a tentative theory of what determines geographic mobility. Following parts offer hypotheses developed from this theory and present the empirical findings of the Philadelphia study in terms of these hypotheses. A final part restates the principal conclusions and suggests major implications for management and future study.

A TENTATIVE THEORY OF GEOGRAPHIC MOBILITY

The central postulate of the present theory is that geographic mobility for a given household is a product of objectively determined opportunities presented by the environment, and a household's subjective willingness to move. Three secondary propositions follow: (1) few households will have an opportunity to move even once in their lifetime, whether for job, marital or other personal reasons; (2) fewer will have the opportunity to move more than once in their lifetime; and (3) fewer still, given the opportunity, will be subjectively willing to move, particularly between communities. It may be concluded, therefore, that geographically mobile households, particularly long distance mobiles, are likely to be relatively unique. This uniqueness, it might be hypothesized, will be carried through to their marketing attitudes and behavior. Before testing this hypothesis, however, the uniqueness of long-distance mobiles needs to be explored by explaining the two components of the "opportunity-willingness theory."

OPPORTUNITY TO MOVE

The opportunities to move long-distance are internal or external to the potentially mobile individuals or households. External sources of mobility are principally job opportunities offered by new or present employers, including the military. Individuals or heads of household who are likely to have such opportunities are those with (1) proved managerial competence, (2) potential managerial competence, (3) scarce technical or intellectual skill, (4) moral claims on management, such as might be held by workers at recently closed plant sites and (5) positions in large, geographically diversified organizations.[3] From these considerations one would initially hypothesize that most long-distance movers are in managerial or professional-technical occupations and have higher than average education and incomes.[4]

Internal sources of long-distance mobility are principally the physical and financial abilities of the movers. Such abilities would be critical prerequisites when moving is motivated by: (1) dissatisfaction with the present location for employment, aesthetic, or social reasons,[5] (2) positive attraction to some other community for the same reasons, i.e., a better labor market, a more favorable climate for retirement, or nearness to close friends or relatives, and (3) scholastic ambitions. Again, solely from these considerations, one would predict long-distance movers would, as before, have higher status occupations, education, and incomes, and possibly stronger pre-move asset positions.

WILLINGNESS TO MOVE

Moving will always cause the household to change some routine patterns of behavior (life style). In many instances, especially in long-distance moving, effects on life style may be significant. Changes usually entail risks for the moving households; risks that new friends will not be found in the new community or will in some way be inferior to old friends; that the new home will be hard to find or inadequate, etc. Willingness to undertake these risks is referred to here as willingness to move. The amount of willingness necessary for

Table 1
Mobility Status of the Civilian Population by Age, Sex,
and Color in 1960 in Percentages

	Total	Same house (nonmover)	Different house in the United States (movers)							Abroad
		Total	Total	Same county Total	Different county (migrant)					
					Total	Within a state	Between states			
							Total	Contiguous	Non-contiguous	
Both sexes, total	100.0	80.0	19.4	12.6	6.8	3.1	3.7	1.3	2.4	0.6
Under 18	100.0	79.0	20.6	13.6	7.0	3.1	3.9	1.4	2.5	0.4
18 to 34	100.0	66.4	32.3	20.0	12.2	5.5	6.8	2.2	4.5	1.3
35 to 64	100.0	86.8	12.9	8.7	4.2	2.1	2.1	0.7	1.3	0.3
65 and over	100.0	90.3	9.6	6.7	2.9	1.8	1.1	0.3	0.8	0.1
Male, total	100.0	79.7	19.6	12.6	7.0	3.2	3.8	1.3	2.5	0.7
Under 18	100.0	80.2	19.3	12.6	6.7	2.8	3.8	1.4	2.4	0.5
18 to 34	100.0	67.5	32.1	19.5	12.6	5.4	7.2	2.4	4.9	0.4
35 to 64	100.0	86.0	13.6	9.1	4.5	2.3	2.2	0.9	1.3	0.4
65 and over	100.0	90.5	9.4	6.6	2.8	1.7	1.1	0.3	0.8	0.1
Female, total	100.0	80.4	19.2	12.7	6.5	3.0	3.5	1.2	2.3	0.4
Under 18	100.0	78.9	20.7	13.8	6.9	3.0	3.9	1.4	2.5	0.4
18 to 34	100.0	66.9	32.4	20.5	11.9	5.5	6.4	2.1	4.2	0.7
35 to 64	100.0	87.5	12.2	8.4	3.9	1.9	2.0	0.6	1.4	0.3
65 and over	100.0	90.1	9.8	6.7	3.1	1.9	1.2	0.3	0.9	0.1
White	100.0	80.4	19.0	11.9	7.1	3.3	3.8	1.3	2.5	0.6
Non-white	100.0	77.2	22.4	18.1	4.3	1.9	2.4	0.6	1.8	0.4

Source: U.S., Bureau of the Census, "Mobility of the Population," Current Population Reports, Series P-20, 1960.

a given move is directly proportional to the extent of risk involved. This risk, it is proposed, is a function of:

1. The number and magnitude of the changes in household status resulting from the move. These changes would include changes in geographical region, city size, city type, occupation, income, social class, marital status, family size, etc.,;

2. The individual or household's uncertainty (lack of information) about the nature and consequences of these changes;

3. The individual or household's attitude toward risk, generally and for this specific move (i.e., how strong is the motivation to move);

4. The extent to which the individual or household is embedded socially and psychologically in the old community;

5. The extent to which help from relatives, friends, etc., is available in the new community to cushion potential social and psychological shock.

These postualtes about the willingness component suggest a number of hypotheses about the characteristics of long-distance movers and the moving process. The more significant of these are:

1. Geographic mobiles are most likely to move between communities of the same type.

2. They do not change occupation, income, household status in the course of the move.

3. They possess advance information about the new community before moving.

4. Long-distance geographic mobiles have had experience in moving long distance before the present move.

5. They are motivated to move by the chance for improved occupations and incomes.

6. They are motivated to move by their own social class aspirations.

7. They have had minimal social and organizational involvement in their previous communities of residence.

8. Geographic mobiles have personal sources of potential aid waiting for them in the new community.

9. Geographic mobiles are relatively young and thus more willing to undertake the risks of moving because they are more adventurous or they know they have more time to recoup losses from present failures.

THE STUDY DESIGN

The sample for the present study was developed from new telephone listings in the Pennsylvania portion of the Philadelphia metropolitan area between March 1 and July 15, 1964. The original sample had 321 households planning to stay in the Philadelphia area at least one year. From this sample, 162 personal interviews were conducted in the first part of August. However, because of the large scope of this exploratory study, only part of the required data was secured in these personal interviews; additional information was gathered from supplementary mail questionnaires left at each household. Of the mail questionnaires 153 (94.5 percent) were returned within three weeks; five were subsequently eliminated for various reasons, resulting in a final sample of 148 households.

Though the final sample does conform in some ways to the census definition of migrants (i.e., intercounty movers), because it includes military personnel living off base, it does not include people moving between counties in the Philadelphia metropolitan area. The sample is, of course also unusual since it was developed in one metropolitan area at one time of the year using a particular sample and instrument design. The few comparisons with census data that were undertaken indicate that the sample had somewhat higher education, income, and occupational status characteristics and comprised a somewhat lower proportion of non-white respondents.

FINDINGS

Having outlined a tentative theory about what determines long-distance geographic mobility and suggested some hypotheses about household and individual characteristics possibly associated with long-distance moving, we turn to the Philadelphia data to discover whether this sample of long-distance movers have the predicted characteristics. We shall examine the hypotheses in turn. The examination will be brief since the principal concern is not with the opportunity-willingness theory but with the more general market segmentation hypothesis.

1. *Geographic mobiles are concentrated in managerial or professional-technical occupations.* This hypothesis is supported by Table 2 which shows that over 60 percent of the heads of households in the present sample held managerial or professional-technical occupations. This compares with 25.6 percent for all males in the U.S. Labor force [10, p. 228].[6]

2. *Geographic mobiles are above average in education.* This hypothesis is supported by Table 3, which indicates that over 50 percent of the females and 69 percent of the males in the present sample had some college education, and almost 22 percent of the males had at least some post-graduate training. Only 16.5 percent of all persons over 25 in the nation as a whole had attained an education level equal to some college in 1960 [10, p. 112].

3. *Geographic mobiles receive higher than average incomes.* This hypothesis is

Table 2
Occupation in Philadelphia

Occupation	Number of responses	Percent of total responses
Clerk or salesman	14	9.5
Craftsworker or foreman	8	5.4
Managerial salaried	51	34.5
Self-employed	2	1.4
Operative	3	2.0
Professional or technical	38	25.7
Service worker	2	1.4
Laborer	5	3.4
Other or don't know	13	8.8
Retired or unemployed	3	2.0
No answer	9	6.1
	148	100.0

Table 3
Education of Respondents

Education	Female respondents[a]		Male respondents[b]	
	Number	Percent	Number	Percent
Up to 8 years	3	2.1	2	1.4
Some high school	7	4.9	7	4.8
High school graduate	45	31.5	18	12.3
Some college	37	25.9	22	15.1
College graduate	27	18.9	47	32.2
Some postgraduate	4	2.8	15	10.3
Graduate degrees	5	3.5	17	11.6
Trade or technical school	1	.7	9	6.2
Business or secretarial	11	7.7	3	2.1
No answer	3	2.1	6	4.1
	143	100.1	146	100.1

[a] Asked of 143 female respondents.
[b] Education of 141 married males were reported by their wives.

supported by Table 4, which indicates a medium income for the sample between $10,000 and $15,000 with 35 percent of all respondent households expecting to earn over $15,000 in their new community.

Table 4
Expected Household Income in New Community

Expected Income	Number of responses	Percent of total responses
Under $4,000	7	4.7
$4,000 to $8,000	19	12.8
$8,000 to $10,000	29	19.6
$10,000 to $15,000	34	23.0
$15,000 to $25,000	37	25.0
$25,000 to $50,000	15	10.1
Over $50,000	—	—
No answer	7	4.7
	148	99.9

4. *Geographic mobiles are more likely to move between communities of the same type.* In the present study, over 80 percent of the respondents, moved to the Philadelphia area from another urban area, tending to support the hypothesis.

5. *Geographic mobiles do not change occupation, income or household statuses in the course of the move.* Approximately 18 percent of the heads of the respondent households changed occupation in the move, 72 percent changed incomes, and 15 percent changed household status. The third finding tends to support the hypothesis, the first and second tend to negate it. (However, see Hypothesis 8).

6. *Geographic mobiles possess advance information about the new community before undertaking a move.* Eighteen percent of the sample had lived in the Philadelphia area before. Of the remaining 82 percent, 79.6 percent sought advance information through various formal and informal channels.

7. *Long-distance geographic mobiles have had experience in moving long distance before the present move.* Approximately 53 percent of the sample had moved at least once previously, tending to support the hypothesis. A further 25 percent reported previous experience moving locally.

8. *Geographic mobiles are motivated to move by the chance for improved occupations and incomes.* Of the 18 percent who changed occupations in the move, 61 percent improved them. Of the 71.7 percent who changed incomes, 90.6 percent improved them. Both findings tend to support the hypothesis.

9. *Geographic mobiles are motivated to move by their own high social class aspirations.* About 56 percent of the respondent households reported aspirations to move up at least one social class in their lifetime.

10. *Geographic mobiles have had minimal social and organizational involvement in their previous communities of residence.* Approximately 75 percent of the respondents were active in an average of 2.3 formal organizations in the previous communities. Approximately *one-half* of these served as officers recently in one or more of these organizations. These findings tend to negate the hypothesis.

11. *Geographic mobiles have personal sources of potential aid waiting for them in the new community.* Approximately 39 percent of the sample had relatives already living in the new community, 51 percent had friends or acquaintances there and 40 percent business associates, all tending to support the hypothesis.

12. *Geographic mobiles are relatively young and thus more willing to undertake the risks of moving because they are more adventurous or because they know they have more time to recoup losses from present failures.* Table 5 tends to support this hypothesis.[7]

In summary, it appears that the opportunitywillingness theory accounts for most of the characteristics of the sample of geographic mobiles in the Philadelphia study. The major exception seems to be the heavy social involvement of long-distance movers in their previous communities. This characteristic may be found, in subsequent studies, to be associated with the kinds of occupations typical of long-distance movers.

Table 5
Age of Respondents

Age	Female respondents[a]		Male respondents[b]	
	Number	Percent	Number	Percent
18 to 24	36	25.2	17	11.6
25 to 29	26	18.2	30	20.5
30 to 39	42	29.4	59	40.4
40 to 49	23	16.1	21	14.4
50 to 59	10	7.0	13	8.9
60 to 69	4	2.8	3	2.1
No answer	2	1.4	3	2.1
	143	100.1	146	100.0

[a]Asked of 143 female respondents.
[b]Ages of 141 married males were reported by their wives.

We now turn to the main question, namely, whether long-distance geographic mobiles represent a unique market segment compared to local movers and nonmovers.

LONG-DISTANCE GEOGRAPHIC MOBILES AS A MARKET SEGMENT

A summary of the descriptive findings in the preceding sections portrays long-distance geographic mobiles as:

1. Relatively young (and in the early stages of the family life cycle),
2. Well educated,
3. In higher status occupations
4. Having above average incomes,
5. In higher social classes,
6. Socially active,
7. Socially upwardly mobile, with high social class aspirations,
8. Geographically mobile in the past,
9. Having their present move economically inspired.

These findings seem to offer evidence for the initial conclusions that long-distance geographic mobiles represent a quality market segment compared to the rest of the population (a) in present purchasing power because of high incomes and occupational status, (b) in future purchasing power because of high education, youth, high aspirations and willingness to be economically mobile.

We may now ask whether, at a second level, long-distance mobiles represent a quality market segment for marketers of any particular kinds of goods and services.

PRODUCT AND SERVICE NEEDS AND WANTS

It may be hypothesized that long-distance movers have unique product and service wants as a result of two interrelated sets of determinants: first their differences from the rest of the population in age, education, occupation, etc., independent of their recent move; and second, the recent move independent of general socioeconomic and demographic differences.

From the preceding sections alone one might predict that they would be particularly good customers for the more expensive, durable and nondurable goods and for the more expensive and perhaps more sophisticated leisure time services. Geographic mobility experience, in this sense, may act simply as an *index* (as social class does) for a number of other descriptive consumer variables.

The more interesting question is whether moving itself acts as *stimulant* for unique product and service purchase patterns, independent of the effects of the unique socioeconomic and demographic characteristics of long-distance movers. A strong argument can be made for this proposition on both theoretical and empirical grounds.

As noted earlier, moving brings a change in life style for the household, the greatness of the change varying by household and by type of move. No matter how great, the *fact* of change will mean that the household is subject to one or more of three distinct kinds of environmental pressures:

1. The need to revise household inventories of durables and nondurables to conform to new living quarters and to new retail availabilities.

2. The need to conform to a different set of regional norms in attitudes and behavior.

3. The need to adjust inventories, attitudes and behavior to different income, occupational or social class levels (or aspirations) attained in the move.

In addition, moving may simply be a convenient time to replace many dated or outworn items, or may trigger purchase decisions already considered.

Although these forces differ by household, they appear to make geographic mobiles as a group a potentially superior market for furniture, clothing, drapes, slipcovers, other dry goods, and consumer durables such as appliances and automobiles. Data from the Philadelphia study seem to confirm this as indicated in actual and planned purchase statistics shown in Table 6.[8]

Table 6 indicates that over 83 percent of the sample actually purchased, or planned to purchase drapes or slipcovers because of their move. Over 68 percent indicated actual or planned purchases of furniture; over 45 percent purchases of clothing; over 41 percent purchases of at least one major appliance, and approximately 15 to 18 percent purchases of small appliances, automobiles and other items.

"SWITCHING" BEHAVIOR

Finally, the mobile segment may be a unique market in brand purchasing behavior and preferences. Here one can argue that it is likely the long-distance mover will switch brands (and perhaps product types) in the course of the move, or directly following the move for several reasons. First, it seems reasonable to assume that the majority of them migrate from known market environments to ones in which many stores and at least some brands are unknown to them. For this reason, one would expect an amount of store and brand switching simply because old favorites are absent in the new community. Second, since many of the movers (a) are migrating from geographic areas where one set of consumption patterns (clothes, furniture, etc.) are appropriate, to geographic

Table 6
Actual or Planned Purchases of Major Assets
After Arrival in Philadelphia

Purchases	Respondents reporting purchases					
	Actual		Planned		Total	
	Num-ber	Percent of total	Num-ber	Percent of total	Num-ber	Percent of total
Major appli-ances	50	33.8	12	8.1	62	41.9
Minor appli-ances	18	12.2	5	3.4	23	15.5
Furniture	64	43.2	38	25.7	102	68.9
Automobile(s)	16	10.8	9	6.1	25	16.9
Clothing	50	33.8	17	11.5	67	45.3
Drapes, slip-covers	91	61.5	33	22.3	124	83.8
Other	22	14.9	6	4.1	28	18.9
No answer	21	14.2				

areas where they are not and (b) are, in the course of moving, changing from one social status level, where one set of consumption patterns is appropriate, to another where it is not, a great deal of brand-switching will inevitably take place. In the case of changing social status, much of the switching would probably upgrade purchase behavior.

It may be tentatively said that moving may not only precipitate specific product purchases by moving households, but also initiate considerable brand, store, and product switching. Switching may hold not only for the transition between old and new community, but also for the early months in the new area when the household is attempting to adjust to new shopping patterns. It follows that although they are only a small proportion of the total customer group for given products and services, geographic mobiles *may* represent — for many brands, stores, or products — a *high proportion* of the nonloyal, noncore customers "floating" during any market period. This vulnerability of long-distance movers to being switched may make them an important target for marketers interested in improving market shares over time.

A NOTE ON INFORMATION-SEEKING BEHAVIOR

Finding a highly desirable market target, such as long-distance mobiles appear to be, is of limited value to marketers if an efficient and unique means of communicating with it cannot be found. It appears that in the present case a set of efficient and usable channels for tapping the geographic mobile market does exist.

First, it is clear from the study that movers have high levels of media exposure which, by itself, implies an easy task for marketers. Over 60 percent of the sample reported that they regularly read two or more newspapers.

It may be speculated that these newspapers could effectively communicate to this group, particularly during the early period in the new community when other sources of information are unavailable or are thought to be untrustworthy. The study clearly shows that new residents in a community have substantial and salient needs for information, not only about stores and products, but also about many other environment features such as the local political system, recreation, and entertainment facilities. It is likely that newspapers serve as important sources of such information. The need for housing want ad information in the early stages of residence, or prior to final residence, should introduce the local newspapers early to new residents. Newspapers should have considerable influence on the store and product choices and the brand, product, and store switches of these mobiles. Some of the same arguments could also apply to the yellow pages.

It is clear from the study that personal sources of information are particularly important to those who move to a new community. Friends, neighbors (and co-workers in the early days of residence) were the sources most frequently mentioned by movers when describing their new market learning activities.

This is, however, not unexpected when one considers the high levels of risk in many of the marketing-type decisions made during the early days in a new community — such as choosing a doctor, dentist, hairdresser. Unfortunately, the present knowledge about personal information systems of new movers is poor enough to preclude recommending action to marketing practitioners.

CONCLUSIONS AND IMPLICATIONS

The study described in this article has offered empirical evidence for the hypothesis that geographic mobility experience is a useful dimension for segmenting consumers for formulating courses of marketing action. The article has indicated that if the study sample is representative, individuals who have recently undergone a long-distance move, when compared to local movers and nonmovers, are likely to:

1. Be above average in present purchasing power,
2. Be above average in potential growth in purchasing power,
3. Be important customers for particular products and services, such as major durables, household furnishings, etc.,

4. Undertake considerable brand, store, and product switching in the course of the move.

The major implications of these findings for *marketing strategy* would appear to be the following:

1. Measurement of geographic mobility should be used in future analyses of consumer markets to describe both the *positions* in life style at any point in time and *changes* in life style over time.
2. Decisions on appropriate dimensions for market segmentation policies should consider explicitly geographic mobility as an alternative.
3. Marketers should consider price, product, channel, and particularly promotion strategies explicitly directed toward the long distance portion of the mobility continuum, with particular emphasis on product and service needs and vulnerability to brand, product, and store switching promotion.

In addition to these implications for marketing action, the study has raised intriguing and important issues for further investigation, for both practical and basic marketing researchers. Among the more interesting of these issues are:

1. For pragmatic marketing researchers,
   a. What, *in detail*, are the specific product and service needs of long-distance geographic mobiles, not only relative to specific moves but also evolving over the course of their lives in response to their commitment to this type of advancement?
   b. What are the nature and consequences of geographic mobility for the approximately 22 million Americans who move within countries each year? How do their needs, vulnerability, information seeking strategies, etc., differ from both the long-distance mobiles and the stable, nonmover part of the population?
   c. What are the effects of multiple moves on marketing behavior? Are there significant and pragmatically important differences in the needs, etc., of households who have moved long distances more than once? Is there such a thing as a chronic mover? If so, how is his or her individual purchasing behavior, intermarket communication, innovativeness etc., important to marketing?
2. For basic marketing researchers,
   a. Are there significant differences in risk levels and risk reduction strategies *before* leaving the old community? What role does the marketing system play in risk reduction strategies? Is the market an important, or perhaps secondary unknown in the mobile consumer's perception of new community problems? What is the contribution of willingness factors to mobility decisions?
   b. If market risk *is* important, and market learning is a way to reduce *market* risk, what are the different learning styles employed to reduce risk, both before and after arriving in the new community? What specific roles in this learning

process do personal sources, impersonal sources, and personal investigation play?

c. What effects do mobile households have on the marketing attitudes and behavior of individuals or households they meet in the new communities?

d. What effects do differences in historical rates of geographic mobility have on the market structures of existing communities?

e. Finally, what effect does moving have on mobile households? What changes in family roles, individual goals, and behavior are brought about by an event or a history of moving?

Geographic mobility presents a unique and intriguing opportunity for marketing researchers to study consumer decision making, attitude change, family role interaction, learning behavior, etc. The heightened nature of the moving situation — the way it packs a large quantity of high-risk marketing decision making into a short space of time — seems to create an ideal situation for efficient, high-yield marketing research.

REFERENCES

1. "Consumer Dynamics in the Super Market: Part 2, the Movers," *Progressive Grocer* (November 1965), K35-58, 71.

2. John B. Lansing, *Geographic Mobility of Labor: An Interim Report*, Ann Arbor, Mich.: Survey Research Center, University of Michigan, 1964.

3. Alfred Politz — Life Magazine study, *Life Study of Consumer Expenditures*, Vol. 7, 1957.

4. Arnold M. Rose and Leon Warshay, "The Adjustment of Migrants to Cities," *Social Forces*, 36 (October 1957), 72-6.

5. Peter Rossi, *Why Families Move*, Glencoe, Ill.: The Free Press, 1955.

6. Wendell R. Smith, "Product Differentiation and Market Segmentation as Alternate Marketing Strategies," *Journal of Marketing*, 21 (July 1956), 3-8.

7. Gregory Stone, "City Shoppers and Urban Identification: Observations on the Social Psychology of City Life," *American Journal of Sociology*, 60 (July 1954), 36-45.

8. Karl E. and Alma F. Taeuber, "White Migration and Socio-Economic Differences Between Cities and Suburbs," *American Sociological Review*, 29 (October 1964), 718-29.

9. U.S. Bureau of the Census, *Current Population Reports: Population Characteristics* p.-20 134 (March 1965).

10. U.S. Bureau of the Census, *Statistical Abstract of the United States: 1965*, 86th Edition, Washington, D.C.

NOTES

1. These criteria will be explained and developed more fully below.

2. Studies related to the present subject include 1, 2, 4, 5, 7, 8.

3. To the extent that these external factors are responsible for reported mobility statistics, the input-output data for populations of various regions may be explained largely by the supply and demand for labor. For an elaboration of this point, see Lansing, [2, pp. 263-5].

4. One would also hypothesize that the higher the organizational rank, the larger the organization and the higher the income, the longer the average move.

5. Thus, while a move from a depressed labor market theoretically may be described as being produced by a negative external opportunity, it is my feeling that such moves are not undertaken without some minimum household resources.

6. The data reported in Tables 2 through 5 are well supported in the literature on geographic mobility. See also 9.

7. The distribution of reported reasons for the move for the sample were as follows: head of household transferred by present employer, 47.3 percent; head changed employers, 23.6 percent; desire for better employment opportunities; 9.5 percent; desire for better home or community, 3.4 percent; other and no answers, 16.2 percent.

8. These findings are supported by data from [3].

The nation itself is becoming increasingly regionalistic, the region too is changing in character, and will continue to do so.

24

myth of the national market

competition — and a host of variables — has spelled its end

jack b. weiner

In all the annals of marketing, no success story quite approached that of Liebmann Breweries' Miss Rheingold contest. Held once a year in the New York area, the contest enabled the potential beer buyer to vote for one of six pretty girls to be named Miss Rheingold. For all its relative simplicity, the election attracted an average of 20 million votes a year, played a key part in raising sales of Rheingold beer from 675,000 barrels in 1940 to more than 3 million by last year and established itself as one of the classic beer-selling devices of all times.

Except, that is, in Southern California. In truth, Miss Rheingold seemed just the way to introduce Rheingold into what was a new market for Liebmann. For one thing, she had established herself as an all-time winner in New York; second, the first basic lesson in the marketing book is that few pictures sell any product as well as those of a pretty girl. Nevertheless, the voting in California did not go at all the way Liebmann expected. In fact, Miss Rheingold was soundly trounced. She went down to defeat before Brew 102, Hamm's, Bull Dog, Eastside Old Tap and other beers.

Reprinted by special permission from *Dun's Review* and *Modern Industry*, May 1964. Copyright 1964, Dun & Bradstreet Publications Corporation.

But why did Rheingold go so flat in California? As Liebmann's President Phillip Liebmann reconstructs it, the brewery simply failed to realize that the two areas are as different as orange groves and subway turnstiles and that what appealed to one would not necessarily sell beer in the other. As Liebmann notes: New York is "a sophisticated market, where they work like hell so they can live in Scarsdale. In Los Angeles there is a maximum of leisure and casualness. At five o'clock there is a rush to the barbecue, and at home they can live in their backyards."

The experience of Liebmann Breweries (which recently was acquired by Pepsi-Cola United Bottlers) epitomizes the change that has come over one of marketing's most cherished concepts, the national market — with its twin concomitants of the product and the campaign that achieve coast-to-coast success. As a marketing entity, "one nation indivisible" no longer exists. It has become a myth. In its place has sprung up what actually is a series of fragmented, regionalized markets.

Each one of them, of course, is entirely different in its desires and its needs. Phil Liebmann is the first to admit that today. "California," he says, "was a regional lesson for us. We just didn't know enough about the West Coast market." The point is made even more strongly by Pepsi-Cola's shrewd, knowledgeable Vice President Robert V. Cox. "I don't see how anyone," he remarks, "could say the U.S. is one big market."

THE "BENNY DAYS"

But what has changed the United States since the days when network radio was truly national and Jack Benny spelled J-E-L-L-O in every home in the nation? In part, of course, it is geography at work. The maker of a soap, detergent, shampoo or even instant coffee, for example, must be aware that Santa Fe, New Mexico has soft water in the summer and hard water in the winter — and that just the reverse is true of Pittsburgh, Pennsylvania.

But it can also involve what can only be called sociological considerations. If the manufacturer is selling soft drinks, for example, he must know that several communities of American Indians in Wyoming are inordinately fond of strawberry soda, that Omaha residents prefer lemon-lime and that thrifty New Englanders do not care what the flavor is as long as they can buy it by the economy-sized quart.

But why, as so many marketers are finding, are these regional differences becoming greater and more intensified today? There are many reasons, most of them tied to the quickening tempo of the times. There is, for example, the competition in all product lines, which has accelerated at a phenomenal rate. So even with the increase in consumer dollars, the originators of today's new products face imitation much more quickly and competition much more severe than twenty, or even ten, years ago. Most often this imitation and competition comes from local brands. The result is one of the most chilling statistics in all of business: only one out of ten new products put on the market succeeds today.

Added to this is the life-and-death competitive battle that rages impartially across shelves and showrooms alike and such economic and demographic factors as greatly increased consumer mobility, rapidly shifting population patterns and heightened consumer sophistication — all of which make for subtle variations in consumer tastes.

And their impact can be painful. A few years ago, by way for example, S. C. Johnson & Son came on the market with its new Raid House and Garden insecticide. The South, with its warmer climate and its presumably greater, more active insect population, seemed one of the most promising markets to start the campaign for the product.

But Wisconsin-based Johnson went south with a Yankee marketing manual. As it always had, the company placed its wares in variety stores and drugstores. But where the Yankee dislike buying insecticides with his food, the Southerner traditionally purchases them in grocery stores. And where the Yankee considers the more expensive aerosol can worth the price, the Southerner prefers cash to convenience. Worse, spring comes earlier in the South, so Southern wholesalers and distributors "stock up" early. To Johnson's chagrin, it learned these facts too late; by the time it began its costly campaign south of the Mason-Dixon Line, area distributors and wholesalers had already made commitments to Johnson's competitors.

Can such mistakes be avoided? They can be, but it takes a wealth of data to do it. Whether the product is a new one or not, in fact, the marketer should be able to pinpoint its performance on a nation-wide, area-by-area basis, and he should know the reasons behind its showing. As a result, the head of one of the nation's most respected marketing consultant firms believes that the maker of even so seemingly uniform a product as shoe polish should have the following data:

- The total number and types of retail stores in the U.S. carrying shoe polish.
- The number and percent stocking his brand.
- The number and percent stocking the brands of each major competitor.
- The strengths and weaknesses in the distribution of his brand *vs.* competitive brands in each region of the U.S.
- The strengths and weaknesses in the distribution of his product compared with competitive products — in food stores *vs.* shoe stores, in drugstores *vs.* variety stores, and for every other major type of retailer selling shoe polish.
- The strengths and weaknesses in the distribution of his product *vs.* the competition in large-volume stores compared with medium- and small-sized outlets.
- The competitive structure of the market as evidenced by distribution in

large metropolitan areas *vs*. medium-sized metropolitan areas *vs*. small towns and rural areas ("Is the wholesaler getting my brand into the smaller stores in more remote areas or merely skimming the cream off the market?").

• The differences in availability of product by type (*e.g*., cream, liquid, paste, aerosol) by region, type of retailer and other related market characteristics.

Certainly the variety of differing conditions and circumstances across the nation cannot be overstressed. A seller of frozen food, for example, should know that about one-third of the homes in St. Paul have a freezer, compared with less than one-fifth of the homes in Indianapolis. Similarly, a marketer of electric razors should be aware that while ownership of electric razors is virtually the same in St. Paul and Seattle, St. Paul's use of electric razors is growing twice as fast as Seattle's. And the garden-equipment manufacturer should know that rotary lawn mowers are more popular than reel mowers in Duluth, while the reverse is true in Fresno.

Food processors, in particular, must take account of regional differences. This point is emphasized by Aaron Strauss, manager of marketing research for the Best Foods division of Corn Products Co. "More and more," says Strauss, "you have got to target yourself to specific and identifiable groups of consumers. It's becoming almost an impossibility under today's marketing conditions to be all things to all men."

Consider, for example, the fact that milk flavorings and sweeteners enjoy an acceptance in New York City far out of proportion to the area's population. Why? Marketing experts with a psychological bent venture one guess. New York City parents, they feel, are generally more permissive with their children, perhaps because of "their own underpriviledged childhood."

Health, though, can sometimes confuse even the experts. Most food and beverage fads, for example, seem to start on the West Coast; for instance, diet foods got a head start there, and safflower oil remains very strong in coastal California. On the other hand, King Sano cigarettes, with a strong "health" appeal, finds primary acceptance in New York, Chicago and Miami, in addition to Los Angeles.

Moreover, preference for some food products can come very directly from an area's economy. Wesson Oil, a cottonseed product, is extremely strong in cotton-producing areas of the South. But in the North and Midwest, where the big cash crop is corn, Wesson loses its crown to Mazola, which just happens to be made from corn.

"The local branch manager," says Irving Roshwalb, vice president of Audits & Surveys Co., "has been yelling for years that 'my market is different.' he's virtually been ignored. Today, though, in more and more cases his superiors are finding out that he has been right."

PEPSI'S POSITIONING

One who discovered that early in the game is the Pepsi-Cola Co. Pepsi positions new product entries in areas where the preference for a particular variety (colas, flavors, etc.) runs strongest. For example, because the cola share of the Southern market often runs as high as 85%, compared with 60% for other areas, Pepsi recently started test-marketing a new soft drink — Diet Pepsi-Cola — in the southern city of Louisville, Kentucky.

Research, moreover, has taught the firm some interesting facts about the booming dietetic soft-drink market, facts on which it bases its marketing strategy for such products as Patio Diet Cola. "Up to several years ago," says Pepsi's Bob Cox, "low-calorie beverages had a degree of snob appeal. The biggest purchasers, we found, tended to be adult females in the middle-income brackets. Mostly in suburban areas. But as we got into the market we saw the pattern begin to change. Now it's leveled out considerably," adds Cox, "and today just about everybody buys low-calorie products."

The Corn Products Co. also molds its output to regions. Its Karo Syrup, for example, is produced in two viscosities solely because Pennsylvanians, perhaps because of the effect of Dutch cooking, prefer a thicker syrup than the rest of the country wants. Similarly, marketing strategy for Corn Products' Hellman's Mayonnaise is geared to fit the very strong regional preferences between mayonnaise and whip-type dressings.

In similar fashion, Colgate-Palmolive Co. has to bear in mind that its Vel Beauty Bar soap does best in hard-water areas and the Midwest; users of Colgate's fluoride toothpaste tend to be more sophisticated, better educated and in higher income groups than users of Colgate's regular toothpaste; high-sudsing detergents are preferred in the South, yet Southerners, as a rule, prefer liquid bleaches to such products as Colgate's Action Powdered Bleach. "The point is," says Dr. Arthur Koponen, Colgate director of market research, "how we capitalize on these differences on a systematic basis."

By the same token the Ford Motor Co.'s Ford division gears it output to such variables as Southern California's overwhelming preference for its Thunderbird (just twenty markets, in fact, provide 50% of T-Bird volume); compact cars, such as the Falcon, also do better on the West Coast; San Francisco is a "great place for wagons," while New Orleans is not.

Similarly, points out John R. Bowers, manager of the Ford division's vehicle advertising, Ford's so-called "fast-back" hardtop found immediate success in the Southeast, where racing and performance activities are so important. Somewhat perversely, convertibles now sell better in cold climates than in hot; this represents the march of progress, for air-conditioned cars have proved more comfortable in the extremely hot regions. "The whole automobile industry," asserts Bowers, "has seen a tremendous increase in demand for different types of cars in the past ten or fifteen years. This month, for example, the Ford division will be selling 46 separate models, including the Mustang, up from about 10 models only a few years ago. We don't like it, and our dealers don't like it," adds Bowers. "But the public likes it — and that's what matters."

Hand in hand with the rise of regional marketing has come another marketing tactic: the "rifle" approach, or the attempt to pinpoint a company's own customers in the vast area of land lying between the Atlantic and the Pacific. The airlines, for one, have found that more than half of all U.S. passports are issued to people from the four states of New York, Illinois, California and Massachusetts. Moreover, these and five other states (Florida, Pennsylvania, Michigan, Texas and Ohio) account for at least two-thirds of all this country's travelers to Europe.

The "rifle" (in contrast to "shotgun") approach is perhaps best defined by Audits & Surveys marketing Vice President Lawrence D. Gibson. "Rather than design a product to appeal to the majority of the market," says Gibson, "design one for the particular likes or needs of a portion of it. Instead of shooting for 25% of a 100% market, aim for 100% of a 25% market. The end result often is a product so designed and sold that consumer satisfaction and loyalty are extraordinarily high, while price competition is lessened."

This tactic, it must be admitted, is gaining momentum. Indeed, more than 150 national consumer magazines now offer regional editions that are attracting increasing numbers of multiregional (national) advertisers. Magazine regional advertising revenues totaled $93.4 million in 1961; by last year they stood at $135 million.

RISE OF THE REGIONALIST

Recognition by many companies that the so-called national market is no more has also fostered the rise of the advertising agency specializing in the regional approach. In theory, this type of agency can utilize regional variables in a positive way, rather than merely "take them into consideration."

One proponent of this concept is youngish Edward Robinson, owner of Smith & Dorian, Inc., whose billings have risen from $1 million to $13 million in the past two years. As Robinson sees it, advertising techniques have not kept pace with the trend to regional marketing. "For the giant advertisers," he contends, "the shift to regionalism creates few problems money can't solve. But the majority of national advertisers find the changeover more difficult. They don't have the staff or budget to study and develop local marketing and merchandising concepts."

So Robinson has set up a network of centrally directed local agencies, with the emphasis on strong local impact. "Joe Jones," Robinson argues, "an experienced and professional advertising man who lives in Kansas City and knows all the right people there — not to mention local tastes, preferences and so on — can do a lot more in making the regional approach work than the agency man flown in from the home office."

While it remains to be seen whether a move as radical as Robinson's is necessary, there is no denying that regionalism has become very much a part of the marketing way of life. It is, moreover, a trend that shows no sign of slowing down; if anything, it would appear that consumers may well become increasingly regional in their tastes and buying desires as time goes on.

There are two good reasons for this. First of all, consumers will have $180 billion more to spend by 1970 than they had just three years ago, and as the booms in scuba diving, "floorstick" cars, World War I airplanes and similar items have already proven, the consumer's taste tends to become increasingly individualized, not to say bizarre, as the level of his disposable income rises. What is more, the consumer will have the time in which to indulge in his whims. For as the surveys show, given the present trend, the average person will be working a three-hour shorter work week by 1970.

In sum, then, while the nation itself is becoming increasingly regionalistic, the region too is changing in character, and will continue to do so. By way of proof, look again at Liebmann Breweries. Lately the company has found that its Miss Rheingold contest holds little more attraction for Manhattanites than it did for Californians. Indeed, from being the platform of the whole Rheingold advertising campaign just a year or so ago, Miss Rheingold has been relegated to the very bottom of the barrel.

Reason? The radical change in the nature of the highly fragmented Manhattan market. In recent years the population of Manhattan has become nearly 25% nonwhite, one of the largest such markets in the world (it also has, incidentally, one of the largest Spanish speaking populations of any city in the world). Given that consumer mix, then, Manhattan simply lost interest in the Rheingold girls — each of whom was chosen for embodying what was supposedly the typical New York beauty.

Clearly, then, today's successful marketer must keep its corporate fingers, brand by brand and in every product category, firmly on the pulse of that restless, changing phenomenon known as the American market place. It must take into account the fact that every twelve months some 40 million American families move to a new home, rarely on the same block, and take their tastes, preferences, concepts, culture and prejudices with them.

Businessmen, to be sure, are becoming increasingly aware of this changed climate. But marketing postures among them vary greatly. And the degree of their success — the separation of the men from the boys — will be determined, as usual, not by fate but by sagacity.

The "National" Brand: Anatomy of an Anachronism

To a manufacturer of surfboards, it is obvious that his product will find little acceptance in the Iowa corn belt. In today's highly segmented market, however, most regional differences are considerably more subtle. The marketers of the Sixties, more and more, must target themselves to specific and identifiable groups of consumers. The tables below were prepared for Dun's Review by Audits & Surveys Inc. Based on actual brand studies for five product categories, the tables clearly reveal that brand preference varies sharply, not only region by region but city by city.

A Packaged Food Product

Perhaps the most extreme cases of regional marketing problems are found in food products. For not only is the diversity of tastes in food products especially marked; so is the competition of local and private brands (usually at lower prices). As the table shows, for example, although metropolitan New York accounts for 19% of the total volume of this packaged food product, Brand A places 34% of its volume there, while Brand D places only 6%. Yet Brand D places 28% of its volume in the Central region, which accounts for only 15% of total volume, while Brand A places 13% there.

	New York	East	Chicago	Central	South	Los Angeles	West
Total Volume	19%	26%	6%	15%	16%	8%	10%
Brand A	34	22	7	13	12	6	6
Brand B	24	20	8	11	12	16	9
Brand C	15	31	6	15	15	8	10
Brand D	6	13	5	28	26	10	12

A Woman's Cosmetic

Drug products are perhaps less regional than food products, but only in degree. As the figures show, although the Northeast accounts for 9% of total volume of this cosmetic, Brand C places 17% of its volume there; in contrast, Brand B does rather poorly (8%) in the Northeast but does extremely well (20%) in the West. Also noteworthy: Brand F places 24% of its sales in the South although the region accounts for only 17% of national volume.

	North East	North Central	South	South West	West Central	West
Total Volume	9%	29%	17%	8%	22%	16%
Brand A	11	31	20	5	22	11
Brand B	8	29	14	7	22	20
Brand C	17	27	14	6	18	18
Brand D	11	31	18	8	21	11
Brand E	9	28	23	6	21	13
Brand F	11	20	24	8	19	18
All Other	7	29	15	10	22	17

Cigarettes

One might not expect so pervasive a product as cigarettes to show sharp regionality; the marketers are national, the advertising budgets are huge, and there are no local brands. Yet, as the figures below show, strong regional tastes do prevail. Metropolitan New York, for example, accounts for only 12% of total cigarette volume, yet for 15% of Brand A, 21% of Brand B and 24% of Brand C. In contrast, in the South, which has 32% of national volume, Brand B places only 19% of its sales but Brand C places 51%.

	North East	New York	South East	South Central	North Central	West
Total Volume	19%	12%	16%	16%	20%	17%
Brand A	19	15	13	12	23	18
Brand B	22	21	11	8	21	17
Brand C	14	24	23	28	15	16

A Home Appliance

The home-appliance field is strongly influenced by distributor relations
and by distribution problems and opportunities. For example, although
the Northeast accounts for only 29% of total volume for this product,
Brand C gets 40% of its volume there. In the South, on the other hand,
Brand C's volume drops sharply to 5%. Brand E faces the same problem
in the West.

	North East	North Central	South	West
Total Volume	29%	29%	23%	19%
Brand A	32	25	31	12
Brand B	28	26	21	25
Brand C	40	29	5	26
Brand D	33	24	31	12
Brand E	30	43	24	3
Brand F	25	25	24	26
All Other	27	29	26	18

An Automotive Maintenance Product

For this product category, local (All Other) brands are extremely
important. Marketer alertness to climate variables and local habits by
season is especially vital for successful placement of product. For
example, although Brand B surpasses both total volume and volume for
All Other brands in the South, its pattern is totally reversed in the East,
where All Other brands place 35% of their volume.

	East	Central	South	West
Total Volume	29%	24%	27%	20%
Brand A	29	22	29	20
Brand B	20	25	36	19
Brand C	31	22	27	20
All Other	35	26	19	20

Cross-tabulation of image data with a measure of readiness to buy will pinpoint which ideas are held about a brand by those most disposed to buy it.

25

measuring
readiness to buy

william d. wells

When a new promotional campaign is introduced, no one can breathe easily until sales begin to climb and indicate success. But —

• Must we put up with the difficult wait until clear sales evidence is available? Are there no reliable indicators to measure performance before sales data come in?

• Even given sales information, what about the all-too-frequent and unhappy situations when nothing appears to be happening or sales seem to be spinning downward? Has all the promotion gone for nothing; has it contributed *nothing* to the consumer's willingness to buy the product?

• Or, on the other hand, has the promotion just missed the mark, just failed to cajole the consumer into a purchase? Could some adjustment be made which would result in speedier or ultimate sales success?

Author's note: The research described in this article was conducted by the Developmental Research Unit of Benton & Bowles, Inc.

That last question in particular is the important one that every marketing man would like to be able to answer with one peek into his crystal ball.

One way to attack this problem is to think of consumers as predisposed (or not) to buy your product. That is, how *ready to buy* your product are they? Obviously, the consumer who is nearly ready to buy is going to be a lot easier to sell than his cohort who would not want to touch your product under any circumstances. It is the function of advertising to create this readiness to buy, and to move such predispositions into purchase action. Consequently, a reliable measure of consumers' readiness to buy can have importance in evaluating the effectiveness of current or proposed marketing strategies through pinpointing the predispositions of consumers to purchase a given product, thereby highlighting the strengths and weaknesses of the campaign.

PSYCHOLOGICAL CONTINUUM

Naturally, consumers are not equally predisposed to buy a given product, service, or brand. As can be seen in Exhibit I, the range of their predispositions can be thought of as a psychological continuum running from intention to buy the item in the immediate future to a firm intention not to buy the item ever. Between these two extremes, the continuum runs through positive intention not accompanied by clear-cut buying plans, through a neutral area in which disposition might swing one way or the other, and through an area in which attitudes are negative but not firmly set.

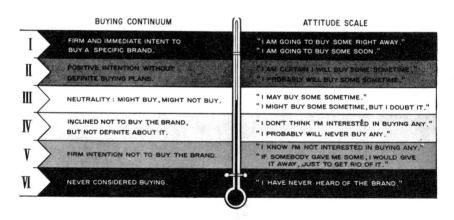

Exhibit I. Range of consumers' predispositions

A consumer's position on this continuum can be measured by giving the respondent a list of brands in a variety of product categories, asking him to select the statement which most accurately reflects his intentions toward each of them, and then expressing the results on an attitude scale similar to the one illustrated in the exhibit. This particular scale is designed to measure the readiness to buy specific brands of frequently purchased items. Other versions measure readiness to buy large ticket items, infrequently purchased items, and services. All scales can be adapted by giving appropriate instructions for use in either personal interviews or mail questionnaires.

Other Attitude Measures

Though measures of readiness to buy are closely linked to scales which show how well a product is *liked*, they differ from such scales by combining a consumer's regard for the item with an assessment of its purchase probability in his over-all buying plans. As a result, the readiness-to-buy measure is closer to purchasing behavior for it taps intention, the mental forerunner of action.

The readiness-to-buy concept also closely resembles the concept of "buying intentions" used in studies conducted by the Federal Reserve Board and the Michigan Survey Research Center. However, there is a major difference in application. Buying-intention studies focus on prediction of long-term purchasing trends; readiness-to-buy studies focus on attitude differences for specific products within the present market. Consequently, readiness-to-buy studies take special note of how far from buying the *un*ready consumer is. For the marketer, information about readiness *not* to buy can be valuable at times.

Finally, readiness-to-buy scales are closely related to questions like "What brand did you buy last?" or "What brand do you usually buy?" when the answers to such questions will be used to classify consumers in evaluating markets. The readiness-to-buy measure singles out prospective customers for special study by examining the predispositions of nonpurchasers toward the product in question.

APPLICATIONS

Examining consumer predispositions makes it possible to think of the marketing process in terms of two broad divisions. The first, measured by readiness-to-buy scales, consists of factors which influence the consumer *before* he reaches the point of sale. Thus a consumer's felt need for the product or service, his past experiences with it, and a variety of other influences (including advertising) can all be summed up by evaluating his readiness to buy the product before he goes out to shop.

The second division contains the conditions which affect the consumer *after* he has reached the point of purchase, and includes such factors as size, location, and attractiveness of display; shelf-space allotment; retailer influence; point-of-purchase advertising or price promotion; and the influence of other shoppers.

Naturally these two divisions of factors interact to determine ultimate purchase action — sometimes reinforcing, and sometimes canceling each other. With this background in mind, let us examine the application of readiness-to-buy scales to marketing decisions.

Trouble Shooting

By comparing consumers' readiness to buy given products with their actual purchases, it is possible to discover which brands are best converting predisposition into action. Such information is important because it helps narrow down the search for trouble spots when sales are disappointing. Exhibit II illustrates the wide range which exists among products and brands in converting predisposition to purchase. But how will such measures help pin down trouble spots?

When sales of a brand are low and readiness to buy the brand is *high* relative to other brands in the same product category, where is the defect in marketing strategy likely to be found? Favorable experience with the product and persuasion by advertising are the major ingredients of strong predisposition; and when such strong predispositions have been created, the advertising and the product itself have done as much as can be expected. Hence the flaw must be at the point of sale.

However, when readiness to buy is *low* compared with other brands in the same category, the marketing deficiency may be in the product, or in the advertising, or in the interaction between them. Brands with this handicap are unlikely to do well; this is true even when conditions at the point of sale are excellent.

Profile Analysis

Obviously, consumers having different demographic or psychological characteristics are not equally ready to buy a given product. It is therefore frequently important to assess the potential of a given product among these different groups. Three such assessments can be found in Exhibits III, IV, and V.

In making such comparisons, it is convenient and more meaningful to group the readiness-to-buy scale statements into larger categories by grouping adjacent statement on the scale. These categories allow for speedier comparison of the predisposition to buy for various groups, and thereby allow formulation of marketing strategy for these groups.

Category I combines the *top two* readiness-to-buy statements ("I am going to buy some right away," and "I am going to buy some soon"). Consumers who use either of these statements are as predisposed to buy as they can be; follow-up studies reveal that they actually do buy the designated brand in substantially greater numbers than do consumers in any other category. Again, Category II combines the *next two* statements in the scale ("I am certain I will

Exhibit II. Converting Readiness into Purchase
(Base: 900 housewives)

	Toilet goods item				Grocery item		
Brand	Readiness score*	Purchasing score†	Purchasing/ readiness‡	Brand	Readiness score*	Purchasing score†	Purchasing/ readiness‡
A	41%	23%	56%	A	37%	23%	62%
B	29	16	55	B	16	7	44
C	22	13	59	C	13	7	54
D	18	8	44	D	12	3	25
E	17	8	47	E	12	8	67
F	5	2	40				

*Readiness score: Per cent of respondents who chose one of top two readiness-to-buy scale statements about the brand.

†Purchasing score: Per cent of respondents who actually purchased the brand within four weeks after making rating.

‡Purchasing/readiness ratio: Per cent of respondents choosing one of top two statements who purchased the brand within four weeks. When this ratio is high, a large proportion of those with intent to buy have actually done so. When the ratio is low, something has interfered between predisposition and purchasing.

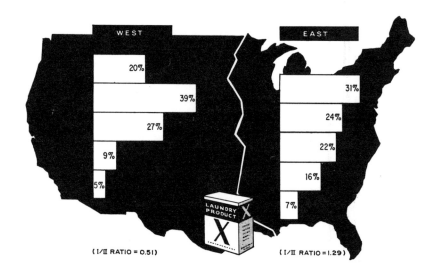

Exhibit III. Regional profiles with different I/II ratios

buy some sometime," and "I probably will buy some sometime"). The attitude of consumers in this category is one of favorability without immediate purchasing intention. Some comparisons:

● The ratio of Category I to Category II is a measure of the degree to which favorable disposition has been converted into actual purchase intention. A high I/II ratio means that many who are favorably impressed by the brand actually intend to buy it. A low I/II ratio means that a "reservoir of good will" remains to be exploited; that a large supply of favorable disposition still remains to be converted into firm intent to buy.

● In Exhibit III, the low I/II ratio in the profile of western consumer opinions of Laundry Product X indicates that the potential in this region is unexploited. Similarly, the high I/II ratios for counties with lower population in Exhibit IV indicate that for this food product Z, the greatest unused opportunity is in the highly populated counties.

A second source of important information in profile analysis is the relationship among Categories III, IV, and V. Exhibit V contains profiles with similar proportions of consumers with immediate intention to buy, but with different distributions in the remaining profile categories. Profiles which differ in this way indicate sharply different marketing problems. Thus:

▲ Profiles with the bulge in the middle indicate concentrations of consumers who have said, "I may buy sometime," or "I might buy some sometime, but I

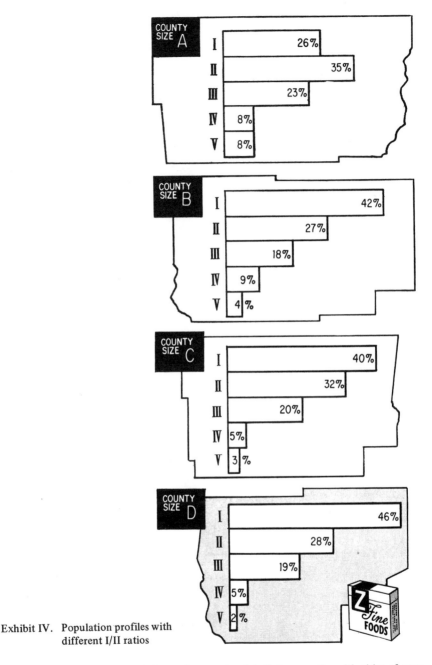

Exhibit IV. Population profiles with
different I/II ratios

Note: County sizes are as follows: County size A includes counties with cities of over 500,000 population plus counties included in metropolitan areas of these cities. County size B includes counties in which the population is over 100,000 and counties included in metropolitan areas of cities in these counties (excluding all counties previously defined as "A"). County size C includes counties in which the population is between 30,000 and 100,000 (excluding all counties previously defined as "A" or "B"). County size D includes remaining counties under 30,000 (not previously defined as "A," "B," or "C").

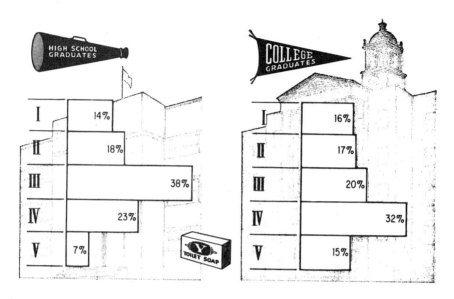

Exhibit V. Profiles with different distribution in Categories III, IV, and V

doubt it." Consumers in this frame of mind are still psychologically accessible because their intentions are not firmly set.

▲ Profiles with the bulge at the bottom indicate concentrations of persons who have strong, preformed negative intentions and are therefore likely to be quite difficult to persuade. They may require different appeals; or given attempts are likely to be much less successful than similar efforts directed at consumers in Categories I, II, and III. Groups of consumers with such negative intentions can often be isolated by demographic breakdowns.

NEW BRAND PROGRESS

If all is going well in a new brand introduction, predisposition to purchase will show a steady increase as the advertising begins to take effect and as experience with the product confirms established expectations. Exhibit VI illustrates just such a happy progression. If the point-of-sale activities are also functioning effectively, such increased predispositions will be converted into rising sales.

However, if all is not going well, predisposition measures will help locate the trouble. For example:

• Failure to establish ready recognition of the brand name appears in profiles as a failure of respondents to move out of Category VI ("never heard of the brand").

● Failure to convince consumers that the new brand is worth trying appears as a movement of respondents from Category VI into Categories III, IV, and V instead of into Categories I and II.

● Dissatisfaction with the brand appears as a migration into the lower categories by those who have already tried it.

● Deficiencies at the point of sale appear as a failure to convert predisposition into purchases.

True, not all segments of the consumer population respond equally well to initial advertising or to initial experience with a new product, and different segments of the population convert predisposition into purchase at different rates. However, segmentation of the sample will readily show which consumer groups are responding most favorably, which are converting favorable responses into purchases (and which are not), which need a little more convincing, and which are responding so unfavorably that they might as well be written off, at least for the time being.

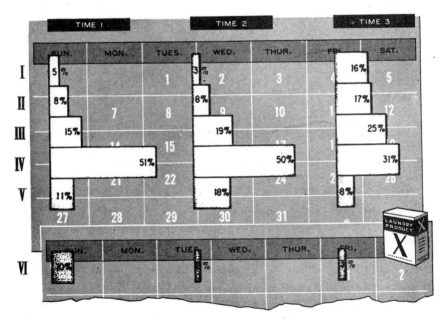

Exhibit VI. Buying readiness profiles for Brand X at six-week intervals

EVALUATING YOUR IMAGE

Given the many techniques at our disposal today, it is relatively easy to discover clear images for many brands and many products. But unless some aspect of the image is obviously negative, it is difficult to decide what changes should be made, if any should be made at all. Cross-tabulation of image data with a measure of readiness to buy will pinpoint which ideas are held about a brand by those most disposed to buy it, which are held by neutrals, and which are held by those with negative intentions.

Exhibit VII illustrates just such an application. In the first graph, the relation between image and predisposition is such that high readiness to buy is associated with the idea that the brand is used by intelligent people, while low readiness to buy is associated with the idea that the brand is used by the unintelligent.

Unfortunately, not all image elements are associated with readiness to buy in such a straight-forward manner. Thus:

● In the second graph, the association between readiness to buy and image variables is neither strong nor clear. Being modern is presumably a desirable characteristic, and it is strongly associated with readiness to buy for some products, but not this one.

● The third graph depicts a curvilinear relationship. Middle values of this image picture are associated with higher readiness to buy, while lower values are associated with the extremes of the image. In this product category, the most wanted brands are thought of as being used by people in the middle age brackets. In this way, image elements can be positioned in terms of their association with buying disposition. A strategy can be subsequently developed.

CONCLUSION

The uses of readiness-to-buy measures outlined above suggest that a shift in emphasis in the use of predisposition measures is needed. So instead of such measures being viewed solely as predictors of behavior, they should be viewed both as predictors *and* as market data worthy of independent consideration. This is not to suggest that predisposition measures can replace sales figures as evidence of final outcome. However, they can be used to give an advance sign of the success or failure of a marketing plan or to "trouble shoot" when sales are not responding as expected. In this way the marketing strategy, brand image, advertising, or other elements of the marketing mix can be adjusted or shaped to meet the specific market.

AVERAGE READINESS-TO-BUY SCORE OF CONSUMER WHO REGARDED "TYPICAL USER" AS—

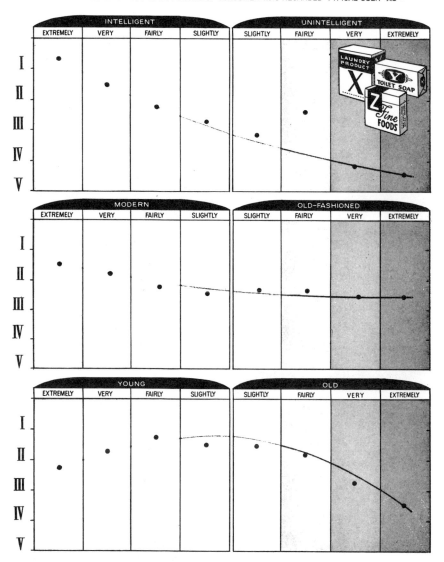

Exhibit VII. Three kinds of relationship between readiness to buy and image variables

Although the concept of market segmentation has captured the imagination of marketers, the results of studies to date have not been very encouraging. This paper reviews some of the findings and implies that the very recent multidimensional approaches to Marketing Research show much greater potential than previous univariate techniques.

26

an overview of market segmentation

john c. bieda and harold h. kassarjian

Not unlike the fad of Motivation Research in the post World War II period, the concept of market segmentation has produced a phenomenal proliferation of articles, studies and papers in the past decade. The concept, itself, was first clearly articulated by Wendell Smith in a 1956 *Journal of Marketing* article[1] a paper that by now has become a classic. And perhaps this should be so, for market segmentation has permeated the thinking of theorists, researchers and managers perhaps more than any of the other fashions and fads that marketing has passed through. Until very recently the controversial nature of the issue has been not whether or not segmentation leads to meaningful analysis as much as on what basis to segment.

To the earlier marketing manager, the natural segments of population were related to the socio-economic and demographic variables found in U.S. Census of Population. From these variables one could distill out *social class*, the ultimate conglomerate in the determiniation of consumer behavior in the view of many. But the field was not to be left to the census analysts alone; for soon after, personality variables such as gregariousness, authoritarianism, inferiority, risk

Reprinted from Bernard A. Morin (ed.), *Marketing in a Changing World*, Proceedings of the National Conference of the American Marketing Association, published by the American Marketing Association, June 1969, pp. 249-253.

taking and self esteem were to make their impact; and finally such concepts as usage rate, brand loyalty, channel loyalty, advertising susceptibility and even price sensitivity were to make their debut.

The usefulness of any given technique for segmentation, of course, is the ultimate one of applicability. "In other words, a crucial criterion for determining the desirability of segmenting a market along any particular dimension is whether the different sub-markets have different elasticities . . . ."[2] The determination of this criterion, according to Kotler,[3] depends upon several conditions.

The first of these is measurability, ". . . the degree to which information exists or is obtainable on various buyers' characteristics. Unfortunately many suggestive characteristics are not susceptible to easy measurement." The size of each segment that purchases toothpaste because of health fears, dislike of dentists, sex appeal or because of habitual patterns inculcated by parents is difficult to measure.

A second condition is that of *accessibility*, the degree to which any given segment can be differentially reached. Unfortunately those starved for self-esteem, the hypocondrical types, or heavy users of toothpaste do not cooperate by differentially exposing themselves to specific media, purchasing from different outlets or necessarily willing to pay different prices.

Kotler's final condition is that of *substantiality*, the degree to which the segments are large enough to be worth sub-dividing for separate marketing activity.

TWO APPROACHES TO SEGMENTATION

As one reviews the literature on marketing segmentation, two approaches seem to emerge. On the one hand, the researcher starts with an existing product. The function of the researcher is to study the customers of that generic product to determine if there are differences between buyers of different brands. In this case the particular segment of the market that the brands are aimed at is determined empirically. Once such information is gleaned, better marketing decisions presumably are made, and perhaps further product differentiation is possible.

A great deal of the commercial research is undoubtedly of this sort answering such questions as, "Who is our market? and how can we better reach them?"

Evans's now often quoted study on the psychological and objective factors related to Ford and Chevrolet owners is an example of this type of approach. Starting with owners of Fords and Chevrolets he collected demographic and personality data and by the use of discriminant analysis attempted to predict the buyers of each make of automobile. His results parenthetically indicated that demographic variables did a better job of predicting brand choice than did the personality variables.[4]

The second type of segmentation research approaches the problem from the opposite direction. The researcher starts with pre-conceived notions of what the critical segmentation variables are — social class, personality, cultural variables, age and sex. Members of each group or segment are one way or another isolated, and product usage, brand and channel loyalty, or media exposure data, are then collected and analyzed. The question the researcher asks is of the sort, "How do young marrieds differ from older persons?" or "What products do southerners use as compared with northerners?" Rainwater's study on the Workingman's Wife is an example of this approach. He collected masses of data on the behavior of working class and middle class housewives relating to their purchasing activities, attitudes, and so on, and made a number of significant comparisons.[5]

Another example of the pre-categorized approach to segmentation is Joel Cohen's study relating purchasing behavior to personality characteristics. Based on Karen Horney's tripartite conceptions of complaint, detached and aggressive styles of life, Cohen developed a questionnaire and attempted to divide his sample into these three groups of persons. Next he searched for and found some differences between groups on brand preference, usage rates and media exposure.[6]

The following overview of the literature in market segmentation includes further examples of both approaches.

AN OVERVIEW OF RESEARCH FINDINGS

Demographic Characteristics

That demographic variables are a useful method of segmentation has become almost axiomatic in marketing, and yet the research evidence is not at all clear. Evans, in his study on Ford and Chevrolet owners concludes, "The linear discriminant function of demographic variables is not a sufficiently powerful predictor to be of much practical use. . . .(They) . . . point more to the similarity of Ford and Chevrolet owners than to any means of discrimination between them. Analysis of several other objective factors also leads to the same conclusion.[7]

On grocery store products, the Advertising Research Foundation study in 1964 compared toilet tissue purchasing behavior with 15 socio-economic characteristics. The predictive efficiency of the characteristics was virtually nil.[8] Koponen, using the same J. Walter Thompson panel data but on beer, coffee and tea, found very similar results,[9] while Frank, Massy and Boyd using the Chicago Tribune panel data compared 57 product categories ranging from food to household products with demographic characteristics. The results were again similar with a very small portion of the variance being accounted for in the regression analyses.[10] Unfortunately, study after study throws doubt upon the direct usefulness of demographic characteristics as a predictor for product purchase.

Of course, this is not to deny that sanitary napkins are primarily purchased by women, razor blades by men, the influence of the purchase of sugar coated breakfast cereals by children, and canned boiled peanuts in brime primarily by Southerners. But nevertheless, other than very specific products aimed directly at a specific group, the empirical evidence seems to indicate that demographic measures, outside of education, are not an accurate predictor of consumer behavior.[11]

Social Class

Perhaps some of the most extensive work on market segmentation has been done in the area of social class.[12] Some differences do seem to emerge in spending patterns, product preferences and shopping habits. Martineau for example found some clear preferences between the lower and middle classes for types of retail stores.[13] Glick and Levy found preference differences in television programs with the middle classes preferring current events, drama and audience participation shows while the lower classes preferred soap operas, westerns and quiz shows. However the degrees of overlap is so great that a statistical prediction would be most difficult.[14]

Further, many of the social class studies are now several years old. By the 1970's what we will mean by lower class is perhaps not an income-occupation-education type of differentiation but more specifically Negroes, Indians and Mexican-Americans. Whether there is such a thing as a Negro market that is in fact different from the white market is still a controversial and not sufficiently researched issue. However, our expectation is that no such market exists. In any case, because of more exposure to the mass media consumption behavior differences between classes probably are disappearing.

Personality

Personality studies have been similarly disappointing. Westfall was able to find differences between convertible owners and sedans but the relationships were weak.[15] Kamen found no evidence to ascertain the consistency of food preferences among personality groups.[16] Koponen in the study mentioned above using J. Walter Thompson data found some minimal differences between smokers and non-smokers on such variables as sex, aggression, achievement, dominance and compliance. However the percentage of variance accounted for both by personality variables and demographic variables combined was less than 12%.[17] Brody and Cunningham on reanalysis of the same data indicated that the personality variables measured by the Edwards Personality Preference Scale on both men and women heads of households accounted for a mere 15% of the variance.[18] Tucker and Painter, similarly found significant but very weak relationships between measures such as responsibility, emotional stability, sociability and ascendency and product preference. Among the products studied personality variables only differentiated between users of deodorants and cigarettes.[19]

Gruen found no relationship between product preference and inner- and other-direction[20] and Kassarjian could not find differences in media exposure between inner and other-directed subjects.[21]

To sum up the literature, personality as a variable has not been a useful mode of market segmentation. Perhaps it is too much to expect the forces of personality to be powerful enough to differentially produce the purchase of Colgate Toothpaste over Crest or Gilette razor blades over Personna. Also it is possible that marketing has not yet found the right variables to measure, having no personality instruments of its own.

Buyer Characteristics

Finally turning to buyer characteristics such as brand loyalty and usage rate, the findings are not dissimilar. For example, Frank and Massy found no significant difference in elasticity between brand loyal and non-brand loyal buyers.[22] Although Twedt did find that heavy and light users can be moderately well distinguished on the basis of their different demographic characteristics, his findings, at best, indicated that the relationships are relatively modest.[23] Again using the J. Walter Thompson panel data, Massy, Frank and Lodahl indicated that heavy and light buying households had virtually identical demographic and psychological characteristics.[24] To continue, Farley could not segment the brand loyal customer,[25] and Frank and Boyd could not differentiate between the private label and manufacturer brand customers.[26] And finally Cunningham found little relationship between rate of purchase and brand loyalty.[27] However Brody and Cunningham found in a two brand discriminant analysis they were able to correctly identify 80% of brand choices.[28]

In general, the consistency of the results tends to indicate that the research to date in market segmentation has either been unsuccessful or if a relationship is shown, quite weak.

Turning back to Kotler's criterion for market segmentation, measurability, accessibility, and substantiality, it is clear that at least some of these conditions have not been met to date. In those cases where segmentation variables are measurable they do not seem to be related to purchasing characteristics. Or, even if the relationship is verified, too often the second condition, *accessibility*, is not a simple matter. Unfortunately media exposure, channel loyalty and purchase rate are not differentiated along the same variables as purchase behavior. To the everlasting frustration of the segmentation specialist readers of *Argosy Magazine* and *True Experience* too often buy Cadillacs, while upper income professionals and businessmen too often shop at Macy's or Gimbel's in New York.

Perhaps then, the usual modes of segmentation are not sufficient. For example, Yankelovich argues that the analysis of various product markets should be made on the basis of several modes: patterns of usage, values derived from usage, preferences, aesthetics, and buying attitudes and motivations.[29] This view is enticing. Perhaps there are sufficiently substantial groupings of people who on a multi-variate set of dimensions can be considered a market segment. Unfortunately, Yankelovich does not present us with a method for such an analysis.

PROSPECTS

Although the results, to date, from studies on market segmentation have not been very encouraging, we might speculate on why so much of the research has been negative when the theory seems so logical and sound on a priori basis. Perhaps the major problem of past research is that in an effort to segment markets we have lost sight of the basic premise of the theory: that different people have different needs and at different times these needs may change. Hence, a company's marketing program will have different elasticities when directed to groups of people where the needs in each group are relatively homogeneous and when the needs between groups are relatively heterogenous.

Consider for a moment the methodological logic of the past research. First, the researcher has arbitrarily selected a group of products or brands that *he* thinks are serving the same market. Then data on purchase behavior is collected for analysis. The analysis consists of using demographic, socio-economic, and psychological variables as independent variables in either a regression or discriminant analysis. The objective is to find out if buyers of different brands are related in any way to the independent variables. If a strong relationship is found a circular argument is used to establish cause and effect, i.e., because the person jointly had the characteristic and bought the product and because the person would not have bought the product unless he needed it, therefore, the characteristic must be the cause of the need for the product. But we never bother to extrastatistically establish the cause and effect relationship. We might ask at this point 1) what kinds of assumptions are made when this type of analysis is carried out and 2) are the assumptions realistic or are other assumptions more plausible?

First, it is assumed that because people have bought the same brand, they have bought it for the same reason, i.e., the same need, desire, tension. The alternative assumption that people buy the same product for different reasons seems more realistic. For example, one family might buy one brand of potato chips because the kids like ridges in them. Another family might buy the same brand because ridged potato chips do not break quite as easily as straight potato chips when served with a dip.

Second, it is assumed that all people perceive the same set of brands to be alternatives from which to choose. Some recent evidence would tend to indicate that this assumption may not be justified. Green, Carmone, and Fox[30] have shown that television programs were clustered differently, on the basis of similarity, by three groups of people. This would tend to support an alternative hypothesis that all consumers do not perceive the same set of products as competing with one another.

Third, it is assumed that each person has the same set of alternatives (brands) available from which to choose to satisfy his needs. But it is common knowledge to every housewife that all stores do not carry the same brands, therefore this assumption does not seem to be justified.

Fourth, it is assumed that people with the same set of characteristics, the same values of the independent variables, have the same needs, wants, and desires. This assumption may be reasonable; however there has been little, if any, systematic research to justify making this assumption on a priori basis.

One final problem with past studies centers on the complete lack of integration into the segmentation analysis of information on the marketing mixes of the products and brands under study. This omission may have contributed to past negative findings if one or both of the following situations occurred.

Situation 1. Suppose that two brands, A and B, were essentially appealing to one set of needs and two other brands, C and D, were essentially appealing to another set of needs. If information on the marketing strategies of the four brands were not incorporated prior to using regression or discriminant analysis then the buyers of each of the brands would be considered a separate group, e.g., we would have a four way discrimant analysis. This being the case, the regression or discriminant function would not be able to distinguish between the buyers of brands A and B nor between the buyers of brands C and D. In this situation we would probably conclude that the results were negative because we could not predict which brand consumers would buy based on the independent variables.

Situation 2. Suppose that one brand was appealing to several segments using different marketing mixes for each segment. If this were the case then we would expect to find the brand satisfying a unique set of needs for buyers in each of the segments. When one or more companies follow this practice a discriminant or regression analysis would not be able to identify purchasers for the different brands because the buyers for each brand are aggregated even though they may belong in different market segments.

A next logical question is: What might we do to obtain more meaningful results on the subject? We would suggest attacking the problem as follows:

1. Determine what **products or brands appeal** to which set of needs, wants,

and desires by the following two-stage procedures. First, apply multivariate analytical techniques to similarity data, i.e., that data obtained by asking the consumers what products or brands they consider similar; then determine homogenous groups (= clusters) of consumers that perceive the market in a similar manner, i.e., that see the same set of products as being similar. Second, for each of the homogeneous groups again use multivariate techniques to cluster products that are perceived to be similar. Then find out what basic set of needs are being met by each cluster of products. The works of Barnette and Stefflre,[31] Green, Carmone, and Robinson,[32] and Green, Carmone, and Fox[33] are significant contributions in this direction.

2. At this point it is proposed that preference data from the consumers be incorporated into the analysis, i.e., the data obtained by asking the consumer which product(s) he prefers. The preference data, in conjunction with the similarity data provides a method of determining an ideal point for *each* individual in the homogeneous group obtained in the previous analysis. The ideal point for an individual would represent a product whose characteristics would be most preferred by the individual.[34] The ideal point for an individual would also serve an additional function as a reference point for determing how closely other sets of needs, represented by the clusters of products, match the needs of the individual. The degree to which the individual's needs and the needs being served by any cluster of products coincide should be an inverse function of the distance of the cluster to the ideal point, i.e., the more similar the two sets of needs the shorter the distance between that cluster and the individuals ideal point. Finally we should cluster the ideal points within each of the homogeneous groups. It would then be appropriate to determine if certain charactertistics could meaningfully describe the consumers in each of these groups. This information would, of course, be used in determining future strategy for marketing to these segments.

It should be noted that the current approach takes into account differences in individuals' needs whereas previous work in this area has aggregated individuals over the entire market making it impossible to identify how different products or even the same product is related to individuals' differing needs.

The advantage of this approach is two-fold: first, we can study the basic needs of the consumers as they are currently being served by the market and, in doing so, we make no restrictions on the number or interdependence of the needs each brand can service; second, we can incorporate information on the marketing programs of the brands under study to determine the differential elasticities for each brand in each of the sub-markets.

SUMMARY

In summary, although the concept of market segmentation has captured the imagination of marketers, the results of studies to date have not been very encouraging. Univariate studies on demographic, objective and psychological factors related to consumer behavior have on the whole leaned towards indicating that product choice cannot be predicted from these types of variables.

However, in recent months a series of multivariate studies have emerged that indicate a real potential for a better understanding of the concept of market segmentation.

NOTES

1. Wendell Smith, "Product Differentiation and Market Segmentation as Alternative Marketing Strategies." *Journal of Marketing*, Vol. 21 (July 1956), 3-8.

2. Ronald E. Frank, "Market Segmentation Research: Findings and Implications," in Frank M. Bass, Charles W. King, and Edgar A. Pessemier (eds.), *Application of the Sciences in Marketing Management*, New York: John Wiley & Sons, 1968.

3. Philip Kotler, *Marketing Management*, Englewood Cliffs, N.J.: Prentice-Hall, 1967.

4. Franklin B. Evans. "Psychological and Objective Factors in the Prediction of Brand Choice," *Journal of Business*, Vol. 32 (Oct. 1959), 340-369.

5. Lee Rainwater, Richard P. Coleman and Gerald Handel, *Workingman's Wife*, New York: Ocenana Publications, 19.9.

6. Joel B. Cohen, "An Interpersonal Orientation to the Study of Consumer Behavior," *Journal of Marketing Research*, Vol. 4, (August 1967), 270-278.

7. Same reference as note 4.

8. Ingrid Hildegaard and Lester Krueger, "Are There Customer Types?" as quoted in same reference as note 2.

9. Arthur Koponen. "Personality Characteristics of Purchasers," *Journal of Advertising Research*, Vol. 1 (Sept. 1960) 6-12.

10. As quoted in same reference as note 2.

11. Education taken as a uni-variate measure does seem to hold up as a segmentation variable as indicated in several studies and cannot as easily be brushed aside as most other demographic measures.

12. e.g., James M. Carman, *The Application of Social Class in Market Segmentation*. Berkeley: Research Program in Marketing, Graduate School of Business Administration, 1965.

13. Pierre D. Martineau, "Social Classes and Spending Behavior," *Journal of Marketing*, Vol. 23 (October 1958). 121 130.

14. Ira O. Glick and Sidney Levy, *Living with Television*, New York: Aldine Publishing Co., 1962.

15. Ralph Westfall. "Psychological Factors in Predicting Product Choice," *Journal of Marketing*, Vol. 26 (April 1962) 34-40.

16. Joseph M. Kamen, "Personality and Food Preferences," *Journal of Advertising Research*, Vol. 4 (Sept. 1964), 29-32.

17. Same reference as note 10.

18. Robert P. Brody & Scott M. Cunningham, "Personality Variables and the Consumer Decision Process," *Journal of Marketing Research*, Vol. 5 (Feb. 1968). 50-57.

19. William T. Tucker and John J. Painter, "Personality and Product Use," *Journal of Applied Psychology*, Vol. 45 (1961), 325-329.

20. W. Gruen, "Preference for New Products and Its Relationship to Different Measures of Conformity," *Journal of Applied Psychology*, Vol. 44 (1960), 361-366.

21. Harold H. Kassarjian, "Social Character and Differential Preference for Mass Communication," *Journal of Marketing Research*, Vol. 2 (May 1965) 146-153.

22. Ronald E. Frank and William Massy, "Market Segmentation and the Effectiveness of a Brand's Price and Dealing Policies," *Journal of Business* (April 1965), 188-200.

23. Dik W. Twedt, "How Important to Marketing Strategy is the Heavy User," *Journal of Marketing*, (January, 1964), 71-72.

24. As quoted in same reference as note 2.

25. John Farley, "Brand Loyalty and the Economics of Information." *Journal of Business*, Vol. 37 (October, 1964), 370-381.

26. Ronald Frank and Harper Boyd, Jr., "Are Private-Brand Prone Food Customers Really Different," *Journal of Advertising Research*, Vol. 5 (December 1965), 27-35.

27. Ross M. Cunningham, "Brand-Loyalty-What, Where, How Much?" *Harvard Business Review*, Vol. 34 (Jan.-Feb., 1956) 127-137.

28. Brody and Cunningham, *op. cit.*

29. The conclusion is stated by Norman L. Barnett, "Beyond Market Segmentation," *Harvard Business Review*, Vol. 47 (Jan.Feb., 1969).

30. Green, Paul E., Frank J. Carmone, and Leo B. Fox, "Television Programme Similarities: An Application of Subjective Clustering," *Journal of the Market Research Society*, Vol. 22 (January 1969), 70-90.

31. Norman L. Barnett and Volney J. Stefflre, "An Empirical Approach to the Development of New Products," Unpublished manuscript, 1967.

32. Green, Paul E., Frank J. Carmone, and Patrick J. Robinson, *Analysis of Marketing Behavior Using Nonmetric Scaling and Related Techniques*, Technical Monograph (Interim), Marketing Science Institute, March 1968.

33. Same reference as note 30.

34. Same reference as note 30.

OPERATIONS - SUGGESTED ADDITIONAL READINGS

Lee Adler, "Symbiotic Marketing," *Harvard Business Review*, 44, November-December 1966, 59-71.

Fred C. Akers, "Negro and White Automobile-Buying Behavior: New Evidence," *Journal of Marketing Research*, 5, August 1968, 283-290.

Robert W. Baeder, "General Electrics Scientific Method for Helping Salesmen Generate More Sales," *Business Management*, November 1968, 30-33.

Frank M. Bass, Douglas J. Tigert and Ronald T. Lonsdale, "Market Segmentation: Group Versus Individual Behavior," *Journal of Marketing Research*, 5, August 1968, 264-270.

James E. Bell, Jr., "Mobiles — A Neglected Market Segment," *Journal of Marketing*, 33, April 1969, 37-44.

Warren Blanding, "Organizational Structure for Effective Distribution Programming — Case Studies," Charles H. Hendersman, ed., *Marketing Prescision and Executive Action*, Chicago: American Marketing Association, 1962, 473-482.

Steven C. Brandt, "Dissecting the Segmentation Syndrome," *Journal of Marketing*, 30, October 1966, 22-27.

"Celanese Puts Marketing Planning on the Grid," *Sales Management*, 99, November 1967, 34-38.

Blaine Cooke, "The Do-It-Yourself Marketing Information System or an Innocent Abroad in the Land of Or," Charles H. Hendersman, ed., *Marketing Precision and Executive Action*, Chicago: American Marketing Association, 1962, 139-151.

Ronald M. Copeland, "The Art of Self-Defense in Price Discrimination," *Business Horizons*, 9, Winter 1966, 71-74.

Daniel F. Cox and Robert E. Good, "How to Build a Marketing Information System," *Harvard Business Review*, 45, May-June 1967, 145-154.

C. Merle Crawford, "A Shotgun Marriage of Mathematics and Marketing?" *Business Horizons*, 9, Summer 1966, 37-48.

Irving Crespi, "Use of a Scaling Technique in Surveys," *Journal of Marketing*, 25, July 1961, 69-72.

Ernest Dichter, "The Operational Use of Motivational Research," George L. Baker, ed., *Effective Marketing Coordination*, Chicago: American Marketing Association, 1961, 563-570.

Roger Dickinson, "Game Theory and the Department Store Buyer," *Journal of Retailing*, 42, Winter 1966-67, 14-24.

Warren Dusenbury, "CPM for New Product Introductions," *Harvard Business Review*, 45, July-August 1967, 124-139.

Richard A. Feder, "How to Measure Marketing Performance," *Harvard Business Review*, 43, May-June 1965, 132-142.

Sidney Goldstein, "The Aged Segment of the Market, 1950 and 1960," *Journal of Marketing*, 32, April 1968, 62-68.

Morris J. Gottlieb, "Segmentation by Personality Types," Lynn H. Stockman, ed., *Advancing Marketing Efficiency*, Chicago: American Marketing Association, 1958, 148-158.

G. David Hughes, "The Measurement of Changes in Attitude Induced by Personal Selling," Stephen Greyser, ed., *Toward Scientific Marketing*, Chicago: American Marketing Association, 1964, 175-185.

Philip Kotler, "A Design for the Firm's Marketing Nerve Center," *Business Horizons*, 9, Fall 1966, 63-74.

Albert R. Kroeger, "Test Marketing: The Concept and How It Is Changing," *Media/scope*, 10, December 1966, 63-84.

William F. Massy and Frederick E. Webster, Jr., "Model-Building in Marketing Research," *Journal of Marketing Research*, 1, May 1964, 9-13.

John McDonald, "The New Game of Business," *Fortune*, 79, May 15, 1969, 143-145; 273, 276, 281, 286.

William A. Mindak, "Fitting the Semantic Differential to the Marketing Problem," *Journal of Marketing*, 25, April 1961, 28-33.

William H. Reynolds, "More Sense About Segmentation," *Harvard Business Review*, 43, September-October 1965, 107-114.

J. S. Schiff and Michael Schiff, "New Sales Management Tool: ROAM," *Harvard Business Review*, 45, July-August 1967, 59-66.

Edward W. Smykay, "The Role of Physical Distribution in the Marketing Organization," George L. Baker, ed., *Effective Marketing Coordination*, Chicago: American Marketing Association, 1961, 387-392.

Abe Shuckman and Michael Perry, "Self Confidence and Persuasibility in Marketing: A Reappraisal," *Journal of Marketing Research*, 6, May 1969, 146-154.

Stanley F. Stasch, "System Analysis for Controlling and Improving Marketing Performance," *Journal of Marketing*, 33, April 1969, 12-19.

Lawrence X. Tarpey, "Advertising Theory and the Capital Budgeting Model," *Business Horizons*, 8, Summer 1965, 87-93.

Harold Weitz, "The Promise of Simulation in Marketing," *Journal of Marketing*, 31, July 1967, 28-33.

"The Computer in Marketing - Part VII Test Marketing, High Hopes for Those Go/No Go Decisions," *Sales Management*, 97, September 1966, 75-82.

"What's a 'Market' to a Media Planner?" *Media/scope*, 10, June 1966, 64-72.

Daniel Yankelovich, "New Criteria for Market Segmentation," *Harvard Business Review*, 42, March-April 1964, 83-90.